Gravyland

Gravyland

WRITING BEYOND THE CURRICULUM
IN THE CITY OF BROTHERLY LOVE

Stephen Parks

SYRACUSE UNIVERSITY PRESS

∞ The paper used in this publication meets the minimum requirements
of the American National Standard for Information Sciences—Permanence
of Paper for Printed Library Materials, ANSI Z39.48-1992.

Credits:

"Strategic Speculations on the Question of Value: The Role of Community Publishing in English Studies" previously
appeared in *College English* 71 (no. 5), May 2009, as "Texts of Our Institutional Lives: Strategic Speculations of the
Question of Value: The Role of Community Publishing in English Studies." Copyright 2009 by the National Council of
Teachers of English. Used with permission.
"The Insights of Everyday Scholars: New City Community Press" contains material by Ken Finkel, Tameka Blackwell, Lorene
Cary, and Ann Marie Taliercio previously published by New City Community Press. Used with permission.
"The Insights of Everyday Scholars: New City Community Press" contains an introduction by Gil Ott previously published in
No Restraints: An Anthology of Disability Culture in Philadelphia, New City Community Press and copyrighted by Gil Ott's
estate. Used with permission.

For a listing of books published and distributed by Syracuse University Press,
visit our Web site at SyracuseUniversityPress.syr.edu.

ISBN: 978-0-8156-3242-9

Library of Congress Cataloging-in-Publication Data is available from the publisher upon request.

Manufactured in the United States of America

To Lori, Eliot, Sadie, and Jude

Stephen Parks is an associate professor of writing and rhetoric at Syracuse University. He is author of *Class Politics: The Movement for the Students' Right to Their Own Language* (2000). He is also executive director of New City Community Press (newcitypress.org) and editor of *Reflections: A Journal of Writing, Service-Learning, and Community Literacy* (reflections.syr.edu).

Contents

Illustration

Acknowledgments

LORI SHORR has been my writing partner for more than twenty years, although she would probably not think this was the case. Without her, however, the best chapters of my life would not have occurred. And without my children's witty and generous suggestions on how to revise some of my ideas about writerly authority, life would be much less of an adventure. Finally, my parents offered me a strong sense of the basics—the happy childhood that made all else possible. To my primary writing community, then, thank you.

Over the past ten years, I have also been fortunate to participate in a rich community of writers and writing groups in Philadelphia and, later, Syracuse. I am grateful for many conversations with Vera Beaton, Lorene Cary, Ann Marie Taliercio, Yolanda Johnson, Mark Lyons, Gil Ott, Margarita Rojas, and August Tarrier. From these folk, I learned to be a better writer as well as to develop a deeper understanding of the political importance of writing. As will be evident in the pages that follow, I have always felt fortunate that many of their voices ultimately became part of the publishing history of New City Community Press.

It was always my hope that this book would become part of these writers' collective publishing history. Too often, however, the academy and the community exist along different publishing tracks—one track destined for professors, the other destined for local neighborhoods. For that reason, I am very grateful to Mary Selden Evans and Alice Randel Pfeiffer for bringing New City Community Press into the Syracuse University Press family, supporting its many writers, and developing a writing community that draws the academic and the organizer, the disciplinary and the communal into dialogue. They have created a wonderful home for those committed to the possibilities of writing.

My colleagues at Temple University deserve a hearty thanks as well. If not for the good nature of Eli Goldblatt, Susan Wells, Dennis Lebofsky, Vanessa Allen Smith, and Nicole Meyenberg, much of the work described in this book would not have occurred. Indeed, Eli Goldblatt deserves a particular note of gratitude for responding to even my most grandiose ideas with enthusiasm and trust—the best response of a true friend. Finally, I want to highlight the importance of Lynda Hill, who introduced me to the Federation of Worker Writers and Community Publishers and who offered the initial intellectual framework for much of the work that would mark both the Institute for the Study of Literature, Literacy, and Culture and New City Writing. I hope all of these individuals see their impact in the work described here.

My colleagues at Syracuse University have been the best of friends for the past five years. In a world where too many of us can tell departmental horror stories, my experiences at Syracuse are a healthy blend of intellectual debate and collective compassion. That such moments often occur over a blend of drinks and nachos just makes them that much more fun. For that reason, I want to express my gratitude to Eileen Schell for convincing me to make the leap to Syracuse University, Carol Lipson for making this leap possible, and the rest of my colleagues for the community they allowed me to enter: Lois Agnew, Adam Banks, Collin Brooke, Rebecca Moore Howard, Anne Fitzsimmons, Margaret Himley, Kristi Johnson, Krista Kennedy, Chris Palmer, Iswari Pandey, LouAnn Payne, Gwen Pough, Minnie Bruce Pratt, George Rhinehart, Jeff Simmons, Marybeth Sorendo, Louise Wetherbee Phelps, and Beth Wagner.

My department is also fortunate to have many talented graduate students from whom I have learned much over the past five years—both about our field and about the insights that will shape its direction for years to come. I want to offer a particular note of gratitude to Brian Bailie, Collette Caton, J. Haynes, Gale Coskan-Johnson, Carolyn Ostrander, Patricia Serviss, Zosha Stuckey, and Dianna Winslow.

Many years ago, in what seems a different life, I was fortunate enough to become friends with James Seitz. Through the years and many Conference on College Composition and Communication meetings, Jim has been a consistent guide in how to understand the twists and turns of an academic career. I am very grateful for his consistent support. Other individuals have also been important influences on the work described here: John Burdick, Ira Shor, David Jolliffe, Malea Powell, Nick Pollard, Richard Ohmann, Cristina Kirklighter, William Thelin, Tiffany Rousculp, Tom Deans, Paula Mathieu, Marc Bousquet, Keith Gilyard, and Linda Flower. A more immediate influence on this manuscript was exercised by Annie Barva, whose meticulous copyediting saved the manuscript from some tangled prose and helped to clarify the importance of these individuals in shaping the work described in *Gravyland*.

Finally, I thank everyone whose collective work is discussed in these pages. Although I often mask their identities, I hope they understand how vivid their voices and insights are in my daily life. Without their support, the following tales about my adventures in the City of Brotherly Love could not be told.

Entering Gravyland

Breaking Bonds and Reaffirming Connections

If all my luck ran out tomorrow
And I fell back to where I began
With a spirit poor and a need to borrow
I'll know that who I was is who I am
. . .
All the rest is just like gravy on the table
And I've poured and passed as long as I was able
And I know it took some time to understand
The rules of behaviour here in gravyland
Here is gravyland.

—JOHN GORKA, "Gravyland"

IN MIKE HUCKABEE'S ADDRESS to the 2008 Republican Convention, he told the story of a teacher who did not allow her students to have a desk until they could figure out "how to earn it." After many days in which the students failed to provide the correct answer, the teacher finally relented. As military veterans carried the student desks in the classroom, she announced: "You don't have to earn your desks . . . these guys already did." Within the context of a national election, the story was intended to connect the goals of education with a love of country and support for military victories past and present. As part of a strategy to brand Democrats as weak on national defense and, potentially, socialist, Huckabee's story was widely considered to be a success.

I, too, want to tell a story about classroom desks, a tale about my attempt to engage students in the local social and political forces that earned them

xiii

seats in the classroom. The story I want to tell, however, is markedly different from Huckabee's. Rather than see members of the local community walk into the classroom, put a desk in place, and leave, I want to tell about classrooms where the community takes a seat and becomes part of the conversation—sharing their knowledge and unique historical perspectives. Rather than see the teacher as the locus of understanding, I want to speak about a classroom that understands the power of knowledge generated through dialogue with the larger community—a dialogue whose insights can support the goals of both a neighborhood and a university. Finally, I want to share classroom stories where students come to understand that the right to sit in a classroom is not just the result of war, but of peaceful civil disobedience, of community struggles to gain self-recognition, and of collective efforts to seek social justice.

I am hardly alone in attempting to create such a classroom. The struggle to maintain the possibility of a progressive education during a period of conservative dominance transcends the particulars of my own teaching or personal experience. Over the past thirty years, university and community activists have made a consistent and collective effort to resist conservative attempts to reduce education to a diluted and restricted sense of national identity and purpose. National organizations such as Teachers for a Democratic Culture, think tanks such as Rethinking Schools, and individual battle zones such as the case of Ward Churchill have served as important nodal points in such efforts. Taken together, these struggles speak to the commitment of university, community, and public-school activists working to create a network of political, social, and curricular institutions that expand literacy practices in concert with progressive political action.

Complementary to such national efforts are smaller and more local moments. Moments where faculty create service-learning classrooms that provide expertise to a neighborhood's struggle against corporate attempts to build box stores or sewage-treatment plants (or other toxic enterprises) in their community. Moments where, against conservative visions of U.S. history, academic programs have created courses that attempt to develop innovative and inclusive senses of our national past. In one sense, then, I agree with Huckabee regarding the need to focus on such stories from our teaching, for I believe that by studying the contour and shape of the stories that emerge from our classrooms, we can gain a better sense of the tactics and strategies required to create seats around a common table of knowledge and activism—even if the activism is pointed in a markedly different direction than Huckabee's.

It is for this reason that I use the pedagogical stories that emerge from my own classroom to focus on the particular case of composition/rhetoric as one site from which to develop a progressive pedagogical and institutional practice. Although composition/rhetoric's modern roots can be traced to the liberal-radical politics and open-admissions policies of the 1960s and 1970s, its full emergence as a discipline occurred during the period of conservative politics' modern ascendance—a period during which the discipline saw the appearance of numerous tenure-stream career opportunities (always with the shadow of part-time exploitation), a rising status for the field's journals, and the beginnings of a power shift toward composition/rhetoric programs within English departments. As articulated by Maxine Hairston (1985) during the height of Reaganism, the question was no longer whether our field was a respected discipline, but whether it would remain in English, develop its own department, or create some new hybrid entity.

It was within this expanding sense of power that a central question for composition/rhetoric became how (or if) the field would retain its commitment to the working-class and working-poor students from diverse and international backgrounds whose bodies initially filled the basic-writing classrooms of the 1960s and 1970s. As the conservative political paradigm took hold during the 1980s and 1990s, the field's commitment to the *traditional* composition student was being rearticulated by larger university and national political trends. Basic-writing courses at research one universities were being eliminated, renamed, and outsourced. Composition/rhetoric's disciplinary success, it seemed, did not translate into university success (or access) for its traditional students. For progressive scholars, the question increasingly became how to develop a set of pedagogical, curricular, and institutional strategies that would support marginalized students and their community's self-defined educational and economic goals. The venue for such work became articulated under terms such as *service learning, community partnerships,* and *writing beyond the curriculum* (terms I explore in greater depth through the course of this book). To reframe Hairston's formulation, the question became whether classrooms freighted with such a community-based pedagogy should take place within traditional English departments, newly formed composition/rhetoric departments, or an entirely new set of structures.

This question still remains. To enter the composition/rhetoric classroom today is to be placed at the nexus of an ongoing struggle to restrict or open opportunities for individuals to attend our classes, to reduce or enlarge the types of voices that make up an individual's education, and to support or deny the conservative politics that have so marked the past thirty years. Of course, I recognize that in the immediacy of our local moment, the dilemma might not appear in such stark political terms—Republican or Democratic, conservative or socialist, and so on. For many of us in composition/rhetoric, the decisions often mutate into questions of what book to teach, course to offer, program to support, community partnership to pursue. We work across spectrums, boundaries, and divides. Pragmatism can become our overarching political philosophy. Nevertheless, at every moment we are also part of the larger debate structuring the contours and context in which education as a national (and nationalist) project is constructed. And although we might not speak at national conventions and create scenarios where the literal figure of literacy sponsors carry our larger social vision of education into the classroom, we are always already implicated in these debates. The thousands of microdecisions that make up our day also make up our politics.

For this reason, I believe we can learn a great deal about how to interact with the national context by focusing on how local classroom moments, existing within larger institutional structures, enact a political positioning of our discipline in the current moment. As we move through our work, considering pedagogical strategies that link our classroom's desks to projects that create a progressive vision of change, we must continually ask ourselves: Out of what set of personal, disciplinary, and political insights do we create our writing classrooms? How do these commitments translate into a strategic institutional practice? How are these decisions an attempt to alter the dynamics of such a conservative age? Or perhaps, more accurately post–Bush II, how can these decisions move in strategic alignment toward a period some believe might be the beginnings of a new liberal age?

Framing the questions this way, however, begs the issue of how we earned our university desks in the first place. Who were we before we had the position to ask such questions and to work toward such answers? How did we earn our desks? The answer, of course, is that we didn't. Perhaps more than any particular academic article we might have read or critiqued in school, it was the actions of our neighbors and our communities that earned them for us. To properly begin the story of this book about my teaching or my writing classrooms, then, I need first to recognize how my own working-class community's collective efforts and wisdom provided me not just with a desk, but also with an ethical compass through which to move into the university and into the field of composition/rhetoric. To do otherwise would be to leave these voices at the door instead of inviting them to sit down and talk.

Earning My Desk: One Community's Lesson in Progressive Values

Every morning during my high school and college years, my father, Clint Parks, left the house by 7:00 A.M., got into his truck and began his day. Traveling from Pittsburgh to places such as Elizabeth, Pennsylvania, and Wheeling, West Virginia, he climbed aboard the boats that carry coal and supplies throughout the East Coast. His job was to maintain the radio and sonar equipment that allowed the boats to navigate their way north—a skill he learned during twenty years in the air force. He had done this work across economies once based in steel and now based in service, as well as across generations once able to succeed with a high school diploma and now having to succeed in college. My mother, Carol Parks, navigated a similar terrain, moving from a clerk at a department store to assistant branch manager of a local bank. Their daily labor was always invested with a sense of hope for their children—hope for a future yet undefined.

Writing a dissertation in graduate school in the early late 1980s and early 1990s, I found it difficult to maintain that hope. Years of balancing university classes with delivering hoagies, working in retail, and busing tables had mutated the utopian ideal of intellectual growth into an act of economic struggle. Now cut loose from course work and financial aid, much of the time I spent writing the dissertation seemed more an act of faith than an act of scholarship. What kept me and my friends moving forward was a sense that the dissertation served as a tool to speak back to our institution, drawing in voices and ideas that seemed to have been too often ignored within our university. Although the "diss" might never see a public audience, our work could serve in its local context as an argument of values that needed to be reaffirmed. In my case, I was a student at the University of Pittsburgh, a traditionally working-class institution rapidly moving toward a more suburban and affluent population. In the process, a cultural shift was occurring that reoriented discussion away from the local student and toward the national rankings. In deciding to write my dissertation about the Students' Right to Their Own Language Resolution as a collective effort by progressive faculty to recognize African American and working-class identities, I felt I was making an argument about my home institution's responsibility to the sons and daughters of Pittsburgh steelworkers—a population that should not be left behind.

Despite the pride many felt as Pitt moved up the rankings, I saw how a lack of resources for working-class students was altering the very possibility of their even attaining a college education. My progress through Pitt from an undergraduate to a doctoral student was premised on federal and state supports that seemed to be vanishing for students just behind me—we were on a collapsing ladder of upward mobility. Each passing year seemed to mark an additional raise in tuition costs and an additional cut in federal grants. Indeed, loans and long-term debt were becoming a hallmark of students' educational experience. As a parent of two children, I also knew firsthand the impact of cuts made to federal programs that traditionally supported working-class students' having access to childcare and health care. With each new academic year, many of my working-class friends were being replaced with their more affluent counterparts.

The changes at Pitt went beyond a university's shifting commitment to its working-class students, however. Working-class communities as a whole were also being abandoned. My high school and college years intersected with the final collapse of the steel industry in Pittsburgh (and in the Northeast as a whole). Former steelworkers were now bagging groceries or working in the kitchens of fast-food restaurants. Neighborhoods that had developed sustaining networks of support were now suddenly being dispersed through corporate downsizing, outsourcing, and plant closings. In the process, the system of personal and communal obligation that had sustained the educational aspirations of each generation was now being fractured. This fracture was most evident in the plight of the public schools in Pittsburgh, Duquesne, and Clairton. The sudden collapse of the tax base devastated educational opportunity. Parents and residents actively attempted to support their children, but in a world of out-of-date books, closed libraries, and transient teaching staff, personal effort could accomplish only so much. As a result, high school graduation rates fell as unemployment rates rose.

It is clear now that we were experiencing the latest wave of globalization—a tsunami that was carrying the working class's manufacturing jobs and community tax base to South Korea, Japan, India, and China. Although hundreds of thousands of lives were affected, the federal government seemed to offer little assistance. By the 1990s, conservative politics had begun to reframe the public sector into a network of private and corporate business opportunities. The effect of these policies is now well known. Government unionized jobs were outsourced to nonunion private companies. Politicians shifted tax dollars from ailing public schools into vouchers for private-school students (or simply cut funds for urban districts). For-profit organizations stepped into the mix, attempting to take over public education as a whole—creating for-profit universities and public-school corporations.

And yet there was hope. Not the hope that Paula Mathieu so effectively describes as a wish—a desire without a sense of agency or collective action, but rather the hope in which one is able "to look critically at one's present condition, assess what is missing, and then long for and work for a not-yet reality, a future anticipated" (2005, 19). This latter form of hope became a sustaining and organizing principle of daily life for many families in Pennsylvania in the 1980s and early 1990s. Parents bore witness every day to the possibilities of education through their own labor. In a place where jobs had vanished, families committed scarce resources to keep their children in college. Union members and community activists staged protests and campaigns for economic justice. Theirs was a hope that liberal and progressive politicians should have tapped and turned into effective collective action. But, of course, this did not happen. From eight years of Reagan to four years of Bush I, conservative politics dominated the horizon.

Trying to write a dissertation about the Student's Right to Their Own Language Resolution and progressive faculty activism while witnessing parents' labor and community advocates' efforts, I began to wonder about the university's role in supporting the collective vision of a working-class community. Historically, the university has had a deeply ambivalent relationship to the working class. Prior to the federally supported GI Bill, many universities were not structured to support large populations of working-class students. When the initial access provided by the GI Bill was expanded through the creation of state and community college networks, some of the necessary structural supports emerged. Yet even these moves were marked by uneven commitments, both in terms of curriculum and resources (see Shor 1992). Moreover, the expansion of support to students (often framed in terms of *individual* students) did not necessarily translate into a commitment to the communities and neighborhoods from which the students emerged. Tuition dollars and public-sector resources were invested in the universities, but the collective payoff for working-class communities, not just its students, remained unclear. I began to wonder what theoretical and institutional models would allow the university to take on systemic support of these communities.

At this particular historical juncture in the history of English departments, cultural studies was becoming the dominant paradigm through which to address such questions of social justice and progressive politics (see George and Trimbur 2001.) As initially framed by British theorists such as Raymond Williams, cultural studies appeared to be making a series of theoretical and pragmatic promises that aligned the work of English studies with a broader vision of a progressive education and democratic practices. Cultural studies was seen as

• committed to a vision of scholarly and pedagogical inquiry that was interdisciplinary; scholars and students were expected to take full advantage of the myriad of theories in the humanities to understand how a particular cultural phenomena worked within larger economic and political structures;

• committed to a sense of scholarship that was linked to political arguments and struggles that transcended the immediate research agendas of any one academic discipline and, in doing so, created a sense of scholarship that was not simply linked to community service, but also not disassociated from pragmatic community need;

• committed to sense of a professional life connected to organizations and institutions outside the academy that worked on issues such as community rights, radical democracy, and postcolonial struggles; and, as such, committed to understanding all residents of an area as part of broad educational community to which everyone was responsible;

• committed to a vision of democratic politics that worked to balance the need for a collective state within the framework of individual and group rights, with an emphasis on a community's ability to define its own interests and to be able to seek collective support.

Such were the origins and possibilities of cultural studies.

The actual history of cultural studies, however, presented a more complicated picture. At first, its political and progressive possibilities seemed to find institutional traction. As it traveled to the United States, it became one element in the larger social-protest activities that began during the 1960s and 1970s. Its emphasis on breaking down disciplinary divisions and traditional canons worked hand in hand with progressive protest movements actively rearticulating the social and political contract in the United States. Media studies courses that were focused on the representation of women and African Americans, for instance, emerged out of the political practices of feminist and Black Power struggles. The two movements were joined at the hip. As the larger social protest movements waned, however, the vision of a cultural studies linked to actual social movements waned as well. Cultural studies turned toward traditional definitions of professionalism. Within English departments in the United States, cultural studies became more focused on transforming the university faculty's curricular and publication agenda. With this more limited goal, a form of success followed. New courses, curricula, and programs were put in place. Interdisciplinary and media studies developed a larger presence in the academy. Tenure-track jobs began to appear (although not at the rate tenure-track jobs were being replaced with adjunct laborers) (see Pfister 1996). Despite these developments, the pragmatic commitment to a world outside the academy still seemed diminished.

This diminishment of political vision was not as clear within composition/rhetoric, however, a field to which I soon shifted because of its commitment to the local students and local neighborhoods. As I traced the history of modern composition studies for my dissertation, I began to understand how, like cultural studies, composition/rhetoric also grew out of the social and political protests of the 1960s and 1970s. (This dissertation was later published as *Class Politics* [Parks 2000].) These roots had remained most evident in critical pedagogy, where its blending of cultural studies and composition/rhetoric classroom practices provided a powerful venue to recast the daily work of teachers as embedded actors in larger struggles for community justice. The work of Henri Giroux (1988), Ira Shor (1992), and Paulo Freire (2000) provided models by which many of cultural studies' stated goals could find traction in the education of students. Through such work, the writing classroom could be seen as a vehicle that would enable students to use their local experiences as the initial lens to trace how larger cultural and political structures had shaped their identities. Within critical pedagogy, there emerged an image of the composition teacher as creating a space that modeled a new form of democratic cultural politics.

Indeed, this initial intersection of composition/rhetoric and cultural studies has continued to produce progressive scholarship that speaks to our local responsibilities. It has provided a theoretical model that has enabled scholars to demonstrate how a student's critical agency emerges from skills learned in their home community. In *The Struggle and the Tools* (1998), for instance, Ellen Cushman uses an extended ethnographic study of a resource-poor urban community to show that individuals employ multiple literacy strategies to work against oppressive and intrusive bureaucracies. In doing so, Cushman highlights the strong network of community-based self-education that sustains these efforts. Throughout her work, she also demonstrates an activist sensibility that indicates how the academic researcher can support neighborhood residents' individual goals.

In *Tactics of Hope: The Public Turn in Composition* (2005), Paula Mathieu has extended this vision of an activist and community-based academic to include efforts that attempt to provide vehicles for an entire community to represent its interests. Working with newspapers published to support the rights of the homeless in general and of homeless individuals in particular, Mathieu provides models for how the interdisciplinary insights gained from cultural studies figures such as Michel de Certeau and critical pedagogy activists such as Giroux enable her to create classroom practices linked to these larger systemic efforts. Indeed, there is a direct intersection between Cushman and Mathieu in the belief that the university's resources should be opened to the larger public. Both represent powerful models of individual commitment to a community-based university.

And yet as a graduate student I wondered if this vision of progressive academics from the 1960s and 1970s (even the work of modern scholars of critical and community-based pedagogy) was adequate to the current moment. If there was any critique to be made, it rested perhaps on the limited impact that individual efforts can have on an institution as a whole. It had become too easy for the university structure to incorporate faculty members' individual efforts, often under the rubric of "service," while leaving many other aspects of its institutional workings untouched. For instance, when I first attempted to introduce critical pedagogy into my classroom, the effect on the students was profound. From an initial recognition of their individual abilities, larger issues of community rights soon emerged as a central theme in the class. Research projects on home communities and local problems were formed. That the institution could authorize such discussions even while actively purchasing most of the land surrounding it for campus expansion, however, seemed a troubling limitation. It was becoming clear that more than an innovative class was necessary. A larger sense of partnership was required.

The nature of this partnership, however, was unclear. Mathieu has argued that the university is not the place to form systemic partnerships with community organizations. Its calendar and myopic self-interest necessarily create structures that are unresponsive to community organizations' immediate and often quick-changing needs. When the university is understood as a collection of individuals or disciplines, I find this argument compelling. However, as Giroux has written,

> We should not be resigned to the roles that universities assign us. The transformative intellectual can develop a collective, counter-disciplinary praxis within the university that has political impact outside of it. The important tactical question at this moment in the history of North American universities is how to get cultural studies established as a form of cultural critique.

Our suggestion has been the formation of institutes for cultural studies that can constitute an oppositional public sphere. (1988, 156)

Giroux and his colleagues are arguing for the creation of interdisciplinary counterinstitutional spaces. Rather than a traditional bureaucracy of departments or majors and minors, these spaces would be marked by mobile and ad hoc organizational structures. In fact, Lawrence Soley (1999) has demonstrated that such entities already exist on campuses, are currently funded by conservative foundations, and support pro-corporate, antiliberal causes (also see White and Hauck 2000). Progressive campus-based institutes seem an obvious response.

Rather than embed the progressive elements of composition/rhetoric further within English departments, then, I came to believe that progressive academics needed to create their own counterspaces within universities that would be systematically directed against the conservative efforts to privatize and corporatize public institutions of literacy. What needed to be created were structures that recognize working-class communities' right to "their own language" as well as venues that would enable these communities' understandings of social justice to challenge the emerging common sense within the university and larger culture about what counts as social justice. Only when the logic of "common sense" changed would the university feel required to shift resources into alignment with the long-term systemic social and political needs of working-class communities.

I knew if I were lucky enough to get a teaching job, I would devote my time to building such a progressive institute, to recognizing the intellectual value of the voices that had surrounded me throughout my whole life. I was aware that my own teacher's desk would be the result of my parents' and my community's labor—a labor that spoke to a collective set of working-class values. I understood that to honor that labor would mean more than simply achieving a professor's job, more than just publishing academic articles, more than gaining tenure. It would entail a different type of academic career. With no money and two kids, I had never actually expected to finish, let alone have a career.

I should have had more faith in the power of the community behind me. In 1994, a year after I received my Ph.D., Temple University offered me a seat at the table—a position as an assistant professor of English, with a focus on composition/rhetoric.

How, I wondered, would I carry these community values into the university? What would it mean to take these values into the heart of "gravyland"?

Inventing the (Counterinstitutional) University: From the Personal to the Professional

Within two years of being at Temple University, I was appointed director of the Institute for the Study of Literature, Literacy, and Culture. In that role, I was part of a collective effort to build sustained partnerships that spoke to the local and immediate needs of Philadelphia's diverse working-class and working-poor communities. Over the course of eight years, the institute would receive more than $2 million in grants to support this work. As a consequence, its reach grew from an on-line writing project emerging from a university writing classroom to a network of public schools, arts organizations, and community literacy programs. Out of this network of activity, the institute established its own publishing house, New City Community Press, which brought the community voices involved in its programs into university, public-school, and community classrooms. The institute's beginnings, however, were more modest and mostly reactive in nature.

When I first arrived at Temple, the English department was not a happy place. Insufficient hiring by the university had forced many faculty to be assigned teaching loads in the general requirement track, such as a year-long great-books course. The First-Year Writing Program had also only recently become an official part of the department, having just emerged from a multiyear reform effort that resulted in a new basic-writing course called Introduction to Academic Discourse (see Sullivan et al. 1997). In the then-current context, this recent inclusion of required composition courses into the department threatened to move faculty even farther away from the literature classroom. It was beginning to appear as if half of a faculty member's teaching schedule might be outside of his or her disciplinary field. If this were to be the case, there would be little support among the traditional literature faculty for expanding composition/rhetoric throughout the department.

In the midst of this larger departmental struggle, a definition of writing as a social activity that transcended disciplinary and classroom-based boundaries had brought together myself, Eli Goldblatt (newly hired as university writing director), and Lynda Hill (African American literature and cultural studies professor) into an emergent alliance. We felt such a view of writing could draw together cultural studies and composition/rhetoric scholars who imagined their work being directed outward to the community and could blunt efforts to diminish such work within the department. Such a vision could also serve as the launching point for an ambitious program to move our writing program into partnership with both North Philadelphia writers (broadly defined) and progressive nonprofit organizations.

That said, there was no money for such endeavors within the department. Budget cutbacks that had already eliminated faculty hires also eliminated most discretionary money. (There was no speaker budget for the department, for instance.) During my first year at Temple University, however, the College of Arts and Sciences had received a Fund for the Improvement of Postsecondary Education (FIPSE) grant to study whether the products that emerge from community service should be regarded as scholarship and, as a consequence, be counted for additional merit pay. The goal was to support engaged scholarship. Because I had spent a year at an education-reform center, I was asked to chair a committee to investigate this question—a committee that featured the department, graduate, undergraduate, and creative writing chairs. As the new university writing director, Eli Goldblatt was also invited to participate.

Initially, I believed that the grant might provide leverage to support the many efforts imagined for our community-based writing program. From the opening moment of the meeting, however, this possibility was quickly put to rest. A majority of the committee members had already decided that working with public schools and community groups or implementing expansive service-learning pedagogies should *not* count as scholarship. To support such an idea would further turn the English department (already housing basic-writing courses) into a service department. Instead, scholarship, it was felt, should remain defined as articles and books written in academic and creative discourses, published and reviewed in academic and creative writing journals, and read by other academic and creative writers. This position is hardly radical or unsupportable; tenure is based on such standards. It was, however, clearly a blow to the work that composition and aligned cultural studies faculty were currently doing or were about to undertake.

With the primary elements of my colleagues' and my own vision for a community-based writing program hemmed in by university budget/tenure policies and my department's response to them, I suggested we form a free-standing institute, à la Giroux, housed within the university writing program and aligned with the entire college. The argument would be that such an institute would bring in its own resources (not tapping funds marked for merit, etc.) as well as allow the department to have endorsed (in some fashion) the FIPSE grant's goals. The committee quickly voted for the compromise. After discussion with the arts and sciences dean, who also quickly agreed, the Institute for the Study of Literature, Literacy, and Culture was born. I was appointed its director.

It was at this moment that cultural studies reentered my life. At the prompting of a senior faculty colleague, I was asked to create a graduate certificate in cultural studies, the first major effort undertaken by the institute. As discussed earlier, the linking of cultural studies and composition/rhetoric was one of the institute's goals. The draft of the institute's cultural studies certificate was the proposed vehicle. To complete the certificate, students would be asked to take courses in multiple departments, studying traditional cultural studies theorists. They would also, however, be required to work at community-literacy organizations in order to produce materials for use by each organization. The long-term goal was also to expand the population of who could obtain the certificate by also offering the program through the university master's in liberal arts program, which had traditionally attracted nontraditional and underrepresented adult students. The overarching aim, then, was to create classrooms that had traditional and nontraditional graduate student populations linked to community-based projects.

Although there was initially strong faculty interest, the certificate failed to gain traction within the college committee structure. In disciplinary terms, the College Curriculum Committee was divided between social sciences and humanities faculty on what it meant to "study culture." Social science professors would not authorize English department faculty (with philosophy allies) to sponsor cultural studies. Instead, a certificate in "literature, literacy, and culture" was passed. This still might have been an interesting moment to reimagine the humanities relationship to community politics, if budgetary issues had not arisen. New budgeting procedures focused on responsibility-centered management led many graduate programs to refuse to allow their students to take courses outside of their departments. Many departments also would not count community service as a course, denying students summer funding. Budget priorities and professional identities had effectively nixed a degree component to the institute.

After many similar experiences attempting to work across disciplinary lines, those involved in the institute gravitated toward Tony Bennett's thoughts on cultural studies. Although recognizing Bennett's troubled relationship to critical pedagogy (see Giroux 2000, 341–60), I agreed with him that cultural studies needed to be more

> circumspect and circumstantial [in its calculations] about how and where knowledge needs to surface and emerge in order to be consequential. . . . [The] field of culture needs to be thought of as constituentively [*sic*] governmental [and] to suggest the need for forms of cultural theory politics that will concern themselves with the production and placing of forms of knowledge—of functioning truths—that can concretely influence the agendas, calculations, and procedures of those entities which can be thought of as agents operating within, or in relation to, the fields of cultural control. (1992, 32)

The goal to develop a certificate now seemed to represent the dream of professionalism and not an active engagement with culture or cultural politics. For it was not clear that such a certificate would help produce the knowledge needed by communities working to rebuild and regain their collective agency. Indeed, as far as I was aware, North Philadelphia residents were not protesting for graduate students to learn cultural studies, but for their home cultures to be respected and supported economically as well as politically.

Instead of attempting to embed cultural studies scholarship further into the university, providing increased opportunities for students to learn to speak *like us*, my colleagues and I came to believe that it was more important to create a venue for writing created in response to local community concerns to speak *to us*. In doing so, we would be disrupting paradigms that imagined the community as knowledge receivers and the university as the only place where culture is studied. In this sense, the institute's work would be to develop a model of writing and activism that was committed less to becoming *legitimate* in the academy (our goal with the certificate) and more toward creating new local forms of *legitimacy* (a goal of every project that followed).

More than a disciplinary or interdisciplinary vehicle, then, the institute, I hoped, would attempt to facilitate the daily practices within a community that can overcome a

> widespread public cynicism regarding the need to develop schools and other educational sites that prepare young people and adults to become active agents of democratic politics; to develop vigorous social spheres and communities that promote a culture of deliberation, public debate, and critical exchange; and to encourage people to organize pedagogically and politically across a wide variety of cultural and institutional sites in an effort to organize democratic movements for social change. (Giroux, 2000, 350)

The chapters in this book detail the extent to which that vision was achieved.

Gravyland: A Tale of Tactical Interventions and Strategic Communities

The creation of the Institute for the Study of Literature, Literacy, and Culture and New City Community Press represents one attempt to use community and university partnerships, infused with cultural and composition/rhetoric theories, to help organize a local progressive politics that transcends the actual for a hoped-for future (Mathieu 2005). This book represents the brief period of the institute's full existence (from 1995 to 2004) and the continued importance of such efforts as New City Community Press. As such, these pages document my entry into the "gravyland" of the academy and my attempts to "pour and pass" its resources to the working populations that surrounding its campus.

The opening chapters trace the difficulties of the institute's initial strategies to support community-based educational reform. In chapter 1, "Writing

Beyond the Curriculum," I focus on how a service-learning class grew into a multischool community-writing project. I use this moment to demonstrate how our original model based on a limited view of community partnership and a consent concept of hegemony ultimately proved inadequate to our actual goals. Chapter 2, "Edge Politics," focuses on the Philadelphia Writing Centers Project. Initially an institute project within one school, the writing center model expanded into multiple schools and gained districtwide support. It was when the school district was taken over by the state and partially privatized that the value of an expanded vision of political activism and an alternative sense of hegemony became evident. To represent this shift, the institute's name changed to New City Writing.

Subsequent chapters focus on the development of New City Community Press and on the value of community publishing as representing the actual work of "edge politics." In "Strategic Speculations on the Question of Value," I use a community-publishing project in a Philadelphia neighborhood (and the resulting protests it engendered) to argue that a reconception of Marxian concepts of value offers the best model of a community partnership focused on working-class community struggle. In "Writing Within and Beyond the Curriculum," I use a New City Community Press publication focused on the Philadelphia disabled community's fight for recognition to bring together discussions of exchange value and "edge politics," showing how the publication represented our most articulated model of a progressive-university/community-based partnership. Here I also demonstrate the value of such partnership work for students involved in a writing classroom. In the following chapter, "The Insights of Everyday Scholars," I provide excerpts from community writing published through New City Community Press. Here the reader will hear the voices of those who took part in our community literacy work.

If the previous chapters detail the difficulties and possibilities of writing beyond the curriculum as both a political and a pedagogical undertaking, the final chapter traces how the community voices and projects that represented New City Writing's success were unable to exist within a university that had moved toward an alternative sense of partnership—a model that moved faculty back into the classroom and moved community partnerships to the margin of the university's mission. Here I trace the decline of New

City Writing and the creation of the North Philadelphia Community Arts and Literacy Network as its replacement as well as the decision to remove New City Community Press from the university context altogether.

One final note. In undertaking to record this history, I found myself unable to disentangle my experiences from what occurred. I entered this work as someone who believed that the university should be about more than disciplinary knowledge—that the university owes something to the communities in which it sits. As I stated earlier, to gloss over the personal education this work provided me (or to frame it simply in terms of scholarly articles) would be to shut out the many faculty, community, and student voices that mentored and guided me. It would also imply a mistake-free existence and fail to represent the many lessons I learned from my coworkers and partners.

Indeed, once I made the move to turn theories into practice, I quickly learned the value of humility. I came to see that calculations made in response to rapidly changing social and political contexts can (and often do) go wrong. Partnerships can be damaged. Hard conversations must (and do) take place. At those moments, it is the ability to listen to others' advice and insights that ensures long-term success. So this book does not offer a smooth story leading to a heart-warming conclusion. It is, however, an honest account of my attempt to learn the rules of the world I was entering, to derive the necessary lessons, and to listen to the individuals who knew more than I, so that in remembering my roots, I could enact the values they represent.

I have certainly made many mistakes along the way. I am grateful, however, for the individuals and organizations that have used such moments to help me develop not only as a professional, but as a citizen as well. It is in that spirit of gratitude that the following pages were written.

Gravyland

1

Writing Beyond the Curriculum

The Hybrid Nature of University/Public-School Partnerships

> Indeed, I would go so far to say that it is the critic's job to provide
> resistances to theory, to open it up toward historical reality, toward
> society, toward human needs and interests, to point up those concrete
> instances drawn from everyday reality that lie outside or just beyond
> the interpretative area necessarily designated in advance and thereafter
> circumscribed by every theory.
>
> —EDWARD SAID, *The World, the Text, and the Critic*

VOICE IS A CENTRAL CONCEPT within composition/rhetoric studies. Centrality, however, does not necessarily imply consensus. For more than thirty years, there has been an on-going debate in the field regarding whether an individual's voice is an intrinsic personal attribute or the result of larger social and political narratives—a difference underlying the Peter Elbow and David Bartholomae dialogue over the nature of personal and academic writing (Bartholomae 1995; Bartholomae and Elbow 1995; Elbow 1995). Nor is there consensus over whether one position is necessarily more conservative or progressive than the other: Is Elbow, whose expressivist pedagogy enables students to bring their community experiences into the classroom, somehow less progressive than Bartholomae, who designed a constructivist pedagogy to benefit working-class students in Pittsburgh? Given a situation with oppositional paradigms and contradictory politics, Joseph Harris (1996) goes so far as to argue that these differences over voice cannot be resolved within our field.

This state of affairs does not mean that voice cannot be a useful concept, however. Rather, I want to argue that the seemingly oppositional logic of

1

voice can be productively deployed within the context of university/public-school literacy partnerships. Instead of trying to imagine that the resolution of the voice debate can occur within any piece of student writing or classroom practice, I propose that when voice is understood as necessarily hybrid, as placing itself in two different domains simultaneously, the seeming contradiction might be understood as operationally enacting a complete form of literacy politics, a politics that can transform the relationship among composition classrooms, university students, and local public schools.

For although the Bartholomae and Elbow dialogue frames the issue of voice within the university curriculum, the dialogue surrounding voice within composition/rhetoric now takes place within the context of our field's *public turn,* a term Paula Mathieu (2005) uses to mark the emerging network of university, community, and public-school partnerships that now exist within universities and university writing programs. In this way, the work of composition/rhetoric has come to include not just the professor/student dynamic discussed by Bartholomae and Elbow, but public-school students, K–12 teachers, and neighborhood activists. In this chapter, then, I want to explore how the concept of "voice" enables a full engagement with the work of the *public turn.*

To this end, I will continue to focus on the development of the Institute for the Study of Literature, Literacy, and Culture by discussing one of its initial projects, *Urban Rhythms,* a project that would place itself within the seemingly oppositional logic of voice as one means to create systemic change within a public school's curriculum. For although debates on voice have been contentious in the field, there also seems to be a pretty unified front that the effects of standards-based education on public-school students has diminished both the personal and curricular diversity of student voices. The difficulty is in understanding how to use those student voices to alter the emergent social and politically conservative definitions of literacy being dispersed in a standards-based environment. This chapter tries to speak to that difficulty.

Urban Rhythms I

During the first years of the institute's existence, I taught an Advanced Composition course that served as one of the initial entry points into the complicated relationship between voice politics and public-school partnerships. It did not start out this way. Instead, the course was initially focused on popular music, with an emphasis on how it could be read as a communal and political response by the working class to mainstream cultural values. Students were asked to read studies of folk music and the blues as well as to study protest music from the 1960s. The end point of the class was to be an examination of politically motivated rap music—for example, the music by Public Enemy—as a current incarnation of class politics.

My thought was that such a course would connect the music most immediate to my students, rap, with a longer tradition of social and political musical expression. The goal was to broaden the historical horizon through which students could understand the political sensibilities and aesthetic actions of working-class culture—here defined as an intercultural and interracial phenomenon—because this diverse sense of their culture most reflected the urban world in which they existed. Ultimately, I wanted them to begin to recognize the role of language in creating a different set of values from the commodity-driven lifestyle being produced by mainstream culture.

In addition to reading about musical history, students were also asked to consider how different composition scholars framed a student's voice in relationship to academic writing. Here, Bartholomae's focus on how the best student writing echoed "improvisation" by both existing within a song structure and manipulating that structure was an important framing of the work the students would undertake. In a Bartholomae-esque move, students were also asked to consider how cultural theorists, such as Dick Hebdige in *Subculture* (1979) and Raymond Williams in "Culture Is Ordinary" (1989), had framed a tradition that valued and analyzed working-class communities as legitimate sites of knowledge production. In their writing, then, students were asked to improvise their own stance within these texts. The course was, I believe, a pretty typical instantiation of composition and cultural studies courses during this time period, the mid-1990s.

The course, however, also drew off of the practices of critical pedagogy. Rather than following a set syllabus (although one was provided), the class also used the texts as prompts to develop their own research agenda. This agenda moved the course in a different direction than intended. As students discussed how music represented a "truer" picture of their home communities, it became evident that a principle site of conflict in defining the value of their home communities had been their urban public-school education. From the experience of teachers who resented their style of dress and vernacular code switching to a school curriculum that seemed designed to keep at bay the beliefs they learned in their home communities, these students considered "schooling" a crucible for turning individuals against their everyday working-class values. Like Paul Willis in *Learning to Labor* (1981), the students in my course told stories of intentionally embedding themselves further in an urban musical culture that valued their voices, their families, and their home lives, often at the risk of their own academic success. Beyond any actual classroom, they also believed that the local media had framed the very categories of their existence (urban, working class) in a negative light.

Although the course was not originally conceived as being connected to the surrounding community, the students began to develop a space where public-school students would be able to write in their own personal voices, à la Elbow, and publish their own vision of urban youth culture. (Notably, publishing a magazine of student writing was an element of Elbow's classroom pedagogy [see Elbow 1995].) The idea was to create a counter-space where the positive nature of the public-school students' lives could be recorded. The result was *Urban Rhythms,* an online journal focused on everyday culture in Philadelphia. As part of that project, some students from my class would travel each week to a local middle school or high school classroom to work with a set of designated writing groups on themes such as music, community, and neighborhoods. They would then publish online the writing produced by these groups. Given the paucity of funding for creative writing in the public schools, teachers dedicated in-class time and provided supervision of the public-school students in exchange for being able to participate in the project.

By directly intervening in the school day, the university students hoped to create a space where public-school students could use their personal experiences and voices to show how their official education failed to provide them with tools to understand urban culture, its concerns, or its rebuilding efforts. Implicit in the project was the belief that through literacy work focused on students' personal voice, a new sense of collective cultural identity could be constructed that could become a vehicle to organize at the school itself for a positive image of urban-ness to become part of the classroom. (To this extent, the early part of the project represented a somewhat traditional view of expressivist conceptions of the political efficacy of voice.) At this point, then, our work as a class became less about the three hours a week spent in a university setting and more about creating the institutional partnerships with public schools that would support this project.

Although this experience was new to my students, it was not new ground within composition/rhetoric. Established studies such as Shirley Brice Heath's *Ways with Words* ([1983] 2006) already provided models for how university and public-school teachers could share knowledge on developing classrooms that brought in the home literacy practices of working-class communities of diverse backgrounds. At that time, other work by Geneva Smitherman (1986), Victor Villanueva (1993), and Ellen Cushman (1998) had or would soon create paradigms through which to understand the ethnic and economic cultures that inhabited the school. This move to connect the university classroom to the public schools also had many existing theoretical and disciplinary paradigms. As Thomas Deans notes in *Writing Partnerships* (2000), the field's ability to perform such work in the present was the result of historical efforts by activists such as Jane Addams and educators such as Thomas Dewey—names unknown to my students, but in whose footsteps they were walking. Indeed, Linda Adler Kassner, Robert Crooks, and Ann Waters's *Writing the Community* (1997) records some of the earliest moments in the reincarnation of such partnerships in the late 1980s. Much of this work was funded by emergent organizations, such as Campus Compact or, later, Imagining America. These forces created an existing pedagogical pathway through which the students and I could legitimate our actions within the department and college. Within this framework, my students were part of both a historic and a current effort to bring university resources to public-school reform efforts.

Yet if the pedagogical and disciplinary tradition authorized an inherent respect for home cultures and for establishing a student-centered inquiry, the progressive sensibilities of *Urban Rhythms* was quickly recast as it entered actual public-school classrooms. Despite meetings with participating teachers, where the writing goals, pedagogy, and overarching project framework were agreed upon, two of my students began to report the difficulties they faced in fully articulating the project in a middle school classroom. They argued that many of the teachers in the program were consistently resisting their students' attempts to portray a complex view of their communities or to connect their experiences to collective efforts for change. Instead, the teachers were moving the students toward defining their experiences in very nationalist or individualistic terms.

This tension was most evident when students were asked to respond to the theme of multiculturalism. When the *Urban Rhythms* project began, the cultural politics of school reform had become dominated by conservative arguments about the centrality of a traditional U.S. culture. Figures such as Lynne Cheney, William Bennett, and E. D. Hirsch had argued for a return to a national cultural literacy that stood against both the progressive politics of the 1960s and, seen as its latest manifestation, identity politics. This cultural push was aligned with a generalized attack on progressive working-class institutions, such as unions, where "American individualism" and "Puritan work ethics" were seen as being stifled by "needless regulations," "unnecessary workers," and "affirmative action." The net effect of this dual strategy was to slowly degrade the cultural underpinnings that had supported the political success of progressive working-class and minority struggles during the late 1960s and 1970s. Indeed, Heath ([1983] 2006) and Smitherman (1986) noted even in the 1980s the potential impact of conservative standards on communities' ability to have an effective voice in their own education. Although there still might be a Black History Month, the daily onslaught of conservative attacks on curriculum and the production of local, state, and national standards embedded any such focus within a larger conservative political context than might be intended—a focus that might be more "bootstraps" than "civil disobedience."

Herein lay the problem with a focus on students' voicing their cultural backgrounds in personal narratives. Given the cultural politics of the United States in the 1990s, a curricular engagement with multiculturalism should have been a progressive gesture, focusing on the struggles of different identities to form collective struggles for recognition. At a time when a narrowly defined U.S. culture was once again being held up as the normative standard, a time when individualism was seen as the collective solution, however, the teachers in the program provided a conservative vision of multiculturalism, a vision that seemed to reinforce negative conceptions of the urban environment rather than call such concepts into question. For instance, teachers actively reinterpreted brief prompts such as "Tell us about your community" as a request for students to provide nostalgic or sentimental portrayals of their heritage—often at the expense of the students' own complex understandings of the values and difficulties of their home culture. For instance, when students were given a framework to write about their ancestry, the following type of poem, written by a sixth-grade student, was often produced:

When I was 5 or 6
I sat in my dad's car.
We'd sing a favorite song of his . . .
"Too-ra-loo-ra-loo-ra
That's an Irish lullaby."

My dad tells me
that his mother sang it to him.
My dad taught me this song
and tales
and rituals
that my ancestors taught his mom.

Today kids like rap music
But me
I sing lullabies
from Ireland.[1]

Here multiculturalism performs two pieces of work. First, Irish ancestry is linked to family values in a fashion that is unthreatening to mainstream

1. Although this poem and other works from *Urban Rhythms* were published under the writers' names, for the purposes of this chapter I have decided not to cite the authors' names. In part, I am discussing the work as common types of writing produced and do not want to implicate individual writers into this critique. In addition, given that this writing occurred when the writers were still in elementary or middle school, I don't want a piece of writing done for school to stand for or be representative of their own unique journey into adulthood.

beliefs: Can anyone really critique a father's singing a lullaby to his child? Rap music, on the contrary, is portrayed as clearly different in values and separate from such familial moments: "Today kids like rap music / But me / I sing lullabies / from Ireland." Here the teacher has clearly interpreted a writing prompt that uses multiculturalism as a way to reaffirm a general conservative aesthetic that devalues urban culture. The active dialogue between teachers, public-school students, and university students and faculty imagined by *Urban Rhythms* had become an enforced and traditional vision of community.

In addition, my university students stated that their public-school counterparts were often directed to reframe their personal stories in terms of the American Dream. Here the teachers' intention was to provide the students with a cultural model that implied that the students, despite their being in a poor urban school, could succeed in life. As one teacher said, "There are no social movements for these kids today; they'll have to do it on their own." To some extent, this view was clearly understandable. Yet the overall effect of teacher participation was to create limitations on what students felt they were able to write (as opposed to discuss with the university students). For this reason, the student responses often parroted the teachers' conservative viewpoint. A sixth-grade student wrote the following typical response to a prompt asking, "Where will you be ten years from now?"

> Ten years from now I will probably have a part-time job and be going to college. I will have my own house and my own car. Ten years from now I will be twenty-two. When I graduate college I would want to get married and have one baby in a year or two. After I graduate I will still have a part-time job just for extra money. I would want to move to a place far away and be able to raise my child in a safe and non-violent environment. When I turn twenty-nine or thirty, I would like to have another child. By that time I will have enough money to raise and support two children. My children will go to catholic school and catholic high school. I will pay for my children to go to college. My life should be very nice.

Clearly, no one would want to discourage the student from such goals or to denigrate the ambition expressed in this piece of writing. Instead, the question should be asked: What image of the urban environment is being created that such an "up by your bootstraps framework" is seen as necessary? Like the ancestry piece, this response portrays the urban environment as unsafe and violent. Things have to change. Yet urban cities appear to possess no individuals and organizations dedicated to revitalizing the area. No entity is mentioned that might aid the student to achieve his goals, nor were any such organizations aligned with the work of the class. As a consequence, the only imagined future for the student (and for his imagined future family) is one outside of the neighborhood, a location reached by individual effort alone. Here I do not mean to critique the student's individual goals, but to highlight how the curriculum and individual comments by a teacher reinforced the idea that the urban environment does not (and cannot) provide such a future life.

My students and I soon learned that simply providing an opportunity for public-school students to write about their culture was inadequate. Despite the sense of equality and power imagined as resulting from transplanting a voice-centered pedagogy into the public-school classroom, a real power difference existed. In the face of teacher resistance, a different strategy was required. The *personal* had clearly failed to become the *political*.

Institutional Framework I

No singular class could be expected to carry the full weight of institutional reform. To understand the imagined value of such a class and to understand how its difficulties reframed the institute's sense of university partnership, the connections between this pedagogical moment and the larger institute must be articulated. For this reason, I want to spend some additional time discussing the development of the institute as the product of composition's growing alignment with cultural studies and its focus on working-class culture and writing.

Much of the institute's work occurred under the heading "writing beyond the curriculum," which was also the title of an article I coauthored with Eli Goldblatt that was designed to locate the institute within the field-specific debate of "writing across the curriculum" (Parks and Goldblatt 2000). The goal was to demonstrate that writing beyond the curriculum represented the next institutional step for writing programs as the influence of cultural studies further integrated itself into composition and as university presidents and administrators were increasingly taking up service-learning/ community partnerships.

Writing beyond the curriculum, then, was a recognition that university writing programs had moved beyond their traditional structure—a structure typically marked by first-year writing, upper-division courses, student support, and faculty development. Writing programs now existed within a larger framework that also included public-school partnerships, community writing groups, literacy research projects, and service-learning courses. The institute, as its mission statement explained, was an attempt to recognize and organize the new writing-beyond-the-curriculum paradigm at a local level:

> The Institute for the Study of Literature, Literacy, and Culture is an alliance of university, public school, and community educators. Housed in the Department of English, the Institute sponsors courses, seminars, workshops, and lectures designed to bring together the educational community surrounding Temple University around a common set of principles:
>
> Every student should have the support necessary to achieve at high standards and gain an understanding of the social context of literacy instruction.
>
> A collaborative relationship should exist among knowledge-producing institutions and disciplines.
>
> Communities should have the means to produce and distribute written and artistic materials that can present and shape group identity as well as forward civic debate.
>
> These goals are based upon the belief that an integrated and productive educational environment requires an active dialogue between educators, neighborhood members, and students about the future of their region.
>
> The Institute is governed by an advisory board, fellows, and a director. The advisory board is structured to ensure representation from all aspects of the educational community surrounding Temple University. At present, the board has representatives from the city school district, a network of community-based teachers, the arts community, Temple's School of Education, and faculty from the humanities and social sciences. Their role is to consider how a particular project from one site can be "braided" into other existing projects or goals. . . .
>
> Institute Fellows are responsible for the actual work of producing interdisciplinary and inter-institutional programs. They create and oversee

projects that bring different elements of the community into contact with each other. For instance, one fellow organized a national conference on Alain Locke, the African American scholar of the Harlem Renaissance. . . . The work of Fellows is supplemented by the work of institute-affiliated faculty and teachers, whose research, disciplinary knowledge, and classroom practice serve as the basis for much of the Institute's programmatic development. The director is responsible for maintaining alliances with community and school organizations, providing support for Fellows, exploring new connections, and discovering funding sources.

The *Urban Rhythms* project was designed, in part, to foster the imagined dialogue and insight into the social construction of literacy among different community members (students, teachers, faculty) and result in a publication that would circulate those insights across the school and larger community. What was almost immediately evident, however, was that the institute was not operating within a theory of community writing and publishing that would foster the development of a collective sensibility among the participants. Instead, the *Urban Rhythms* project seemed to have created a community of individual parts, each operating with its own sense of purpose and ambition. For the institute to become fully operational, to support the goals of writing beyond the curriculum, a community-based theory of writing would also have to be initiated.

The United Kingdom's Federation of Worker Writers and Community Publishers (FWWCP) became the model through which to address this need. Founded a couple of years after the Students' Right to Their Own Language Resolution (see "Students' Right" 1974) was written and published in *College Composition and Communication,* the FWWCP imagined itself as an organization whose practice rested on the radical possibilities of working-class culture. It consisted of more than eighty independent small writing groups located across the United Kingdom and focused on issues of class, race, disability, and immigration. These groups would meet on a regular basis, sharing what they had written for response and critique. Once a set of writings had reached the point where it should have a public audience, readings took place in local spaces, such as pubs and community centers. Finally, the work was often published for distribution within a local neighborhood, although some gained a national audience. (For a history of the FWWCP and its writing strategies, see Woodin 2005.)

It was in the publication process that the progressive elements of the FWWCP became most overt. Unlike in large publishing houses, in the FWWCP the writer became central to the actual layout and production process of any published work emerging out of a writing group. That is, where possible, the FWWCP groups intentionally involved writers in all parts of the writing process, from first draft to laying out text for publication. The book was then distributed through membership groups across the country. In addition to modeling a more egalitarian form of cultural production, this effort was also seen as a direct attack upon capitalist forms of the division of labor:

> It has taken labour and thought to move away from the forms of work of
> the publishing industry—one of whose characteristics is the division of
> labor to the point where responsibility for the shaping of the whole work
> gets removed from the writer, dispersed and lost. In the beginning . . .
> some of the publishing groups in the Federation worked in much the same
> way as conventional publishers as far as the author could see. . . . But as the
> movement developed we learned how to work with writers at every stage of
> making the book. (Maguire et al. [1982] 2010, 39–40)

These strategies were also seen as a response to the growing representation of working-class life in the mass media. Because the writers themselves took control of all aspects of the writing and distribution process, the representation of working-class life remained solely in the hands of the working class. (As discussed in a later chapter, the institute's attempt to replicate this strategy was through its press, New City Community Press).

In its daily practices, then, the FWWCP was committed to rearticulating the connection between the working class and cultural production. In its constitution, the FWWCP defined its relationship to working-class writing in overt political terms: "By 'working-class writing' we mean writing produced within the working-class and socialist movements or in support of the aims of working class activity and self expression" (Coles 2001, 192). The FWWCP's first published collection, *Writing,* states: "We would argue that the energy which powers social struggle is not, in the end, separate or separable from the energy needed to write or paint or compose music: art and politics subsist on the same fuel—a feeling for life and a desire to make something of it. Socialism is rooted in a feeling of life" (1978, 246).

To understand how the FWWCP's writing practices and publications are linked to political advocacy work (beyond the politics of the process), a slight detour into the work of British cultural studies theorists Richard Hoggart and Raymond Williams is necessary. In *The Uses of Literacy* ([1957] 1991), Hoggart wrote from the belief that prior to World War II, working-class culture had developed a unique set of collectivist, anticapitalist value systems—values that were under attack in the new media-saturated and consumer-based economy. In making this argument, Hoggart was attempting to frame the value of working-class culture against the elitist impulses of the Leavasites as well as against the leveling tendencies of the newly infused American consumerist popular culture in Great Britain. (To some extent, the Advanced Composition class from which *Urban Rhythms* emerged echoed elements of this belief by initially choosing to focus on noncommercial folk music as a lens through which to understand the "politics" of modern rap music.)

In "Culture Is Ordinary" ([1958] 1989), Raymond Williams continued Hoggart's line of argument that traditional working-class culture had developed a set of collectivist and egalitarian institutions. He argued that this culture could serve as the basis for a reconfiguration of society in terms of equitable distribution of resources and more environmentally sound economic policies. According to Michael Green, both Hoggart and Williams saw "in strategies of cultural and community politics—the self-making of classes and fractions—the 'speaking' of values inimical to capitalism." And in an age when political parties seemed incapable of adequately supporting working-class rights, "Both were concerned not so much with classes or parties but with cultures of resistance. To put it another way, an adequate political understanding, for both, would require a knowledge of the values and motifs and knowledges generated through the forms of everyday life" (1996, 53).

Indeed, like the FWWCP in its earlier invocation of socialism, British cultural studies scholar Stuart Hall would build on Hoggart and Williams's cultural work to argue in the 1980s that it was also deeply implicated in the production of a new progressive politics. According to Joel Pfister, Hall believed that "the rebuilding of a cold war socialist movement [required] 'cultural and social' as well as 'economic and political' strategic critique [and he] stressed that the study of the cinema or teen-age culture . . . is not for the purposes of appearing trendy but must be grasped as indispensable to a knowledge of 'imaginative resistances of people who have to live within capitalism.'" Hall was "convinced that politics, too narrowly conceived, has been a main cause of the decline of socialism in this country." Attention to the actual theories and resistances of marginalized populations was required (Pfister 1996, 288; see also Hall 1982, 1996). In this sense, the FWWCP was participating in Hall's belief that a focus on culture was also a focus on socialist politics.

The FWWCP's practice of supporting working-class writing and publication was one means by which a collective practice of resistance could evolve from the grassroots. In this way, the baker who spends his day in a bread factory and her nights writing poetry about that work is engaged in *cultural* production and the production of a working-class *political* vision. Indeed, many FWWCP writers produced work wherein their personal experiences are in constant dialogue with the large-scale forces of production shaping economic relations and, as such, reflect a response to that larger context. This conjoining of individual experience with economic narratives is captured in Olive Rogers's "Once I was a washing machine":

Once I was a washing machine
Or was it a cooker? I'm not really sure.
I think I alternated every second day
One thing is certain—
I required very little maintenance.

When did I stop being a washing machine?

Well now, that's a fine question.
I believe it was when I realized
that when my parts wore out
they couldn't be replaced.

But I, as a whole, could. (Rogers 1989, 34)

It is the ability of this personal experience to become enmeshed and reflective of a collective experience that the FWWCP believed captures the common underlying unity of workers spread across Britain. In its anthologies and individual publications, then, the FWWCP consistently presents writers who move from their personal experiences to larger structural issues in society (or vice versa) as a form of social and political critique.

Further, the publication of group members' personal voices was often linked to grassroots political activism by FWWCP member organizations to reestablish control over their neighborhoods, often in opposition to cultural or educational organizations. Universities and public schools were not partners, but opponents. In Brighton, for instance, the local tourist commission initiated a plan that would have favored business in the center of the city over neighborhood businesses. In response, FWWCP members created maps that highlighted the personal histories of neighborhood residents, personalizing the area and drawing tourists to local and family-owned businesses. In the case of Stepney, school children's personal experiences were used as a tool to highlight the educational inequities in the private (in U.S. terms, public) school system. On a national level, in the 1970s the FWWCP became engaged in a struggle with the Arts Council of Britain to fund their organization and, in effect, to fund the counterhegemonic vision of working-class writers. In response, the Arts Council famously described the FWWCP's work as having "no literary merit." Yet, by continuing to seek funding, the FWWCP aimed to directly attack elitist conceptions of what counted as "culture" in Britain. (For a full discussion of the FWWCP struggle with the Arts Council of Britain, see Maguire et al. [1982] 2010.) In this way, the writer's authentic personal voice was interjected into the larger collective struggle to construct a community with an enhanced political and economic entity.

Clearly, such a writing model had allegiances with how composition had framed student voice during the late 1960s and early 1970s. In the most famous example of such pedagogy, the Black Caucus and New University Conference pushed in 1974 for the Students' Right to Their Own Language Resolution, which argued that writing classes were best served by being a forum for students to recognize and validate the dialects of their own communities. In supporting such work, progressive organizations, such as the Conference on College Composition and Communication Progressive

Caucus, had used this same resolution to articulate the student's voice even more directly into the social, arguing that a focus on community languages would produce class alliances among students as well as support larger social and political movements. Such emphases have been further developed in light of a new focus on university and community partnerships. Linda Flower's partnership with the Settlement House in Pittsburgh was beginning to use rhetorical strategies based on the concept of rivaling to create a community dialogue on issues such as neighborhood curfews. Here, students partnered with community members to develop an evening forum where multiple perspectives of the problem, drawn from personal experience, were articulated in front of political and nonprofit organization leaders.

The concept of voice that organized the initial formulation of *Urban Rhythms,* however, had failed to give the writers access to this more collective sense of a writerly identity. Indeed, Bartholomae hints at much when he argues that the turn to "individual identity" in composition studies represented an attempt to put aside issues of social identity. Addressing Elbow, Bartholomae writes,

> I would argue that our current conversations [in the 1990s] are very much a product of an important moment in composition in the early 1970's—one in which Peter played a key role. At a time when the key questions facing composition could have been phrased as questions of linguistic difference—what is good writing and how is that question a question of race, class, or gender?—at a time when composition could have made the scene of instruction the object of scholarly inquiry, there was a general shift away from questions of value and the figure of the writer in a social context to questions of process and the figure of the writer as an individual psychology. (1995, 68)

As detailed earlier, the limits of such a framing became most evident when attempts were made to bring the composition studies framing of "voice" into alignment with its work in the public schools.

I do not, however, want to position Bartholomae as having *won* the debate. As he states, "There is a good bit of common ground here" (1995, 84). Indeed, both he and Elbow ultimately share a common focus in the debate on the "individual voice" and collective identity. Even though both acknowledge that personal voices exist within larger traditions (such as personal narrative for Elbow and academic discourse for Bartholomae), they carve out a space for the student-writer voice to be heard as "individual." Through the difficult work of revision, that is, the student writer ultimately gains a position where she can claim that this is her work against any other individual or tradition of speaking. The result is that the writer is seen to be part of a larger tradition, but his or her value as a writer comes from his or her unique position within that tradition. That is, both Elbow and Bartholomae locate their writers within writing traditions where the individual voice is prioritized as a form of membership—autobiographical and expressivist writing and academic discourse.

The FWWCP's work, however, demonstrated how the Institute for the Study of Literature, Literacy, and Culture would need to change its practice if it were to work fully within the hybrid nature of voice politics. As with Elbow and Bartholomae, one of the institute's pedagogical goals was to produce writing environments that would enable the student to gain an identity within writing traditions—personal or academic. Unlike either figure (or the programs their work represents), however, the institute was also attempting to position itself within a collective tradition of social change. As a potential partner with community organizations, the institute's ultimate goal was to participate in a tradition of collective political action—where the individual voice represented common economic and political concerns or stood for a base of power from which to act. As evidenced by the FWWCP's work, this sense of voice required not just a particular form of writing or particular type of curriculum, but a collective sense of identification across a set of communities—public school, university, community—designed to alter not only what counted as literacy, but what systems supported that literacy. Here the goal was not to stand out within a tradition, but to stand with the community for collective success.

The hybridity of voice, then, is not so much between individual voices and the individual authorial traditions in which a writer stakes out a particular territory. Nor is it the difference between taking on a voice to be "listened to" versus a voice through which to create "individual readings of established traditions." Rather, the hybridity of voice stands for the dual desire both to create a sense of individual identity within traditions existing within a classroom space (expressivist or constructivist or both) and to place that voice within traditions of collective action—sites where individual identity is subsumed under a community's collective needs. "Voice," therefore, can come to stand as a hybrid relationship between individual need and collective action. In developing such work at the institute, those involved in forming community-based writing projects would need to exist both within and beyond the pedagogical and curricular goals set by university writing programs.

Under the rubric of "writing beyond the curriculum," the FWWCP strategy began to provide a solution to the binary construction of voice as existing within composition/rhetoric, and, more directly, within the institute. As modeled by the FWWCP, the purpose of writing beyond the curriculum was not to choose between the authentic/constructed binary embedded within individualist traditions, but to recognize how voice operated on an individual and collective register, requiring the need to work within that binary for the mutual support of both. Supporting both elements of a person's voice was necessary in local communities' long-term struggles for increased local, state, and federal support of their public schools. For the institute, then, the work of its courses would be to create spaces where individual personal voices could gain authority and then, modeling after the FWWCP's publication strategy, to attempt to circulate the collective sense of these voices within the political and social networks that were both defining and delimiting the students' and the community's collective power. In this way, the British model, drawn into dialogue with emergent trends in composition/rhetoric and community partnership models, provided both theoretical and practical sets of tools to recast conceptions of voice toward a broader sense of cultural activism by local communities.

Urban Rhythms II

As the *Urban Rhythms* project began to encounter resistance to allowing public-school students to write about their own experiences in their own terms, it began to adopt a form of publication strategy like the FWWCP's. The students' written work would now be cast within a larger network of urban writers with the intention of demonstrating how urban culture contained both strong communal values and a critique of larger society. Here, the project was enacting the belief of figures such as Raymond Williams that working-class culture should be understood as offering an important set of values on which to reform society. As the introduction to *Urban Rhythms* states,

> Penn Treaty teacher Joel Moore asked his 8th Grade students a blunt question: Who should be the one to write about their homes, photograph their community, represent their lives? Who should collect the fables and tales that make up their past? Who owned their community?
>
> He answered his own question by giving the students cameras, tablets, and pens.
>
> In doing so, they began to collect the tools necessary to take control of their history.
>
> *Urban Rhythms* is committed to publishing the poetry, fiction, and insights of the urban writer and artist. Our belief is that the traditional power of writing and the new technology creates the opportunity for individuals and communities to intervene in the negative representations of urban life. Beneath these harsh stereotypes are children, students, adults, and elders using language and art to revitalize their communities. We hope our journal will be a tool to create a more complex vision of urban existence and, in doing so, participate in the formation of new and progressive communities.
>
> This first issue, then, is also a call to community writers and artists of all ages to share their work. *Urban Rhythms* should publish the voices of parents, aunts, and grandparents; it should publish the voices of public school and university students. It should tell the stories of families that have lived here for generations and families of recent immigrants. *Urban Rhythms* should demonstrate the collective folk and community wisdom that infuses urban life.

As the project began to move toward actually publishing student work, then, we developed a new strategy to highlight how an individual student's personal experience was part of a collective identity and that this collective identity could become part of an effort to build on a community's existing strengths to work toward a better future. Although the project initially was to feature only the writing of public middle school and high school participants, it began to collect writing from a range of individuals in the hopes of demonstrating a common vision that would emerge from working-class urban culture across age, race, and educational backgrounds. The goal was to create linkages between the limited vision allowed to the students and an overarching vision being developed in alternative sites, such as community centers, university classrooms, and academic journals.

(This move to juxtapose vernacular, academic, and community writing was also made in response to Temple's Office of School and Community Partnership K–16 initiative. As one means to encourage urban students to attend college, the director, Lori Shorr, had asked faculty to develop projects that would enable urban school students to imagine what work they might do in college. By expanding the type of writing being published, *Urban Rhythms* demonstrated how the inherently political aspects of the public-school students' writing, which seemed separate from their schools' official curriculum, was actually the topic of study across the city—from aunts and uncles to tenured university faculty. As such, one of the project's goals was to attempt to reframe the meaning of "becoming educated" for the students. By highlighting how this "extracurricular" work was central to university and community research, *Urban Rhythms* was also providing a justification on why continuing one's education was potentially so important.)

From this emphasis, an *Urban Rhythms* Web site was developed in which different voices commented on each other and indicated a larger and more productive urban environment. For instance, the second issue of *Urban Rhythms* opens with an adult college student's stream-of-consciousness narrative that takes the reader through different aspects and neighborhoods of Philadelphia, ultimately arguing that to understand Philadelphia one must first see it as a foreigner would. Ancestry poems follow, but not just the poems that present a soft vision of multiculturalism. These pieces also feature the larger "political context" of ancestry, such as this poem by a fourth-grade student:

> I eat at the Russian breakfast table,
> Grandma serves casha, I complain,
> this is not breakfast food.
> But since Bella worked hard I'll eat it,
> "The Russian way."

Anita and Bella are teaching me about . . .
the appalling losses of WW2 for Russia,
the fundamentals of life,
funny things in the past,
gory things in the past,
and most importantly,
about that time when
Nikita Khrushchev tapped his shoe on the table during
SALT.

In life most people
take the SEPTA train to work.
I take the
Transsiberian Express to Novosibirsk.

The introduction of a larger political context (Khrushchev pounding his shoe) both complicates the simplistic notion of ancestry and opens up a larger conversation about the political nature of ethnic heritages shaping the urban environment. In a sense, it plays on seeing Philadelphia through a foreigner's eyes. This work is furthered by a university undergraduate student's poem that metaphorically connects the flawed origins of the United States to the current situation of urban residents of Philadelphia. Beginning with a reference to the slave labor that helped to build the United States ("cobblestone bones" and "cracked liberty bells"), the reader is provided an image of Philadelphia as a working-class town:

city built on
cobblestone
bones
cracked
liberty bells
chiming in
each time
the sun
christens camden
beginning its
daily commute

across the delaware
avoiding bridge
traffic and tolls
calling it a day
hanging out at
dusk in
west philly
billy penn
chillin with
bird shit
on his nose

Ancestry is not romanticized here. Instead, as the sun travels across the city, it highlights a flawed origin's connection to the present day—from the cracked Liberty Bell to a statue of William Penn (which sits atop city hall) with "bird shit / on his nose." This complex shifting of key images from Philadelphia's history to its current urban culture would be replicated in other work featured in *Urban Rhythms*. In this sense, the published work in *Urban Rhythms* might be seen as enacting Bartholomae's sense of irony—an attempt to take formulaic images (such as the Liberty Bell) and invest them with a meaning particular to that context. Khrushchev's shoe and the Liberty Bell are being invoked to make a specific intervention into how students' literacy education was asking them to speak about their multicultural urban culture. Philadelphia is a diverse city, but it is not the city seen in the nostalgic vision encouraged by a teacher's ancestry assignments.

This intervention was about more than presenting a negative image of the city, however. The university students also recruited and found longer fictional pieces where the urban environment is seen as possessing individuals who are actively working to support each other as they struggle to achieve a successful life in the context of their neighborhoods. Like the ancestry poems, these fictional pieces are also somewhat formulaic; they deploy standard images and the clichés within them to draw the reader into the narrative. What is important about the inclusion of such pieces is the way in which urban life is portrayed. The formulaic writing is actually an intervention into a context that would not authorize productive images of urban culture. In such writing, neighborhoods are not seen simply as places of violence where individuals are alone, but as places that contain a sense of collective support that fosters individual and community development. In a piece by an adult student returning to the university, a young welfare mother is represented as attempting to create a better life for herself. She is supported in this effort by an older woman who looks after children in her home:

The nursery school was actually the home of a six foot tall, middle aged widow named Mrs. Jackson, in whose deep brown arms the two toddlers were enthusiastically intercepted by, the moment they walked through the door. "Good morning, babies!" Mrs. Jackson rained kisses on the twins, but included their twenty-year old mother in her greeting. "How're doing, Mrs. Jackson?" Billie asked as she set the two diaper bags on the floor by the door. "Doin good, real good now that I have all my children here so that we can get started with our day," the caregiver replied, in her distinctively resonant voice, while peering through her bifocals at the five children that were tumbling in her spacious sunken living room. Her gaze, which contained the same clear quality of her voice, then focused on Billie. "Billie, I know that you're concerned about being able to pay me to watch the children, but girl I've told you that's not the reward I get from minding these children, and you know that I am not hurting for any money." Billie shifted her weight on the gleaming hard wood floor of Mrs. Jackson's foyer, "I understand that Mrs. Jackson, but it wouldn't be responsible or fair for me to expect you to take care of the twins if I can't pay you." They both stood silent for a moment, each having nothing to say, for this was a conversation that they had had for the past few weeks, since Billie had lost her Welfare Privileges to paid child care. "I have to go now, I know you all will have a good day," Billie said breaking the uncomfortable silence between the two of them, while turning towards the door. "All right honey, you have yourself a good day, and don't waste any time worryin about those two," Mrs. Jackson said softly, indicating Billie's two contributions in the frolicking group of five that had not yet ceased tumbling. Billie blew kisses, unnoticed by her children that had already begun their school day that promised to be filled with crayola drawings and nursery melodies. While savoring the pleasant images of her children's happy faces, Billie grabbed her backpack and walked out the door.

Such a narrative acts as a corrective both to the teacher ideology of the individual's "having to do it on her own" as well as to harsh portrayals of the urban environment often seen on local television and media outlets. What such a story begins to represent is the unacknowledged social networks that exist within a neighborhood and from which a community-based progressive politics could emerge. As Susan Hyatt argues in "Service Learning, Applied Anthropology, and the Production of Neo-liberal Citizens" (2002), one of the failings of previous urban-reform efforts was the inability to recognize and to build from the community's vernacular support network. The inclusion of such stories embeds public-school students' individual struggles within a larger supportive environment. As *Urban Rhythms* continued, it thus produced a rhetorically important moment for public-school students in that it demonstrated that a *collective* sensibility was being formulated and enacted within their own communities.

It is important to note that as this collective sensibility was being recognized, Temple University professor Richard Shusterman was translating a concept of community into an academic study of rap culture. In *Urban Rhythms,* following the piece about the welfare mother, Shusterman asks the reader to complicate their conception of urban community and race politics. In doing so, he also begins to question how the "narratives" within rap music must be examined as potential calls to collective action—arguing that a larger conversation both inside and outside the community must occur. In his piece entitled "Ghetto" and previously published in a popular rap magazine, Shusterman writes:

> But what does it mean in concrete cultural and practical terms? What does being "ghetto music" mean in terms of the important political, social, and artistic issues which rap faces: controversies concerning racial and ethnic purism and the validity of gangster image and the pimpin style? These problematic issues will have to be resolved collectively by the hip hop community through dialogue, debate, and action—on and off vinyl. No individual can provide the answers, and I certainly would not pretend to, especially since, as a white philosopher and fan of rap I am only a very marginal member of the hip hop community. I want, however, to take this opportunity to lay down some knowledge about the concept of the ghetto and to offer some thoughts about what that concept's history means for rap

as a ghetto music with respect to the issues of isolationist black purism and exclusionary ghetto pride. (Shusterman 1997)

Shusterman's piece also reflects back on the previous narratives within *Urban Rhythms,* both questioning representational stories' ability to account fully for the complexity within the urban context as well as their ability to mobilize conversation. In a sense, Shusterman's piece acts as a call for public and university teachers to move beyond acts of writing to create intercultural and intercommunal dialogues and debates. What he suggests needs to occur now, in the context of partial representation of urban experience in popular culture and in journals such as *Urban Rhythms,* is the creation of new sites in which these experiences are examined for their ability to guide and formulate collective politics. (Not unimportant, the trajectory of the published material, from short poem to academic piece, also demonstrates how public-school students can project their interests through school into the university.)

One way to read the trajectory of *Urban Rhythms* is as beginning a forum where a student's personal vision could become part of a collective struggle to create a new educational and urban community. Indeed, over the project's existence, it expanded from one public-school classroom with approximately thirty students to approximately seven schools and hundreds of students. Teacher and school officials from across the school district regularly adopted *Urban Rhythms* assignments and writing prompts, mailing in student work even when their schools were not formally involved in the project. When these micromoments of classroom and curricular change were published in the on-line journal, they were connected to larger efforts to alter the public image of urban working-class culture, for *Urban Rhythms* was read across the city in both classrooms and nonschool locations, by students and parents, teachers and community members. In fact, the legitimacy that *Urban Rhythms* gained enabled the institute to expand the nature of its public-school partnerships into on-site writing centers in many public schools, developing a larger sense of writing that was connected to recognizing and distributing self-generated representations of urban communities (see chapter 2).

In this way, the institute had moved from one upper-division class, Advanced Composition, to advancing and supporting writing that both critiqued the vision of a conservative and standards-based classroom and to assuming a role within the larger community of education-reform movements. We had, in a limited sense, moved beyond the curriculum.

Institutional Framework II

But had we really succeeded? Did *Urban Rhythms* fulfill the community goals of writing beyond the curriculum?

Upon reflection, I do not think so. Instead, I believe *Urban Rhythms* demonstrated the more difficult and expansive nature of the work to be done. To understand why this is case, it is useful to get a sense of how the work of British theorists and working-class organizations invoked at the outset of the chapter fared in its "travel" to the United States. In developing my class and supporting the growth of *Urban Rhythms,* I had imagined that the strategic intervention (à la Bennett) of a community-based writing initiative would activate connections between teachers and students to local community organizations. Given a stronger history of socialist activism in Britain, for instance, writers across age groups in the FWWCP were able to access collective organizations, such as union or cultural clubs, to discuss in their writing and to draw out political responses to local issues. This was not the case for the *Urban Rhythms* project.

Indeed, across the age groups represented, the basis for much of the writing in *Urban Rhythms* lay outside of established theoretical schools or established institutions. No allusions or asides were made to any outside author or community organization, for instance. In the place of such organizations, formulaic (or cliché) tropes were deployed instead. That is, rather than pointing to the importance of a local parents' group in unifying a community or of a local church in reaching out into the community, the students' pieces invoked the sun as a cross-communal force and an elderly woman caring for children. The project had supplied no linkages to progressive organizations that represented an egalitarian or supportive community model within which the writers could embed their experiences. In the place of such organizations, somewhat clichéd tropes were invoked as standard bearers for community organizations or possible alternative political structures. Despite a recognition of the hybrid nature of voice, both personal and constructed, no actual partnerships were developed with organizations politically working toward connecting an individual's *personal* voice to a new politically empowered *community* voice.

Those of us involved in the project were correct, then, in our belief that public-school students felt a disconnect between the messages of the curriculum and their daily experiences. Beneath the shiny surface of ancestry and multiculturalism, a different set of experiences and politics was emergent. As evidenced in the voices of university and community writers, these emergent politics transcended the curriculum and moved into areas of economic and social justice. They ultimately pointed to the need for politics outside of the classroom. What we did not see, or what we came to see, was that the language of writing beyond the curriculum did not adequately capture what work the institute needed to do. That is, it did not adequately engage with the larger political and economic framework to which this writing was attempting to respond.

To wipe the shit off of William Penn's nose would take a transformation not only of a public-school system, but of the school system's relationship with community organizations dedicated to confronting issues of urban poverty and racism. It was not clear that continuing to expand *Urban Rhythms* across schools would address this larger framework. To truly give this writing traction *beyond the curriculum* demanded more than recording experiences or expanded lesson plans. For the project to be successful, a different type of partnership and pedagogical work seemed necessary. The need to produce a productive crisis had emerged.

Here the work of Georg Lukacs and his analysis of reification became a framework to rearticulate the institute's work into a stronger institutional practice. In *History and Class Consciousness* (1971), Lukacs argues that the practice of capitalism is twofold. First, capitalism reduces a worker's full humanity to a singular moment in the process of production, effectively cutting the worker off from himself and others. Second, capitalism creates the belief that the value of commodities exist outside the relations of humankind—they are somehow distinct in their value from the labor relations that produced them. Lukacs uses the term *reification* to name capitalism's ability to divorce labor and social production from time and place. As a result of these processes, collective concepts such as community or history lose their social and political power:

> [T]he [worker's] personality can do no more than look on helplessly while its own existence is reduced to an isolated particle and fed into an alien system.
>
> [Further,] the mechanical disintegration of the process of production into its components also destroys those bonds that had bound individuals to a community in the days when production was still "organic." In this respect, too, mechanisation makes of them isolated abstract atoms whose work no longer brings them together directly or organically; it becomes mediated to an increasing extent exclusively by the abstract laws of the mechanism which imprisons them. (1971, 90)

It was clear that the FWWCP had positioned its own work as a response to this situation—writers actively engaging in all aspects of the writing and publication process. In doing so, the FWWCP appeared to have found "gaps" in the system of reification where a different truth could emerge. This is possible because, as Lukacs argues, although capitalism has successfully integrated its economic workings into almost all aspects of society, it does not do so with a singular totalizing social narrative. Instead, there are thousands of partial narratives through which the goal of capitalist labor relations and commodity production are inscribed into daily workings of modern life. For Lukacs, the work of these partial narratives is simultaneously to control and to contain countercapitalist moments within the narratives' own area of influence.

Herein lies the potential moment to induce an ideological "crisis," for capitalism's ultimate ability to control and expand throughout society rests on these partial narratives' continually being integrated into each other and continually being woven into the fabric of reification. Lukacs states, "The true structure of society appears rather in the independent, rationalized and formal partial laws whose links with each other are of necessity purely formal (i.e. their formal interdependence can be formally systematized), while as far as concrete realities are concerned they can only be established fortuitous connections" (1971, 101). For this reason, capitalism is constantly in the process of having to develop or maintain purely formal connections that attempt to guide individuals' actual movement and beliefs. However, reality is constantly providing fissures through which individuals can see through such formal linkages to the labor relations underneath. Capitalism might try to repress the role of exploited labor in production, but workers experience the effects daily. In the same way, although it may be the case that formal relationships can be drawn between student need and a curriculum, teachers and students' actual experiences often refute such connections. Students might be asked to write about their ethnic identity, problems facing their communities, and a novel on different pieces of paper, but the connections between these things are still there. Or, to frame it another way, teachers might try to have students voice just a personal characteristic, but students know that their voices also exist on a larger communal and constructivist plane. An individual's experiences necessarily contain oppositional knowledge that allows the person to recognize and exploit gaps in the system of reification.

These gaps between theory and practice, between formal and fortuitous, are evident in a second reading of the *Urban Rhythms* selections. What goes unremarked in the previously discussed writing samples is the different social and economic location of each writer's ethnicity. The "Russian" student had only just begun attending a public school after being in a private school previously and, probably not accidentally, was the only student who posed this identity in political terms. He attended a private school the following year, as did the writer of "Irish Lullaby." The writer of the welfare mother piece was a product of the Philadelphia public-school system, where more than 90 percent of the students live below the poverty line and some high schools graduate only 20 percent of their freshman class. The "William Penn" writer is the adult child of a construction worker, returning to college after living in France. The ways in which economic and political location has marked the length, fluency, and content of each writing sample are evident. Each writer's inability to inhabit comfortably the imaginary class-neutral terrain of ethnicity proposed by public-school teachers is equally clear. *Urban Rhythms* had produced insights from which an overarching view could be formulated to produce a *crisis* in the classroom and, if structured appropriately, in the school. The project failed to act on this moment.

As my students noticed right away, the *Urban Rhythms* project too quickly ceded authority to teachers interested in translating student voices into ethnic paradigms of success, which could be rapidly co-opted and commodified for consumption in consumer capitalism—or, in the world of public education, in grants and professional development opportunities. Certainly one aspect of *Urban Rhythms'* early success among teachers lay in the dividends of participation in such work—teachers received extra pay, attended conferences, and funded similar projects that used video. It soon became clear, though, that *Urban Rhythms* needed to take a different tack. It needed to explore how the common set of insights produced by the students might be framed outside stereotypical concepts of success and how they might enable students and other writers to see alternative connections to their communities outside of education-reform networks.

Instead of such connective work, however, a "bootstraps model" became the overarching interpretative paradigm. Although there was a movement to expand the published writings to include alternative viewpoints, it had little or no impact on the participating schools' actual curriculum. These latent connections did not filter out into the ways in which writing or literacy was being taught. Students might write a community piece for the journal, then quickly return to a study of *The Outsiders,* but with no thematic connections between the two moments. Instead, author studies or personal growth essays were assigned. Despite the hopes of all involved, *Urban Rhythms* became an enrichment program—a moment when community became a reified object, not the object of a political struggle for change.

It is in the attempt to move beyond enrichment that the general usefulness of Lukacs's theory for understanding the work of the institute becomes evident. If a practice can be initiated where these partial narratives become rearticulated in their relationship to each other—a relationship that exceeds the bootstraps paradigm, their formal linkages bumping up against a larger sense of reality—alternative actions and insights might occur. Ultimately, that is, I came to believe that the institute should work not only to provide a space that allows alternative personal narratives to gain a hearing, but to do the work of suturing these narratives to alternative practices that institutionally support the work of political and economic empowerment in a community. This was the lesson of *Urban Rhythms.* After writing and publication, grassroots actions outside the public-school framework had to occur for *Urban Rhythms* as they had for the FWWCP.

Taking on this role, however, would position the institute not as *studying literacy and culture* or necessarily as focused on just those two issues. Rather, the institute would have to draw itself into the community struggles being discussed by the writers in its literacy projects. What might this mean in practice? One fifth-grade student participating in the *Urban Rhythms* project had asked for the following sentence to be published: "I like Fat Joe because he represents himself and PR. I like his songs because they are true." Within a context of rearticulating how the voices featured in *Urban Rhythms* relate, it is possible to imagine this short sentence as the launching point for a series of conversations. Students might compare the writing of this middle school student to the writing of a private-school student to gain a sense of how literacy is sponsored differently across race and class lines. Further conversations might examine the Puerto Rican experience in Philadelphia neighborhoods, Fat Joe's lyrics, English-as-a-second-language instruction in public schools, and Puerto Ricans' economic and legal status. The concept of "representation" might be developed to frame a discussion of what it means for a *successful* community member to act on behalf of those communities. In some ways, the conversation might invoke Antonio Gramsci's sense of an organic intellectual. From this moment, larger conversations concerning the necessary work of building mutual support networks or how to community responses into larger policy and social trends might follow.

Each of these conversations might then be brought alive through partnering with nonprofit advocacy organizations or unformalized networks active in the community. This type of work would build outward from the community's insights and demonstrate to students how community organizations disrupt the rhetorical and policy linkages that deny collective political mobilization. For instance, the fact of abandoned cars in some of Philadelphia's poorer neighborhoods had become widely accepted. The cars seemed linked to a larger perception that poor communities did not tend to their neighborhoods. One community organization, however, demonstrated that many of the cars had been abandoned by individuals who lived outside the neighborhood—rearticulating many cultural narratives and demonstrating that it was a citywide rather than a neighborhood problem. The effort led to the removal of more than fifty thousand cars. Working with such campaigns in a conversation that locates personal experience in such networks would

demonstrate how "writing" can move beyond the curriculum and the disciplinary space of composition/rhetoric and its normative curriculum.

For this reason, *Urban Rhythms* became just one moment in the production of a community-based politics. In a limited sense, the project did
create a space where students' cultural production interrupted the school
curriculum's ability to push away students' culture and the references they
use to understand their own life. And despite the teaching staff's attempted
intervention, the project did produce a sense among students of how the
current curriculum failed to address their communities' immediate social
needs. Through expanding the parameters of the program and its writers
to the K–16 context, the project also fostered a sense that every educational
institution had a responsibility to consider and work through issues of
urban identity and culture. These moments are an example, for Lukacs, of
the web of partial narratives breaking down and of an alternative reality
breaking through. What the project should have done next was to create
a structure within the school through which this latent sensibility could
have been expanded and united with both a history and a present of collective action.

I began to see how this work should drive the institute's theoretical production. For Lukacs, an articulation of oppressed workers' personal experience in an understanding of the social terrain, an understanding that leads
to strategic actions, is exactly the work of theory. Theory emerges out of
community-based cultural production. I started to see how the institute's
theoretical work should support a local group's effort to conceptualize the
latent politics of its community within the totality of the social and political
system. Its work should link these politics to institutional practices (such as
curriculum or local policies) that could empower a community in meeting its
political and economic needs. Further, the institute should also work to disrupt the formal connections that attempt to deny the full range of possible
alliances between a community's culture and public institutions; it should
also work to foster alliances across local cultures. The institute, then, should
rest within the "gaps" and "fissures" of the social terrain in order to support "alternative" alliances and collective possibilities. This work would fully
implement the hybrid nature of voice and the beliefs embedded in writing
beyond the curriculum.

The Voices of New City Writing

At this point, the internal debates within composition/rhetoric might seem far afield from the work that the institute was trying to do. I would argue, however, that this is not the case. As discussed at the outset of this chapter, "voice" has been represented as an either/or proposition—authentically personal or socially constructed. What the *Urban Rhythms* and institute experience demonstrates, however, is that voice is a hybrid—both personal (whether the personal exhibits itself within an expressivist or academic tradition) and communal at the same time. Rather than attempt to resolve the debate concerning voice simply within classroom-based pedagogies, the work should be to construct partnerships that simultaneously enact both properties of voice—simultaneously authorize the individual's voiced experience and work collectively to address the larger social and political contexts in which that personal voice exists. In a sense, our responsibility is to work out of both sides of our mouth, for it is this linguistic jujitsu that will produce the political reconstellation necessary to support urban public schools and the communities they attempt to serve.

In generating this expanded vision, *Urban Rhythms* served a vital purpose in the formation of the institute. It began to map out the terrain of local community politics as well as to demonstrate the need for linking the act of writing to active community organizing. But it was now clear that for this type of work to succeed, more was required than diverse voices networked across the World Wide Web. More was required than community-based writing exercises in a public-school classroom. These tactics were necessary but not sufficient. Instead, the possibility had to be created for participants to come to see the ways in which their personal viewpoints were simultaneously part of a web of existing or emerging progressive community-based institutions. Such work would require creating more community-based writing projects within and outside the public schools, expanding the scope and intent of the institute's publishing efforts, and connecting these publications to grassroots organizations.

I came to see that the institute's work was utopian in the best sense—an effort to participate in the creation of a new city that encompassed the literacy and cultural values of its diverse neighborhoods and cultures. Rather than just "studying literacy and culture," the institute needed to be about the work of putting into place practices that would help to develop the progressive alternatives latent in urban community and neighborhood cultures. To reflect this larger vision, we changed the institute's name to "New City Writing." Under this new name, writing beyond the curriculum would continue to support programs that could open up avenues for new experiences and new voices to be legitimated, but it would also begin to work on producing a "crisis" in the larger frameworks that denied the legitimate political claims of those voices. *Urban Rhythms* had ended, but there was much work still to be done.

Edge Politics

Oppositional Strategies and Collective Politics

Unrecognized producers, poets of their own affairs, trailblazers in the jungles of functionalist rationality . . . they trace "indeterminate trajectories" that are apparently meaningless, since they do not cohere with the constructed, written, and prefabricated space through which they move. They are sentences that remain unpredictable within the space ordered by the organizing techniques of systems. Although they use as their material the vocabularies of established languages . . . although they remain within the framework of prescribed syntaxes . . . these "traverses" remain heterogeneous to the systems they infiltrate and in which they sketch out the guileful ruses of different interests and desires. They circulate, come and go, overflow and drift over an imposed terrain, like the snowy waves of the sea slipping in among rocks and defiles of an established order.

—MICHEL DE CERTEAU, *The Practice of Everyday Life*

WHERE DO OPPOSITIONAL MOMENTS come from? How can our daily practice foster such moments and encourage their growth into successful strategies for change? *Urban Rhythms* had imagined itself as a space where student voices could resist their interpolation, à la Lukacs, into narratives that diminished their agency and their community. As the project continued, however, it became clear that a more systemic set of interventions was necessary, that the hybrid nature of "voice" necessitated both a pedagogical and a political set of actions. In this way, *Urban Rhythms* provided insight on the type of work necessary for writing programs premised on progressive social values and committed to expanding literacy rights within local communities. For real change to occur, we learned, an important step was to connect classroom pedagogy to progressive community organizations.

But are community partnerships really enough? The community partnerships typically discussed in composition/rhetoric journals have been with public schools and small and medium nonprofits. Such partnerships are often formed to blunt or stop conservative social policies on issues such as education, homelessness, and welfare. Implicit in these partnership models is a conception of hegemonic change that works by gaining the consent of those in local agencies to expand or broaden the service opportunities offered. Within such a framework, New City Writing could be understood as an intermediary between local literacy teachers and surrounding communities, offering programs that were marked by a broader definition of literacy (and literacy services). Although such work is valuable, I want to show a possible limitation of such a framing and argue that New City Writing and, by extension, writing programs in general need to take on a more expansive view of partnership based on an alternative and oppositional model of hegemonic politics—one that recognizes the need to respond directly to the coercive power of the state.

In speaking of oppositional politics, however, I do not mean to imply a politics simply based on negation—an effort designed just to stop the forward progress of conservative or reactionary politics. Rather, what I hope to demonstrate is the extent to which the category "oppositional" can also come to stand for the development of an organized community collective that can push for progressive social and political priorities. As defined by James DeFilippis, Robert Fisher, and Eric Shragge, such community efforts "stand in opposition to dominant values and power relations while working to extend and protect social and economic rights." "The implication," they write, "is that the organizations do not 'de-responsibilize' the state. They have an understanding of both the relationship between the community and the state as well as the importance of state intervention to either regulate the market or provide programmes to improve social and economic conditions" (2006, 38). The term *oppositional*, as I use it, comes to stand for both working against conservative politics and working toward progressive social and political goals.

To develop this argument, I want to examine the creation of the Philadelphia Writing Centers Project, an effort that positioned itself against educational and political trends that had limited the value of community-based voices at the city's public schools. Initiated toward the end of 1998, the Philadelphia Writing Centers Project was originally located in one middle school and was a classroom-based project designed to restore an engaged and expansive sense of community in the school's curriculum. It soon expanded into a writing center within the school. This single writing center grew into a network of similar centers in seven other schools and supported by three additional university partners. While this was happening, however, the state government took over the school district, and its vision of creating a decentralized district containing a series of private/public partnerships radically altered the status and work of the writing center network. The complicated (and tumultuous) history of this project, then, provides a rich terrain through which to explore the development of collective strategies and oppositional politics.

Oppositional Voices: Rigorous English-Language Rights for All

With more than two hundred thousand students, the Philadelphia public-school system is the largest public-literacy organization in the city. Throughout the 1980s and 1990s, the public schools faced continued budget deficits and, as a consequence, reported poor student scores on standardized tests. When New City Writing began its original partnerships with the public schools, for instance, it was not uncommon for more than 70 percent of students in comprehensive high schools (which draw from their local communities) to score below "basic" in standardized tests or for many comprehensive high schools to graduate less than 60 percent of the original freshman class. Given this situation, there was intense debate within both the city and the state governments over how much funding should go to the district as well as how resources should be restructured to change teachers' work and raise students' test scores. As a result, the meaning of terms such as *teacher, student,* and *community* were being placed in a crucible of political and social debate.

This crisis was particularly clear in the case of writing instruction. The new curriculum standards called for students to write rigorous academic, creative, and personal essays. A study done by Temple's Office of School and Community Partnerships and the Philadelphia Education Fund, however, had found that middle school students were being asked primarily to write about their personal experiences as well as to make those personal experiences the primary interpretative tool of literature (Shorr and Herold 2002). For instance, *Romeo and Juliet* was often studied for how it connected to the student's personal life and not for its cultural history. And even where such personal writing was assigned, it was not uncommon for students to write less than ten pages in an academic year.

This focus on voice and personal writing was not necessarily a result of literature being taught poorly, although a lack of adequate preparation by teachers in literary studies clearly played a part. Instead, here the expressivist drive by public-school teachers was part of a belief system that wanted to value the voices of minority students. Many of the teachers who would become involved in the Philadelphia Writing Centers Project were deeply enmeshed in the local African American community. Almost all students were African American, Asian, or Latino. These teachers wanted students to develop a positive sense of personal voice and community identity as a response to the media's daily images of minority students as criminals or delinquents. They believed it would enable students to push back against some of the urban issues pressing upon them. For this reason, developing a personal voice through writing was seen as the first step in a politics that attempted to recast the value of African American, Asian, and Latino communities. To many teachers involved in the Philadelphia Writing Centers Project, the exact value of reducing writing to a standardized academic discourse was not clear (and remained unclear), particularly when that discourse intentionally removed the student's education from any relationship to her or his home and community network. Personal writing in these circumstances, then, was also a way to hold on to critical political and social questions.

Of course, it would have been nice if academic writing had been seen as the place for such work. In the current testing climate, however, academic writing was being reframed as unconcerned with the local community of students and more concerned with a rote form of apolitical reading strategies for standardized tests—tests that were taking up an increasingly large amount of the school year. In this context, the teachers felt students were being asked to accept an impoverished sense of literacy instruction that would never be allowed in the wealthy suburbs surrounding Philadelphia.

The continued insistence on personal writing was their way of pushing against such pressures until a more engaged model of academic "discourse" could be instantiated.

Demands for particular types of writing instruction also touched on a teacher's sense of professional identity in terms of authority, expertise, and labor rights. Many teachers began to see themselves as moved from being professionals with a curriculum that they helped to develop to being positioned as "providers" of testing strategies. (Formulaic professional development offered by outside consultants reinforced this sense.) Equally important, this reframing of teachers as "providers" was also in effect a demand for more work without compensation. One of the principle complaints by public-school teachers was the increased labor time required to prepare students for the new writing standards and standardized tests without sufficient professional support or economic incentive. For many teachers, the drive toward standards was slowly whittling away a significant percentage of the professional privileges and class markers they had gained by years of labor. (In fact, during the course of the Philadelphia Writing Centers Project, the Pennsylvania state legislature passed a law effectively ending Philadelphia teachers' ability to strike for better labor conditions.)

Teachers were not the only institutional category being redefined by public debate over writing instruction, however. The students themselves were also being repositioned. On one level, the public nature of standardized test scores had been an important lever to demonstrate the need for increased aid from the state and federal government. The drive to raise test scores, however, also had the affect of limiting the school's curriculum. It was not uncommon to defund arts programs to support curricular and professional development work designed to raise test scores. To a great extent, what counted as literacy education was being redefined as test literacy. In the process, any sense of literacy as connected to community or larger social purposes was being slowly pushed out of the room. This loss of social purpose went against community traditions about the importance of "giving back" and, I believe, further alienated both students and parents from the school.

Temple University, itself, had also publicly criticized public-school students. University president Peter Liacouras complained in the local media that accepting Philadelphia public-school students was hurting the university's academic mission and that the university needed to begin to recruit from the suburban schools. An internal study documenting that students who scored at a "basic" level on standardized tests (as opposed to a proficient or advanced level) could still succeed at the university was not allowed to be released because such data contradicted Liacouras's public statements and went against Temple University's campaign to recast itself as a rigorous school. In this case, public relations trumped an overt commitment to public education. It was in this context that admission requirements for the university also began to rise.

In response to these changes, faculty working outside their departments presented strong counterinitiatives and partnered with university administrators to support community/public-school partnerships. During this time, the vice provost for undergraduate studies supported the development of the Office of School and Community Partnerships, directed by Lori Shorr. The College of Liberal Arts later replicated this initiative. In these offices, systemic faculty and community partnerships were fostered. The Office of School and Community Partnerships also created a universitywide service-learning roundtable. Within the university as a whole, then, it is most accurate to say that a conflict was occurring concerning which aspect of the university would take the lead in community partnerships.

To literacy activists in Philadelphia, however, the situation was less conflicted. For many, the set of circumstances outlined here demonstrated various institutions' slow abandonment of a rich literacy education for urban public-school students. In response, different elements of the literacy community began to organize and to create programs where the network linking the categories of teacher, writing, university, and community would be rearticulated within a progressive context. During the fall of 2000, a coalition of university administrators, college faculty, public-school teachers, community activists, and educational consultants met to discuss how to reposition writing instruction as a seminal tool to understand both local communities and larger sociopolitical trends in education. This cross-institutional alliance was designed to create a program that would bring together participants from across the literacy community to do this pedagogical, curricular, and institutional work.

Sponsored by the Philadelphia Education Fund, this coalition, called Rigorous English Language Arts for All (RELA), would embed expert teachers in middle school classrooms as mentors to help improve classroom instruction. In addition, the expert teacher would work with other teachers across the school to reinvent the possibility of engaged writing instruction through an active reading of the required standards. Here, the personal and the academic would be connected through having students produce writing that had a relationship to issues within the community (*Romeo and Juliet* as love story, as tale of family/gang violence, and so on). The initial implementation sites were several middle schools because it was in the sixth through tenth grades that the seeds of Philadelphia's high dropout rate were sown. Such an emphasis also aligned the effort with city, state, and federal initiatives. In this way, the program would touch on many different levels of school reform in Philadelphia.

One of the initial RELA middle schools, which I call Constitution Hall Middle School, was close to Temple University. For this reason, the Office of School and Community Partnerships recommended that the Philadelphia Education Fund and RELA meet with New City Writing. From the perspective of New City Writing, the project was intriguing because of the way in which "All" in "Rigorous Language Arts for All" was being defined. In part, "All" spoke to the belief that every student deserved a rigorous curriculum. Rather than implying that this rigor would result simply in increased pressure on public-school students, "All" also spoke to the belief that every member of the community—student, teacher, parent, neighbor, and activist—had a stake in the success of a person's literacy education. It was out of this collaborative context that New City Writing agreed to participate.

The actual plan was simple. An expert teacher would work with a school's teaching staff on integrating an engaged writing model into their classrooms, a model that deployed a variety of writing genres to focus on cultural and social issues related to urban communities. The most important component of the project at the outset was to demonstrate that academic writing could take on social or community issues in an effective and engaged fashion. Temple University would establish a service-learning component in its entry-level writing classes, beginning with the midlevel courses and working back to basic-writing courses. University students would be asked to study the debates around public education, the nature of literacy, and the history of their own education. In addition, they would provide literacy tutoring to the middle school students through weekly visits to the public school. Community residents and additional university students would provide tutoring during periods when the service-learning students were in class. (It should be noted that the initial model for the program was based on work done by Education Trust's Carlton Jordan while he was a teacher in Montclair, New Jersey. His ability to translate his intellectual insights and moral conviction regarding all students' ability to learn academic writing into practices for teachers to adopt was a primary reason for RELA's initial success in its many sites across the country.)

For the first year of the partnership, the professional development and service-learning support enabled teachers to expand the range of writing available as well as the required increased revision by students. In response to the teachers' work at Constitution Hall Middle School and numerous university tutors, students who had previously produced only a single sentence in response to a novel were now writing five-page analytical papers. As a result, an increasing number of teachers asked to participate in the program. In addition, university student enrollment in the tutoring class went up each term, with students consistently asking to expand the amount of hours spent at the middle school. Public-school student interest eventually strained the ability of both teachers and university students to effectively meet the demand.

Heading into the second year, these systemic issues led to the creation of a centralized tutoring room. With a dedicated teacher and "writing space" in the middle school building, it was thought more students would be able to meet with tutors, who would now include public-school students and community members. As important, the writing center director, a teacher at the school, would act as a nodal point through which all teachers could discuss and share student writing. Finally, set apart from direct classroom requirements, the center would also become a place where alternative and innovative writing based on community experiences could be fostered and supported. The *radical* nature of RELA, then, was in its reestablishment of teacher authority and its call for a writing model that exceeded the standardized curriculum's narrow goals. In this way, the writing center was attempting to become a space that stood in opposition to many of the political forces defining writing instruction for Philadelphia public-school students and that simultaneously provided a progressive vision of academic and community writing.

Implementing the plan, however, required an evolving set of tactics. It was necessary for participants to develop a set of concrete acts that would allow the RELA project to take hold in the school. These acts took on many forms. Within the school itself, teachers and principals had to work against numerous limits and roadblocks. In order to furnish a room for tutors to meet with students, supply categories and classroom schedules had to be reinterpreted. Student teachers were also put in charge of particular classes to allow one certified teacher to work consistently with university tutors in the tutoring room, despite a policy that dictated that student teachers could not be left alone in a classroom. The certified teacher, "rostered" into the class but really down the hall with tutors, was defined as "being in the classroom." Other teachers intentionally slowed the curriculum down to create space for increased tutoring; they dragged their feet on completing newly assigned tasks or reports; they juggled the academic subjects to create time for tutoring during the school day. New school positions were also created to support the work but were classified in such a way as to avoid scrutiny by the district. RELA used professional development funds for teachers on standards-based education to demonstrate how standards themselves could be reinterpreted to allow greater creative freedom and community commitment. (For instance, a standard on public writing was reinterpreted to generate a community history project with parents as participants.)

Students were also key participants in changing the process. In small but persistent ways, they reinterpreted assignments so that tutor help was required. They used hall passes and bathroom passes to leave one class in order to work with a tutor on a paper due in another class. (Teachers, often aware that such practices were occurring, allowed them.) Students would also stand in groups outside the tutoring room until new hours were added to the schedule. They brought tutors into the lunchroom to get help with writing a particular paper. University students also actively redefined the goals of their own university class, arguing that the course itself was research based and that the object of investigation was the school. They insisted that more university class time be dedicated to tutoring in order to support their research on public education. Collaborative writing by students within the class also argued for how the program could be expanded as well as for how such work modeled an activist vision of English classes.

Similar actions also had to be developed within Temple's English department. At the outset of the RELA project, the department did not offer designated service-learning courses or courses with public-school literacy as a topic. Indeed, despite educating a significant number of education majors, the department had historically not taken on public-school education as part of its mission or identity. For this reason, with the support of the English department chair, it was necessary to intentionally reinterpret existing courses. Developing Prose Styles, typically a course on creative writing, was redefined into a course that could be made to speak to the project's goals. Emphasis was placed on *developing* as a code word for both tutoring (developing writers) and helping a particular population—middle school students—grow in a cognitive sense. The course became the study of how different literacy institutions define and enact literacy codes. This initial act of redefinition was further deployed by taking advantage of a revision of the course catalog in the department. Here, the Advanced Composition course description was altered to authorize similar work without having to go through the university committee structure.

After much collaborative work, then, there were significant areas of change in teachers and students' classroom practices at Constitution Hall Middle School. Against narratives of literacy as testing, students were showing remarkable increases in both the amount and the diversity of their writing; against negative images of urban youth, they were actively seeking out more tutoring hours and reinterpreting the curriculum to demand more one-on-one instruction. Teachers who had previously felt like "providers" were now actively working with each other to form new writing assignments that linked the personal and the academic, writing theory and community practice. Finally, public-school teachers and university faculty saw real improvement in both public-school assignments and the students' work. After two years, the central tutoring room was rededicated as a writing center with the goal of allowing more teachers and students to participate.

To many involved, the project had successfully created an oppositional moment for community voices within the literacy politics of Philadelphia.

Defining an Oppositional Moment

At the outset of this chapter, I defined "oppositional politics" as an attempt both to stop conservative-reactionary policies and to create a progressive alternative. At this point in the story of the Philadelphia Writing Centers Project, the key concern becomes how to analyze this particular oppositional moment, a moment where ad hoc actions seem to have created the space for an expanded set of literacy practices. Does such a moment constitute success? If not, what can be learned from it about the development of a fully articulated oppositional politics?

As one way to begin, I would argue that such an oppositional moment stands at the crossroads between a set of successful tactics and a strategic counterhegemonic practice. To make this clear, it is useful to look at how Michel de Certeau's *The Practice of Everyday Life* distinguishes between a tactic and a strategy. Concerning tactics, he writes:

> [A] tactic is a calculated action determined by the absence of a proper locus. No delimitation of an exteriority, then, provides it with the condition necessary for autonomy. The space of the tactic is the space of the other. Thus, it must play on and with a terrain imposed on it and organized by the law of a foreign power. . . . It does not, therefore, have the options of planning general strategy. . . . It operates in isolated actions, blow by blow. It takes advantage of "opportunities" and depends on them, being without any base where it could stockpile its winnings, build up its own position, and plan raids. What it wins it cannot keep. . . . It must vigilantly make use of the cracks that particular conjunctions open in the surveillance of the proprietary powers. It poaches in them. It creates surprises in them. It can be where it is least expected. It is a guileful ruse. (1988, 36–37)

The initial sets of practices associated with the RELA writing center were clearly tactical interventions. There was literally no space within the school for the project, nor was there any space within the existing schedule or testing initiatives for such an alignment of community and academic work to occur. (The fact that such work actually met the endorsed curriculum only highlighted how the curriculum had been high-jacked by testing pressures.) As shown in the previous section, almost every teacher, faculty, or student action could be considered "opportunistic," an exploitation of gaps in "the surveillance of the propriety powers."

These tactics, however, were more than just simple acts. One of the key elements in understanding the development of the Constitution Hall Middle School writing center is how these tactics became associated with different class and race perspectives—perspectives filtered through the language of writing, teaching, students, and community. In looking at such tactics, then, I would agree with James Scott, who argues in his analysis of resistance that it is important "to grasp the nature of the normative filter through which these self-interested actions must pass and how and why they are socially transformed by this passage" (1985, 306). This perspective allows us to understand that African American teachers were not resisting academic writing out of spite or simply refusing to take on new work. Instead, they were attempting to take a certain race politics and embed it in a system they saw as hostile to African American voices. As it developed, the Philadelphia Writing Centers Project's rhetoric of diverse writing styles and community concerns became a means by which to maintain a progressive African American voice in the school curriculum while also engaging in academic writing. The particular action or tactic deployed was an attempt to embed (or maintain) an alternative vision of writing in the school.

This framing of teacher and student efforts unites intellectual intention and tactical action. As such, it changes our focus from a simple examination of results to the larger question of how such acts were also conceptual and theoretical interventions in the ways writing and literacy were framed. Indeed, it is only through recognizing actors' intentions that the value of personal writing or engaged academic writing becomes clear. James Scott's definition of resistance is particularly apropos here:

> At a first approximation, I might claim that class resistance includes any act(s) by member(s) of a subordinate class that is or are intended either to mitigate or deny claims (for example, rents, taxes, prestige) made on that class by superordinate classes (for example, landlords, large farmers, the

state) or to advance its own claims (for example, work, land, charity, respect) vis-à-vis those superordinate classes. While this definition . . . is not without problems, it does have several advantages. It focuses on the material basis of class relations and class struggle. It allows for both individual and collective acts of resistance. It does not exclude those forms of ideological resistance that challenge the dominant definition of the situation and assert different standards of justice and equity. Finally, it focuses on intentions rather than consequences, recognizing that many acts of resistance may fail to achieve their intended result. (1985, 290)

What the RELA project highlights is that everyday citizens individually or collectively use resistant tactics, which are the basis for oppositional politics, to position their vernacular knowledge and value system against hegemonic culture. These tactics are thus wedded to latent and alternative theories of justice and equality. Inherent in oppositional politics, then, is an alternative community-based vision. Oppositional is not simply negative, but positive as well.

I do not accept Scott's definition of resistance in its entirety, however. As written, his attempt to ground all resistance in economic terms, "the material basis of class relations," seems to deny those traditions that do not necessarily have an exclusively or predominantly economic basis. In fact, it is important to note that the material basis of class relations includes not only economic relations, but cultural and social relations as well. Marx writes:

[T]he number and extent of [the worker's] so-called necessary wants, as also the modes of satisfying them, are themselves the product of historical development, and depend therefore to a great extent on the degree of civilization of a country, more particularly on the conditions under which, and consequently on the habits and degree of comfort in which, the class of free labourers has been formed. In contradistinction therefore to the case of other commodities, there enters into the determination of the value of labour power a historical and moral element. (quoted in Rubin 1975, 163–64)

For many people involved in RELA, the material basis for their concerns was a moral commitment to racial and class equality. Indeed, to many in the project, racial equality had become the normative value through which better labor relations were defined. (I often heard from the teachers that the Pennsylvania legislature would never single out for decertification a predominately white union teaching white students, for instance, as it had singled out the minority teachers and their union.) For that reason, issues of educational justice worked within an acceptance of African American culture. In the case of RELA, then, the alternative sense of justice had to do with respecting the diverse culture of urban students as well as with providing them with the same literacy mobility as suburban students.

Certeau makes the point, however, that individual tactics are not wed to any particular discourse (or to any discourse). The wealthy and the poor, the hegemonic and the counterhegemonic can employ the tactics described here for their own ends as well. This point was clear in the counterresponse to the writing center. Despite strong support from many teachers, some teachers felt the writing center director (a teacher in the school) was receiving an easy assignment. They raised questions about her appointment and the process by which the job was approved; and they cited district and union contract rules in an attempt to block such moves in the future. Because of the center's lack of focus on testing, other teachers felt that it was not doing enough for the school's institutional mission—to raise test scores. These teachers, like the teachers who used the tutoring services, slowed down their classes, but to make more time for test preparation. In a tactic similar to the students' "hall pass" ploy, some teachers also used the writing center as a space to send "difficult" students or to take a break in the school day (an indication of the decline in working conditions). Other students came to the center to play on the computers or to skip a class they did not enjoy. Finally, some faculty in the Temple English department, which housed the service-learning courses that trained and supplied tutors, consistently argued that such work was not academic and not tied to the mission of a liberal arts college. There was intense scrutiny and critique of the class, and it was seen as being less "English" than "English education."

The counterresponse to RELA demonstrated Certeau's point that such tactical interventions occur without a firm place for the actors to stand. Or, rather, as Certeau frames it, counterhegemonic initiatives stand on a precipice, on the edge of discourse. For Certeau, this *edge* represents an area outside the immediate control of hegemonic institutions, such as the school district, and contains a hodgepodge of countercultural concepts, resistant tactics, and alternative organizational structures. Indeed, it is exactly the messy nature of this space that poses a threat to hegemonic control. There is the constant threat that these different components might wed themselves together and gain social traction and power within the larger culture. Maintaining hegemonic control, then, means controlling the type of tactics allowed into the center of public debate as well as disassociating such tactics from oppositional theoretical frameworks. As demonstrated earlier, the struggle to maintain control of tactics and to associate them with particular discourses was directly reflected in the struggle to implement RELA.

An oppositional moment is thus the tentative wedding of counterhegemonic concepts to a particular set of resistant tactics as a way to argue for an alternative theory of justice and rights. In the domain of educational politics, oppositional moments stop the expansion of hegemonic practices that oppress or deny individuals' larger literacy rights. Within this context, I would argue that the writing center served as such a moment within the school, drawing together a disparate set of oppositional theories, linking them to resistance tactics, and creating an alternative vision of literacy instruction.

What had occurred at the middle school, however, was a moment— not a victory. It was not even a solidified strategy. Whereas tactics are a set of practices without a solid base, Certeau writes,

> a strategy [is] the calculation (or manipulation) of power relations that becomes possible as soon as a subject with will or power (a business, an army, a city, a scientific institution) can be isolated. It postulates a place that can be delimited as its own and serve as a base from which relations with an exteriority composed of targets or threats (customers or competitors, enemies . . .) can be managed. As in management, every "strategic" rationalization seeks first of all to distinguish its "own" place, that is, the place of its own power and will, from an "environment." A Cartesian attitude, if you wish; it is an effort to delimit one's own place in a world bewitched by the invisible power of the Other. (1988, 35–36)

Although there was now literally a place to write, a writing center *room*, the counterresponse demonstrated that RELA was clearly acting within a much larger discursive terrain dominated by other teachers, the school district, the labor union, state policies, and federal initiatives. The writing center had only just begun to distinguish itself from the environment; it was still clearly a *tactical* alternative in a larger educational terrain.

As an oppositional moment, then, the writing center was a beachhead or incursion into a larger discursive field. It was a momentary resting spot in the struggle to hold onto alternative intellectual practices and concepts of justice by those now outside the central discursive forces shaping educational, economic, and political power. The question became how to move from resting on the edge of discourse to the more solid space of strategy: How, that is, does a project gain strength to last longer than a moment? How does a project move from resisting a previous system to creating a new one? What are the practices that create a counterhegemonic practice?

From Oppositional to Strategic and Back Again

The question of moving from an oppositional moment to a generalized strategy of oppositional politics ultimately touches on the nature of organizational and counterhegemonic practices. At the outset of New City Writing's involvement in the RELA project, the limited scope of the project (one school) and its limited goals (drawing connections between teachers, students, and the community) allowed for a loose organizational structure. The decision-making process among the local partners (Philadelphia Education Fund, New City Writing, Constitution Hall Middle School) was ad hoc, usually face to face, and in response to an immediate issue. In this way, there was no strong push to generalize the rhetoric and tactics being utilized into a new way of speaking or a new organizational structure. Even the establishment of the fledging writing center did not change the dynamic of collaboration as much as provide a space to attempt to draw more individuals into the conversation.

As the project grew, however, pressure to create a more formalized structure for the work emerged. In part, there was a sense that the original ad hoc tactics were becoming unsustainable. There was increased observation of student teachers, which did not allow the primary teacher to leave the room as freely. The English department was not able to staff enough sections of the course Developing Prose Styles to meet the needs of the writing center; too many public-school students were interested. For this reason, there was a growing gap between need and student/community volunteers. In the face of such obstacles, it was increasingly difficult to sustain momentum or to push back against pressures to link the work more closely with the district's call to improve standardized test scores. A lack of funds was also a concern. When the project initially started, there were funds to pay for different partners to spend time in the school, work with teachers, and train tutors. After two years, these funds were spent.

When a federal program approached the project offering funds, it was met with both relief and trepidation. Gaining Early Awareness and Readiness for Undergraduate Programs (GEAR-UP) was a federal grant program housed in the school district whose aim was to prepare public-school students for college. To that end, it funded public-school/university partnerships focused on preparing students academically for college. Given RELA's success in attracting students to engage in academic writing, GEAR-UP asked the project participants to write a grant application to fund the existing middle school writing center as well as to develop writing centers at six other public schools. In fact, what was particularly intriguing was that the GEAR-UP project would pair public and private universities with high schools and middle schools. The collaboration in the initial RELA project would now encompass different age groups and higher-education institutions.

The rationale behind the district's decision to ask for a writing center network grew from its need to fund programs that were based in academic content areas. Too much of GEAR-UP funds, it was felt, was going to non-academic programming. Because the GEAR-UP grant had a surplus of funds from the previous year, there was money to take on the project without having to cut other initiatives. In that way, the writing center network was not seen as taking away resources. Indeed, $700,000 were approved for the network with little or no debate.

The $700,000, however, made it appear that there was strong support not only from GEAR-UP, but from the school district as well. At a time of teacher shortages, the Writing Centers Project was allotted funds for a full-time substitute teacher to staff each writing center. There were specific funds for faculty development across the schools, and additional funds to pay university students to work as tutors. There was also money to foster communication across the partnerships as well as to support student publications. Taken together, the network was clearly an expensive undertaking.

Despite GEAR-UP's offer to provide significant funding to the RELA project, many of the original partners in the project were reluctant to take on the additional work the funding would require. Programmatically, it was not clear that some of the aspects of the first project could be replicated. There was not the same demand for attention to writing in the new schools as in the original RELA middle school. Larger schools did not have the same sense of faculty community as the original middle school. One participant also felt that the writing center model itself did not engage deeply enough in classroom practice. In the end, however, there was consensus that moving from one school to seven, from a small amount of private funding to a district and federal funding source, and from a marginal status in one school to a major initiative in the district would provide increased power and security for the writing center concept as a whole. Through GEAR-UP funding, the RELA Writing Centers Project would become its own strategic entity, à la Certeau, in the district. To many individuals involved in the project, this shift in identity seemed to imply greater power and control.

It should be noted that this replication of the original project and its shift to a central organizing institution is not a particularly unusual move for reform efforts to make. In fact, it can be argued this growth is exactly what often counts as success. In the process, however, the financial need to support the original project became actualized in an organizational structure that was much more involved in the district and its curricular oversight. The first stage of this oversight was the requirement to develop a formal mission statement delineating *who was in charge* as well as *what would be achieved*—a document never produced by New City Writing for the more ad hoc RELA writing center at Constitution Hall Middle School. Having been promised financial support, that is, the project had to develop a common statement of beliefs that closely modeled the goals of the original writing center, but that could also be understood by university policymakers. The mission statement (reproduced here in the form approved) explained:

The Philadelphia Writing Centers Project will establish on-going university and school partnerships dedicated to improving student academic reading and critical writing skills. The grant will accomplish this through the establishment of a school-based academic writing centers and on-going professional development opportunities.

During a one-week summer institute, site teams will learn tools to achieve the following project goals and to develop a year-long plan to implement them.

Goal 1. Establish a school-based academic writing center where students can receive tutoring in rigorous textual analysis and critical writing strategies.
- dedicated room in building with networked computers
- pre-test/post-system to establish assessment of student learning
- university students working as tutors during school hours
- teacher assignments that will enable full staffing of writing center
- record keeping system
- writing instruction materials, course materials, and books.

Goal 2. Provide professional development opportunities for teachers on how to increase the rigor of academic reading and critical writing assignments in the classroom.
- during summer institute site team examining existing curriculum and decide where and how academic writing instruction can be made more rigorous. New assignments and materials may be added.
- bimonthly visits by university members to school classrooms and visits by teachers to university writing centers and classrooms.
- joint site team professional development through school-based study groups. (SIP [Standards in Practice] process will be used on student writing.)
- content workshops by experts on required readings.
- produce a writing handbook for use in classrooms using student writing

Goal 3. Develop programs and publications which highlight the connection between academic writing and urban communities.
- provide expertise and publication assistance to 8th grade classes working on community service projects. Coordinate publication by New City Press on methods/strategies for developing community writing projects.

• link community writing festivals to activities in public school writing centers. Writers from the United Kingdom as well as Philadelphia's Celebration of Black Writing will provide visiting writers to do one day workshops with students.

Goal 4. Develop research and publication agenda
    • teachers will keep portfolios of student work, assignments and logs on best practices
    • site teams will work together on articles suitable for education/composition journals; articles will also be featured in end-of-year notebook.

The language of the mission statement clearly indicates a participation in many of the key terms and rubrics of the standards movement—use of Standards in Practice, rigorous pre- and post-test assessment, and so on—that was driving instruction within the school district. It also indicates that the Writing Centers Project was designed to embed increased attention to academic texts as a means to develop critical writing skills. What remained unspoken but was nonetheless part of the RELA project was the extent to which these critical writing skills were based in a social and political set of concerns, a critical writing and analysis that responded directly to the urban environment.

Indeed, the structure of the mission statement itself represents a narrative about the goals of writing instruction and its place in the urban environment. The document attempts to cast the historical work of the initial writing center in language that the district could comprehend, without locking itself into a narrow constricted vision of literacy. Although goals 1 and 2 are crafted in language very close to the district's official goals, the remainder of the document attempts to embed this language within the local environment. In the larger Philadelphia Writing Centers Project, the endpoint for academic work becomes linked to a community audience. Goal 3, that is, connects academic writing to urban communities. Through goal 4, "Develop research and publication agenda," teachers and professors are asked to reframe their research and publication work around these goals. The mission statement mutates the language of standards into the context of the need for social and neighborhood commitments to mark literacy studies.

Yet in undertaking this clarifying and organizational work, the original partners were both changing their relationship to the original set of RELA tactics as well taking on a different role with respect to the new participants in the project (i.e., the district and additional schools). In effect, they were moving from being equal partners among each other to being a central organizing staff. (Although this notion of "central staff" is not egalitarian in tone, it was partially a natural result of taking on the financial management of district funds.) This transition is not dissimilar to Gramsci's argument about the relationship between a political party and folk culture. Gramsci argued that latent in the daily experiences of the working class are economic insights that often get expressed through or translated by a residual form of thinking, such as religion or superstition. Within the working class, then, there is already a generalized worldview that must be brought out and organized. For this to occur, the folk culture through which this economic situation is expressed must be delineated or formalized; only then can it become part of a general strategy against hegemonic forces. The chaff of superstitious beliefs, for instance, has to be separated from the kernel of economic insights that it masks. Through such work, a coherent vision of working-class power would be made possible. For Gramsci, it is the political party that will combine existing folk or worker concepts and tactics into an overarching intellectual and pragmatic framework for a class-based counterhegemonic struggle (see Gramsci 1985, 206–75).

As stated earlier, the particular frameworks and tactics used to develop the first writing center grew out of the teachers' everyday culture but were presented in more general concepts, such as *writing, community,* and *student.* Embedded in these terms, however, was the latent sense of economic and cultural politics that was at odds with the elements of the school district's reform agenda. This collective vision, however, had developed over the course of many years. The Writing Centers Project was now taking on the work of uniting individuals within each new school and university partnership to this generalized vision of writing instruction. In effect, the original project had taken on the subject position, if not the name, of a political party, an organizing and clarifying force across the multiple new schools' distinct folk cultures. In that sense, the Writing Centers Project mission statement became a manifesto by the original group of participants to be introduced into the numerous institutions now developing writing centers.

As an organizational model, the Writing Centers Project hoped to coalesce the various rhetorical and tactical moves being made in each school around this vision of literacy instruction. The model was based on the belief that similar institutional experiences among teachers could be drawn upon to create a common community. Over the summer, an intensive series of workshops and meetings were held in which each university/public-school partnership met to formalize the work that lay ahead. It almost immediately became clear that by adopting a centralized *party* structure, the project had failed to plan for how teachers at the local level would have to implement the plan. It failed to recognize, as Scott's work demonstrates, the need for resistance to be spoken initially in the voice of the local situation. During the course of that week, then, each partnership developed initiatives that it believed would work at the local level. Different lead teachers were selected to head the project, plans to bring the principal onboard were developed, and potential student leaders were selected to ensure student support. Through working collaboratively to get each partnering institution to *consent* to this project, a collective sense of decision making was articulated. If only in an initial sense, an emergent counterhegemonic nucleus had been created.

But then the conceptual and practical difficulty of such a model of hegemonic change became evident. During the late part of the summer, the power dynamics within the school district were drastically altered. In response to the previously mentioned poor test scores and chronic budget deficits, the Commonwealth of Pennsylvania passed legislation to *take over* the Philadelphia school district. As part of the takeover, universities, such as Temple University, and for-profit companies, such as Edison and Vanguard, were given "management contracts" that gave them complete control of individuals schools. Other schools were marked for reconstitution, which meant fundamental staff and curricular changes would be implemented. The elected school board was replaced with a state-appointed school-reform commission. GEAR-UP itself went through significant change as reporting lines altered, staff left, and funds were redefined. In fact, in the course of one year, the GEAR-UP director alone changed three times.

The net result of these changes was to disperse the schools in the Writing Centers Project across a wide set of managing institutions. Constitution Hall Middle School was assigned to a for-profit educational management organization; another Writing Centers school went to Temple University; two more were reconstituted. Each school now had a different curriculum and a different set of institutional objectives. School staff changed radically as teachers transferred or resigned to avoid being managed by outside entities. Indeed, many of the teachers in the original RELA project went to the suburbs or to schools untouched by reform. Only one school still had the same principal; another school changed principals four times during the course of the school year. Throughout these upheavals, parents and students staged protests at schools and district offices in their opposition to public education's being turned into a profit-making enterprise.

As the school year opened, then, the Writing Centers Project was facing a completely different situation than originally planned. In a context where teachers and students were losing local control, the project once again became cathected with the desire for professional and intellectual autonomy. The mission statement goals of linking academic, personal, and community writing were again rearticulated into a question of a teacher's right not to become a literacy-test provider. In that context, a school's writing center director became a symbol of teacher authority, working across grades and disciplines to organize enriched visions of writing often in opposition to the goals of standardized tests. More than a broad-based oppositional strategy across schools, the project became about creating oppositional moments in each local institution.

Successful implementation of such moments, however, was directly related to each school's new legal status and whether its immediate alignment was with the district, a university, or a for-profit organization. In the chaos of the first year of state management, the Writing Centers Project was able to succeed at the schools most affected by the reform efforts—those that had been taken over by outside organizations or had new principals. In these schools without strong management in place, senior teachers were able to use the status of the Writing Centers Project as a GEAR-UP initiative to take control of the writing center, create a strong alliance of university and public-school teachers, and develop a nodal point of protest against the changes to their professional status and the school's curricular mission. Students at these schools also literally used the writing centers to reclaim control over their own education—carrying furniture into the room and demanding more tutoring, more input from teachers, and more support from the district.

At these writing centers, teachers worked (against the pressure of testing) to embed a variety of rigorous academic and personal writing assignments as well as to produce collaborative and diverse writing pieces. For instance, in a world where Pennsylvania System of School Assessment (PSSA) test scores were the measure of good writing, one writing center director had Black Panther Elaine Brown speak on the political power of writing and asked students to draft their own written responses. In addition, these centers also created a sense of community among teachers that allowed for innovative curriculum to follow. Throughout the semester, teachers expanded assignments to include community writing and nonmainstream authors.

A report from one high school writing center indicates some of the community-based work being done:

> Students come to the writing center to work on writing assignments and projects. They will either come in on their own or a teacher will send them to get help. They may also come in to use the computers for research. We have tutors from [two universities] available to work with students one-on-one.
>
> We recently started a creative writing group that meets for two hours each week to practice writing. We experiment with different techniques, look at different authors' work, critique each other's work and discuss the craft of writing. We are hoping to publish a book of the group's work sometime this summer.
>
> Recently, we have also been submitting student writing to the local paper. . . . Students have had essays or poems published every week. Last week we submitted [a student's] opinion piece about Iraq.
>
> [Two students] are using the center to work with students on compiling a booklet about their experience doing community service this semester. They are transcribing interviews that they did with some of the older neighborhood residents and are writing essays about homelessness and community service work at the St. Francis Mission House.

Such work clearly went beyond overtly and simply preparing students for standardized tests.

In contrast, the Writing Centers Project could barely begin its work in those sites where the school district had strengthened its control, the reconstituted schools. These schools' principals were placed under intense pressure to make sure that every element of the school be directed toward raising test scores. The Writing Centers Project was positioned as an entity that supported the failed policies of the *old* district and that therefore carried no weight in the *new* district. In these schools, both the principal and the teachers were under threat of immediate transfer if the school's test scores did not improve or if the building staff were not seen as supporting the new drive to raise scores. Here it became politically unwise to support the project. Writing center advocates who stayed on at the school consequently focused their energies on maintaining the current faculty community; oppositional tactics, if used at all, were muted and focused on survival.

Throughout this period, the project's central staff attempted to interpret writing center activity in a fashion recognizable to the *new* school district. At first, the dominant strategy was to highlight the extent to which urban school students were literally demanding more time at the writing centers. In interim reports, teachers were quoted who claimed that the project was a "student[-led] movement for educational rights." Student voices highlighting how often they attended the center, the value they received, and the higher grades earned were also featured in these reports. In this context of student interest and achievement, neighborhood writing projects were treated as a real-life connection to the community. Unfortunately, none of these rhetorical attempts to reframe the language of standards and assessment was successful. The district's response was focused primarily on whether the writing centers could be shown to raise test scores. In a world where resources were being shifted to support test score improvement almost completely, progressive visions of critically engaged students or community-based literacy work did not have sufficient traction.

The larger political narratives that were restructuring the Philadelphia School District, then, ultimately reached into the workings of successful writing centers as well. When the project applied for funding in the second year, the rhetoric of cost cutting, resource management, and standards began to alter the program radically. During the summer before the new school year began, the Writing Centers Project, which was the only project directly linked to academic instruction, was continually reassessed and revised for how it fit the district's standardized curriculum then being put into place. Underlying all of these economic measures was a sense that the GEAR-UP funds should and could instead be used to support the district's goals, meaning that any funds in existing GEAR-UP programs should/could be used to support more general initiatives. On at least five occasions, the project was approved but then was held up again for another person's final signature. At each juncture, there were increased calls for the Writing Centers Project to validate itself through raised student test scores.

The situation was not unlike the ones Certeau describes where those in power use tactics such as foot dragging to stop the implementation of programs that do not fit into the existing hegemonic structure. This is not to say that the Writing Centers Project was inherently radical in the stereotypical sense that Marxist-Leninist diatribes were encouraged. Instead, the centers became places where the true diversity of writing came into contact with the limited aesthetic of standardized testing. As the project responded to each foot-dragging moment in an attempt to survive, however, it became increasingly aligned with the project of standardized test scores.

It was not until midway through this second public-school year, in December, that the project was finally approved. Even then, however, the budget was cut from $700,000 to $140,000. To a great extent, this amount was approved only as a result of intense lobbying for at least a residue of programs linked to academic content to continue. In the new situation, however, the goals associated with the academic content were now directly linked to test score improvement. There was now a clear mandate that the future funding of the Writing Centers Project would depend on demonstrating that students who attended the centers improved their test scores on the district's Terra Nova exams and on Pennsylvania's standardized tests. Indeed, the mission statement now directly linked effective teacher practice to test scores, stating that the Writing Centers Project now needed to "[e]stablish assessment models based on PSSA and Terra Nova scores that will provide the writing centers and public schools the necessary data to improve teaching practices."

The cut in funding eliminated many of the structural supports that had allowed the program to succeed. Funds for supplies were cut; space for each writing center was now shared with other initiatives; money for curriculum and staff training was drastically reduced; central money for a summer workshop was also eliminated. One of the most significant cuts was the replacement of each existing public-school writing center director with noncertified part-time graduate students. This single act served notice that the writing centers were no longer in the control of school staff, but were now being restructured around a very narrow goal—test score improvement.

It is at this point that yet another form of oppositional tactics began to be used. Within the individual school cultures, it was clear that teacher participation in the writing center was being recategorized in terms of testing—one of the concerns motivating the original writing center. There were now moves to create test-preparation units for whole classes to use in the center; individual students were assigned to work with tutors based on low test scores; and university faculty were asked to prepare workshops on the PSSA for public-school teachers. In response, some teachers lodged protests to stop the center from even opening. In one school, union representatives tried to block the hiring of noncertified teaching staff to run the center. In other schools, teachers refused to take on the extra work to staff the center and ensure students would have materials to work on. Meanwhile, students tried to lobby for the centers to continue their focus on community writing and creative fiction and nonfiction. In almost every location, the overarching goal became to resist the translation of the writing center into another form of measurement and control.

At that point, the different writing centers as a *network* no longer had the status of strategic interventions. A set of rooms had been provided for the writing centers, but the contours and supporting mechanisms had so radically altered the Philadelphia Writing Centers Project that it would be unwarranted to imagine that any coherent set of strategies organized its workings. Instead, despite the umbrella of a project manifesto, each different center became a place where each constituency attempted to locate its oppositional tactics, unrelated to another constituency. Teachers attempted to shut a center down; students pushed to have it open; university faculty pushed a vision of academic writing unrelated to test-taking strategies; principals saw the center as a place to teach students how to be successful on standardized tests. This is not to say that individual projects based on alternative vision of writing did not survive in some centers. They did. They survived, however, only through the project sponsor's individual will and not as a supported and widening collective of oppositional political action to the narrowing and limiting vision of writing that was taking over Philadelphia public schools. The individual projects were tactical interventions looking to be an oppositional moment, but they were not strategies for change.

The second stage of the Philadelphia Writing Centers Project had been constructed around a traditional reform model that called for centralizing ideological frameworks and embedding the work within a larger institutional structure. It is unclear whether this model might have ultimately succeeded in replicating the best aspects of the original RELA writing center if large-scale school reform had not occurred. It is clear, however, that such a model was thoroughly inadequate as a response to such quick and profound change in the district. This failure demonstrates a fundamental problem with the Writing Centers Project in its GEAR-UP period. The desire to become a larger part of the terrain, a larger blip on the radar screen, ultimately placed the project outside the control of those most intimately connected to its founding objectives. Becoming visible meant becoming an object of scrutiny and control.

The Writing Centers Project also revealed an implicit misunderstanding of the nature of hegemony. For New City Writing, beginning with *Urban Rhythms,* counterhegemonic struggle had been focused primarily on individual classrooms and individual schools. Each moment was infused with a belief that consent was the principle tool of hegemonic practices. RELA continued this model with the strategy of convincing teachers not to consent to one model of teaching, but to endorse a more engaged form of writing instruction. To a great extent, the Writing Centers Project continued this model and did not focus on the forces of coercion—that is, the literal fact of the state's ability to take over and to alter radically the nature of the public schools. In this way, our conception of counterhegemonic struggle had consistently been too limited; we did not consider how persuasion and small changes in practice were unconnected to altering the power of the state to mandate and coerce schools to act in a certain fashion. Perry Anderson critiques such a notion of hegemony by demonstrating how it appears at points in Gramsci's own work:

> [I]n so far as Gramsci at times suggested that consent primarily pertained to civil society, and civil society possessed primacy over the State, he allowed the conclusion that bourgeois class power was primarily consensual. In this form, the idea of hegemony tends to accredit the notion that dominant mode of bourgeois power in the West—culture—is also the determinant mode, either by suppressing the latter or fusing the two together. It thereby omits the unappealable role in the last instance of [State] force. (1976, 45)

Acting as if hegemonic power were ultimately consensual, the GEAR-UP Writing Centers Project inflated its own sense of power, imagining that persuading individual schools (or even pieces of the district) to take on alternative writing practices enacted counterhegemonic work. In some sense, the participating writing teachers imagined their field of expertise as central to progressive political struggle. The state takeover of the district, however, demonstrated the interrelationship between consent and force in maintaining a hegemonic structure of power; it showed the inadequacy of our "political party" as well as of any sense that writing pedagogy should be seen as central to reform politics.

What RELA and the Writing Centers Project can demonstrate for writing teachers is that actual oppositional politics and counterhegemonic practices imply actions that exist outside our local moment of expertise. Rather than assume the centrality of our work, we need to connect our limited expertise (writing, pedagogy) with those projects that are altering the state's ability to coerce conformity. For instance, the writing center network pushed against the state's coercive power by subverting the classroom's relationship to standardized tests; it did not subvert the state's power to require such tests or work to change what was on the test. In that way, it might be argued that the writing center network, even at its most productive, never achieved the status of oppositional politics. Or, to return to earlier language, its attempt to become a strategic intervention in the district was unrealized because of its limited sense of hegemonic power. In the final section of this chapter, I suggest an alternative model of oppositional politics and counterhegemonic struggle: the *politics of the edge*.

Edge Politics: Working Within and Against
the Confines of Hegemony

Given the complexity of the Philadelphia Writing Centers Project, it is per-haps foolish to imagine that any one lesson could have been drawn from it. It is, however, useful to consider how each stage of the project asked New City Writing to enact and respond with a different set of oppositional practices. Such a focus provides a sense of how New City Writing might have more productively engaged in supporting progressive work by local lit-eracy organizations and literacy activists. It also begins to describe a different strategy for such work, a politics of the edge.

Certeau has highlighted how the terrain at the edge of discourse—a terrain described earlier as a contact zone of tactics, alternative beliefs, counterhegemonic practices—is the space where opposition and hegemony meet. The initial RELA writing center at Constitution Hall Middle School grew out of an alliance with individuals whose politics emerged from this context. In the heightened testing environment of the public schools, even certain visions of middle-class literacy and progressive identity politics had been pushed off the map. When working with one school, New City Writ-ing was able to help coalesce these tactics and participate in the production of an oppositional moment within the school. New City Writing might even have been able to support the center's becoming a strong site of local resistant activity.

We made the mistake, however, of imagining that embedding the proj-ect within the larger institution of the school district would strengthen the initiative. In this instance, strategy became not about fostering oppositional moments from the edge, but about adopting a traditional model of reform. I use the word *reform* intentionally. Taking on a reform model of inclusion and replication necessarily muted a more alternative set of tactics and ideolo-gies. The district's support both allowed the expansion of writing practices at the school and placed them under the panopticon of raising test scores. By spreading this work across so many sites, the reform model also pushed the project to the point where New City Writing could no longer be as engaged in each university/school partnership, further ceding power to the district. Indeed, as the project continued, it became clear that New City Writing lacked the resources to marshal the different writing centers (and individuals involved) into a similar ideological and tactical alliance that was created at the original middle school.

Although this says something about the relative strength of New City Writing to the school district, it says something more important about how academics traditionally imagine organizing for resistance through the model of reform. Lacking sufficient funds, university- and community-based efforts often attempt to expand by moving farther into the system; the argument becomes that embedding our work in the system produces both larger structural change and needed financial support. Based on the Writing Centers Project experience, however, I would argue that incorporation is not necessarily success. It does not even take into account the very strengths that university-based literacy organizations, such as New City Writing, bring to such work. Indeed, our strengths lie elsewhere.

Instead of large-scale program management, university-based literacy organizations such as New City Writing (and writing programs in general) should locate themselves on Certeau's edge of social and cultural debates. They should use their resources to enable the advocates of vernacular knowledges to form and organize initial tactical forays into particular institutions. In the process, they can help to formalize and publish materials that represent these vernacular or nonmainstream viewpoints, using the university's status to validate them for community, professional, and political audiences. Once such an initiative becomes established as an oppositional moment, university-based writing programs can become equal partners with a variety of political, cultural, and social organizations. Here, the work with other organizations should be to coordinate the multiple activities occurring into a generalized oppositional strategy that both presents an alternative form of literacy for individuals to enact (or consent to) and simultaneously works to limit the ability of the state (or state testing) to mandate a singular model. In this process, the local moment becomes a nodal point to organize against larger state coercion.

This collaborative strategy is important even when the central issue is writing or literacy. That is, even when writing is our central area of expertise, we should not go it alone. To attempt to expand an oppositional moment throughout a system from the singular vantage point of the university or a university writing program ignores the variety of knowledges that are necessary to enact a truly counterhegemonic project. It assumes that the university writing program or university-based literacy organization, such as New City Writing, has an expertise that simply is not there. For instance, New City Writing did not have the background in school-reform history, the dynamics of public-school union contracts, state and federal legislation, or congressional mandates in order to respond fully to the district tactics. By attempting to establish a network consisting only of university faculty, public-school teachers, and tutors, New City Writing failed to think through all the components necessary to produce real counterhegemonic change (and the time table in which such change could occur) within a school district. Once alternative literacy practices are established within a local moment, a university-based literacy initiative needs to embed itself within the larger social and political network that is resisting attempts to limit literacy instruction; indeed, some of its central work will be to support the larger network's efforts to explain the value of vernacular language patterns that are attempting to be recognized and supported.

For this very reason, at the local moment of decision making, New City Writing probably should not have decided to expand the scope of its expertise to additional schools. Instead, it should have worked to embed the project even more deeply in that one school where the project was started (creating a deep strategic intervention in one site) to establish it as a fully functioning countermodel to testing literacy. Instead of a writing center network, we should have then turned to the work of building an oppositional political network within the district and state—a network of pressure points through which the balance of hegemonic power would be slowly tipped toward a more expansive vision of writing instruction.

In such a scenario, alliances should have been made with alternative non-school-based organizations so that collective pressure might have had more success at producing systemic change. An argument can be made and was made that rather than accepting funds from GEAR-UP, New City Writing should have worked within GEAR-UP to foster alternative visions of how the grant should be spent, providing counterreadings of the federal grant language that would have forbidden its dispersal throughout the district. (Indeed, Lori Shorr, director of Temple's Office of School and Community

Partnerships, did take exactly this approach.) New City Writing might also have worked to support legislative efforts to alter the state's ability to take over the district. The framework of such action, however, would be to see the work of New City Writing not as program management and expansion, but as the use of its expertise to foster the empowerment of the *edge* across the district, city, and state. In this way, community and university partnerships are an initial but not a final step in the effort to produce real social change. In effect, New City needed to be the *strategic* hub within our university, organizing curricular and community partnership efforts that could model progressive literacy work, but be just one *tactical* partner within the larger strategic work of multifaceted coalitions that could effectively produce change.

Such a role can, of course, be cast as a very limited and seemingly modest one. It often seems more important to take on programs, sustain long partnerships, and move them into the system. As expressed elsewhere in this book, we do need to ground our literacy work within a core of primary community partnerships. We need to realize, however, that alternative and innovative literacy practices will be expanded only through traditional political work. Political change is ultimately produced by pressure points across hegemonic systems of power at the local, regional, and state levels. Writing programs can organize vernacular visions of literacy and provide the tools to turn those visions into public discourse, but they should ultimately be part of a larger network of actions that confront the *state's* ability to coerce conformity. We need to recognize our role in these battles and imagine the collaborative oppositional politics that follow.

Of course, implicit here is the belief that university-based literacy programs should foster such work, that our role is necessarily oppositional. The specifics of the Philadelphia case aside, it would be difficult to argue that current popular versions of literacy (or assessing literacy) endorse the range of language and genres most writing programs attempt to foster. It would be difficult to say we are satisfied with how children and adults are being taught to think about and to use language. In the current national context, I would argue that our role is, in fact, necessarily oppositional. We should positions ourselves within this debate and foster myriad strategic interventions, for it is this *edge* that is the battleground for literacy. No matter how good it might feel to imagine ourselves more central, believing ourselves to be central is the ultimate trick hegemony plays. By positioning ourselves on the edge, however, as one partner within a large coalition of players, we undertake the slow work of matching hegemonic incursion with a collaborative counterhegemonic response. It is this form of oppositional politics that should guide our work.

Strategic Speculations
on the Question of Value

The Role of Community Publishing in English Studies

> What I mean by dwelling in the ruins is not despair or cynicism; it is
> simply the abandonment of the religious attitude toward political action,
> including the pious postponement or renunciation of action. . . . Change
> comes neither from within nor from without, but from the difficult
> space—neither inside nor outside—where one is. To say we cannot
> redeem or rebuild the university is not to argue for powerlessness; it is to
> insist that academics must work without alibis.
>
> —BILL READINGS, *The University in Ruins*

VALUE IS A SLIPPERY TERM that permeates our work in English studies.
Within literary studies, value has a long history of being associated with
canon formation and curriculum reform. One way to mark changes in literary studies is to examine the revaluing of formally subjugated writers and
their inclusion in the daily practices of the academy, such as the classroom,
the scholarly journal, and the academic conference. The focus on subjugated
or marginalized voices is not unique to literature, however. Over the past
decade, there has also been a focus in composition studies on connecting
its practices to underrepresented populations through such vehicles as service-learning or community publishing projects. This work has emphasized

An earlier version of this essay appeared as "Strategic Speculations on the Question of
Value: The Role of Community Publishing in English Studies," *College English* 71, no. 5 (May
2009). © National Council of Teachers of English. Used with permission.

including and revaluing formerly excluded or ignored voices. The value of this work is not only the "discovery" of new voices, but also the actual services offered to these communities.

Portraying these two trends within English studies as simultaneous, however, raises the issue of whether these efforts are actually part of a similar project or not. Does the *value* of service learning and community publications intersect with the *value* associated with canon and curriculum reform? If not, what might it mean to bring this work together and to push it to the next level of articulation? How can such work be transformed, to invoke Certeau, from a local tactical response to a strategic intervention in how English studies operates? That is, where can the concept of "value" actually take us?

To explore these questions, I examine one of the early community publishing collaborations between New City Writing and a local Philadelphia urban neighborhood that I will call "Glassville." The goal of the project was to publish an oral history of the neighborhood by bringing together a service-learning course, the community's neighborhood association, Temple's First-Year Writing Program, and faculty from multiple departments. Instead, the project resulted in a community-led protest, where issues of race, class, and power had to be recognized and negotiated. It is in the working through of such a moment, I argue, that a revised conception of value, one embedded in the process of community publishing, can draw together the work of English studies and composition studies.

Partnership

The Glassville project began when a professor contacted New City Writing. The professor had initiated an ethnographic field project and encountered Glassville, a fifteen-block neighborhood that for fifty years had maintained an integrated neighborhood with no apparent racial strife or hate crimes (Bissinger 1998, 89–95). This achievement was notable because an adjacent neighborhood was known for its history of racial conflict. Although Glassville had experienced many of the economic downturns and job losses that confronted the rest of the city, the fact that it had remained an integrated community in the face of such changes stood in stark contrast to the outcome in other areas (Adams et al. 1993).

As a result of the ethnographic project, the neighborhood association expressed an interest in having the neighborhood's history published. The professor contacted New City Writing because I had recently formed New City Community Press (newcitypress.org), a community press dedicated to formalizing much of the writing produced in our literacy and service-learning work with Philadelphia neighborhoods. After discussions among New City Writing staff, the neighborhood association, and involved faculty, a project was soon formed that would bundle these interests together to produce a book of resident interviews, tentatively titled *Glassville Memories*.

Each partner went into the project, however, with a variety of interests. For members of the Glassville neighborhood association, the book would do more than just record their voices. Part of their struggle was to be recognized as a unique entity within the network of city neighborhoods. In that regard, the book would act as a symbol of the community's distinct identity and, as a consequence, validate the residents' arguments for increased political and economic support. One of their goals for the book, then, was political—to document and legitimate the community's needs within the city's urban-renewal plans.

From my perspective, the book would enable the institute to the move farther toward an expanded vision of writing beyond the curriculum. As discussed in previous chapters, New City Writing had attempted to integrate the different literacy and community voices of the surrounding neighborhoods into the writing curriculum through both expanded readings and service-learning opportunities, as well as to form progressive partnerships with community organizations. Much of this internal curricular work had occurred at the upper end of the English department curriculum. *Glassville Memories*, however, would be used in our introductory writing courses. The hope was that such a text would disrupt an introductory writing curriculum that, by focusing heavily on the values of academic discourse, had not paid enough attention to the exclusions that shaped literacy in our city (for a synopsis of this curriculum, see Sullivan et al. 1997). Produced in conjunction with a community organization, the proposed book would make evident how issues of literacy and power were present in a student's "backyard." In this regard, the press and community members would be coming together to form a new community-based textbook for the university's first-year writing course.

To advertise the existence of the community and to expand the reach of the book, the Glassville neighborhood association and the press also agreed to introduce this book into a *network of exchange*. In one sense, we were already doing this in that the book would be assigned across forty sections of the university's basic-writing course, which meant that approximately one thousand students would purchase it in one semester alone. It was also decided, however, that the book would be advertised to other writing programs and disciplines as well as to local and national booksellers. It was hoped that the book would ultimately reach a wide audience of those generally interested in urban life. To ensure that the neighborhood residents were not exploited, a portion of the profits from all these different venues would be shared with the Glassville neighborhood association, returning to the residents some of the economic value of their stories.

The project was to be directed by two professors, each of whom brought unique talents to the project. One professor was a trained ethnographer who had extensive experience in community-based projects. She also had the trust of the Glassville neighborhood association. The other professor had extensive experience working with community writers and had taken a leadership role in our emergent community press. Together they brought a range of expertise and insight to the project.

Difficulties occurred almost immediately, however. As part of the project, the two professors were to co-teach a specifically marked undergraduate course cross-listed between their two departments. A new university budgeting procedure made it impossible to have the course co-taught or cross-listed, however. Instead, the professor with community press experience was assigned as the sole instructor. Moreover, neither was given release time to work on the project. Whereas one was at least assigned to the class, the other faculty member had to volunteer extensive time to working with the students. Despite these complications, the two professors brought the students to the community during the term, arranged for interviews, and discussed interview protocols in class. This project nevertheless depended on their providing sufficient time and support to conjoin their expertise for the benefit of the student ethnographers and community members. Systemically, this did not occur, and gaps in communication began to develop, a fact that soon impacted the project's future direction.

The neighborhood association had never before been involved in such an extensive project. Although some of the residents had the experience of being interviewed for other community history projects, a focus on their particular community was new. In addition, as discussed after the book's publication, many of the residents had been unaware of how their voices actually phrased or articulated ideas in everyday speech and thus would appear in print. Many of the residents interviewed were also senior citizens with a different sense of what it meant to interact with college students in terms of respect and building a relationship. For these residents, the model of students just dropping in to interview them and then returning to their class seemed alienating and, to some extent, rude. (They expressed this sentiment to me personally at the community meeting after the book's publication.)

Finally, particular issues arose around editorial control of the book. New City Community Press had made a commitment to producing books focused on community voices not often represented in mainstream culture and to showcasing those voices with high production values. The belief was that each community should be able to frame and develop its own communal and historical identity as well as to have its aesthetic identity fully represented. Previous publications, such as *No Restraints* (Ott 2002), a book on our city's disability community, had used handwriting, artwork, and graffiti to represent a community's sense of its voice. Our editorial staff had produced books that were well received by the intended audiences and garnered awards from city leaders. Given my goals for this project, however, the Glassville book's audience was more nebulous than the audience for any previous publication. For instance, the potential readers included students in writing programs, the community residents, academics, and an unformalized general audience. In addition, I believed that, unlike any other book produced by the press, the book also had to also represent its connection to an undergraduate course—the specific context from which the book would emerge and, for the university, to which it would return. This meant some of the work would be uneven, representing the different skills students brought to the project.

Consequently, numerous populations and individuals now felt they should have a say in the book's formulation, so it became an open question what conglomeration of interests represented the book's "community." In order to have the book ready for the following academic year, however, we also had to define this "community" very quickly. Despite these radical departures from the press's earlier projects, we did not create any new process to negotiate this new terrain or the competing sense of ownership and authority. To some extent, we did not realize the ways that producing a text for "classroom use" and "community use" would infiltrate and mutate both the project and the workings of the press.

As might have been expected by those more experienced in community-based partnerships, the project began slowly to unravel. The original bundling of interests had failed to create a firm sense of how the competing needs would be negotiated. Communication among the partners, already hindered by a lack of systemic university support, was further damaged by school calendars, faculty leaves, lack of transportation, elderly residents' health problems, the need for students to work extra jobs to stay in school, and other difficulties. Under these conditions, the university course working on the project slowly became cut off from continued dialogue with the community. Imperceptibly, the project's overarching goal became more about representing the work of the students than the voices of the community.

This shift altered both the editorial process and the status of the student interviews. As a product of a service-learning class, the interviews came to reflect the students' uneven commitment to the project. On the one hand, some interviewers were able to grasp the neighborhood's history and asked the residents to discuss the loss of businesses, the attempts to rebuild the job base, and changing demographics within the community. One such student and resident exchange went as follows:

STUDENT: And what were some of the issues that were of concern to the community?

GLASSVILLE RESIDENT: We have things such as the quality of life issues such as too much trash. People come down here and unload big dump trucks in our neighborhood, thinking it is just a dumping ground. We have a lot of light industrial business down there. We have no recreation for our youth whatsoever. We have some homes that are in desperate need of repair. There is a high unemployment rate amongst our teens. There are many things that we just ignored, but we are on the ball now.

In these interviews, the development of the Glassville neighborhood association was represented as an important act of community politics. However, the book also included moments of confusion between the students and the neighborhood residents about important community institutions. At times, this led to awkward and unproductive moments—moments that would come back to haunt the publication.

> STUDENT: St Mary's what?
> GLASSVILLE RESIDENT #1: St. Mary's of Szczecin.
> STUDENT: How do you spell that?
> GLASSVILLE RESIDENT #1: S-Z
> GLASSVILLE RESIDENT #2: C-Z
> GLASSVILLE RESIDENT #1: E . . . you got me. [Smiling.]
> GLASSVILLE RESIDENT #1: [Laughs] Write it down.
> STUDENT: [Handing resident #1 a notebook.] Here, do you want to write it on this?
> GLASSVILLE RESIDENT #2: S-Z-C-Z-E-C-I-N
> GLASSVILLE RESIDENT #1: [Handing his wife the notebook] Here you write it. I'm the Pollack, and she has to write it.
> [STUDENT]: What does that mean, Szczecin? [Laughs.]

In one sense, this exchange was friendly. It also demonstrates, however, that the student did not seem to have the necessary community or historical details to conduct the interview effectively. Other interview questions also remained at a personal level, such as "When was your first kiss?" Here community members had to struggle to create a context for a broader community or worldview to emerge. Although weak in terms of research strategies, such moments were seen as appropriate for inclusion because the book was coming to be seen primarily as serving a pedagogical purpose; in terms of the goals of the writing program, these weaknesses would teach students how to do better ethnographic work.

Pedagogical goals, however, were not the goals of the community. Upon publication, the book immediately became a site of disappointment and anger for Glassville. Many residents were unhappy with the unequal lengths of the interviews, believing certain residents were featured more prominently than deserved. Others felt that important aspects of their own lives or of the community's history should have been included in the book—either through additional interviews or supplementary materials. The book also contained several historical mistakes about the community. Concern was also raised that the student-created interview transcriptions had been used in the book instead of organizing the community voices around themes or categories. Because of this decision, many were shocked at seeing how they "sounded" on the page. (One resident, noting that the interviews were exact transcriptions, complained that she sounded like the "village idiot.") Some comments, casually made in conversation, now appeared to them as racist or antireligious. (For example, it is one thing to refer to yourself jokingly as a "Pollack" in the privacy of your living room; it is another to have that comment read by one thousand students in university classrooms.)

The book's cover also became a site of anger and infuriated elements of the community. The self-image of the Glassville neighborhood association would have been best represented by a cover showing an integrated neighborhood scene. During the term, however, the students had not worked with the community to select a cover, and once the term was over, many of the students were no longer available. In the absence of such input, a cover was designed that was intended to reflect the students' perception that the book was a historical study of individuals. Instead of featuring an integrated neighborhood in the present, the front cover featured a handwritten title, a picture of a white resident on her way to the prom, circa 1960, laid over a set of a city map that bled over to the back cover, where photographs of an African American family, circa 1950, appeared. Many residents did not endorse this attempt to create a continuity of images, however. Instead, as one resident stated, "White on the front, black on the back, of course." In response, the Glassville neighborhood association wrote letters of protest and demanded retractions and revisions throughout the text.

Almost immediately after the book was given to the community, I received a call from the neighborhood association president, who presented the residents' concerns in no uncertain terms. Promising to make things right, I offered to meet with any and all residents to discuss what had gone wrong and what needed to be done to fix the project. A community meeting was called whose sole topic of discussion would be the publication.

Neighbors spoke of being betrayed and ignored. Complaints were lodged against the student ethnographers, who had "suddenly" stopped coming. The university's commitment to be a true partner was questioned.

Prior to the meeting, I had decided not only to apologize for the mistakes in the book, but also to stress the positive value of the publication— how it showed the remarkable nature of Glassville and how students could learn from the residents' voices. No one, I felt, wanted to be told that his or her participation was meaningless. In this sense, I stood my ground on the importance of their voices being heard, even if the process and publication had failed them. I also publicly promised that New City Community Press would fix the book to their satisfaction. As might be expected, folks questioned whether it could ever be fixed. There really was no response to this comment other than to ask for another chance to make things right— whatever that might take.

These dramatic moments, however, do not capture the full response: it was not as simple as the entire community's rejecting the book. Even during the height of the controversy, the book began to integrate itself productively into the community's networks of exchange. Some community members were happy with their interviews and sold the book as a fund-raiser for their church. Some also felt that when seen as a continuous image, the cover was "quite striking." Many residents bought extra copies to give to family members. At the same meeting where anger was so high, some argued that the community simply did not want to admit to some of the features represented in the book. One neighborhood resident offered a prayer of thanks for the book's publication. Community anger also lessened when an involved professor used hard-earned community respect to endorse the possibility of finding a solution. As a result, the attempt to have a retraction or apology put on the cover was rejected. Finally, as discussed later, the association ultimately endorsed the use to which the book was put in our basic-writing classrooms, where, in ways not intended, it served to highlight the difficult and exacting nature of university/community publication partnerships.

Nevertheless, the Glassville project, in light of its own goals, had failed on many counts. The neighborhood association would not use the book to advertise the community or to recruit members. Without the association's support, plans to market the book to other writing programs and to bookstores had to be shelved. Tensions between participants who defined the book's goal as a community publication and others who defined the book as a student research publication reached a point where future collaboration no longer seemed possible. In an attempt to cross the divisions among the university, the community, and the curriculum, a divisive and flawed product had been produced.

Rethinking Value

In retrospect, it seems clear that the Glassville project embedded itself within a particular version of value, one that initially might be explained by Marx's theory of value and its incorporation into the academy. The shorthand version of Marx's theory goes as follows: Individual workers, dispossessed of the means of production, are forced to sell the only value they possess, their use-value as laborers. For this labor, the capitalist provides them with enough wages to sustain their daily existence; this wage is the labor's exchange-value. The capitalist trick is to force the worker to labor beyond the point of his mere reproduction; that is, workers will provide more use-value than they receive in exchange-value. Marx concludes that the worker fails to see this exploitation because of the fetishism of commodities: the worker believes it is the inherent quality of an object, not his own labor, that creates value (see Marx 1977, 1:125–244).

Marx's view that capitalism produced a culture that masks worker exploitation has been translated into an argument that the canon has worked to exclude the full range of writing being produced within a culture as well as the economic and historical context from which that writing arose. The canon has fetishized certain texts and claimed them as "art" by removing them from the context of their production. Under the guise of objectivity, the canon has become a vehicle for representing the desires of the bourgeoisie or middle class. In response, Marxist literary critics have argued that previously marginalized texts, such as those written by the working class, should be placed within the literary canon. Indeed, marginalized writing is often held to possess the progressive values that critics claim the cannon has traditionally denied. This version of canon reform has led to a situation where English studies is asked to choose between two opposing sets of texts (canonical and noncanonical), each seen as possessing opposing moral values (Guillory 1993, 25).

A similar narrative can be made about the integration of nonstandard texts into composition classrooms. As James Berlin argues in *Rhetoric and Reality* (1987), the *canonized* text for composition classrooms is the expository essay embedded within the current traditionalist paradigm. Since the late 1960s, however, nonstandard writing and nonhegemonic voices have become part of the picture. A look at mainstream readers, such as *Negotiating Differences* (Bizzell and Herzberg 1996), or at standard texts, such as Mike Rose's *Lives on the Boundary* (1990), reveals how marginalized identities have been incorporated into a "composition canon." As was the case with the literary canon, these alternative voices are often brought in as a way to represent alternative moral values for students to study. Their inclusion poses the question of which set of essentialized voices (canonical or noncanonical) composition should endorse.

In both composition and literature classes, the *value* of introducing these texts has been seen principally as creating a more representative set of literary and cultural voices. John Guillory argues that in a time of conservative politics, this push for canonical representation stands in for actual political representation. As Guillory notes, including Latino literary voices in a literature course is a poor substitute for ensuring that Latinos can enter the classroom. He states, "What is excluded from the syllabus is not excluded in the *same way* that an individual is excluded or marginalized as the member of a social minority, socially disenfranchised" (1993, 33, emphasis in the original). In this regard, it is not clear how such curricular inclusion has significantly changed the actual political relationship of a university to its local or national partners. Increased representation in the classroom via assigned texts has not necessarily resulted in increased resource sharing with underrepresented populations at the local level.

To return to our immediate context as teachers of writing (whether literary or expository), we might also question whether the introduction of these texts has changed the way we teach the workings of language. James Seitz argues in *Motives for Metaphor* (1999) that the inclusion of alternative texts has not changed the actual writing style expected of students, which is still primarily academic prose. Nor has the inclusion of such texts been used to expand students' vision of how language actually works. For Seitz, we still teach a vision of language wrapped in literalism. In the case of discussing the writing of formally marginalized voices, such as those of Latino, African American, or Queer communities, Guillory argues that we are perhaps even more literal, taking the voice on the page as representative of a whole community and its inherent identity.

Nor has the introduction of these texts necessarily challenged the political relationship of writing that is produced, published, and distributed in partnership with the marginalized communities being studied. Students tend to read finished pieces nicely framed in anthologies or placed within publishing house covers. In such situations, the community's sense of ownership of the writing as well as how the community might have presented its writing are greatly mitigated or even negated. (For an extended discussion of this issue, see George 2003.) In fact, it might be argued that writing programs have adopted Marx's theory of value only in the most limited sense; they have used it to acknowledge exclusion, to detail the history of that exclusion, and to allow the "literal" voice of that excluded population into our curriculum. In the process, however, they have finessed fundamental questions on the nature of language, community, and property.

The Glassville project certainly demonstrated the failings of such a limited vision. The community's voices were included in the curriculum; they were not, however, developed in a context affording the community itself equal control of the book's content or its visual qualities. It was the students, not the community members, who collected and edited (or failed to edit) the oral histories. It was the press that framed the community voices through images, font, and cover design. It was the university writing program that seemed to have the power to decide how the book would be used in its composition classrooms. (As Guillory might have predicted, the book would be made to "represent" a set of progressive community voices that could be held in opposition to traditional and conservative forms of academic discourse.) To a great extent, Glassville residents had stopped being potential producers and readers of the book and had become the new subject for an academic study by students.

Yet through their protests and calls for control of the book's contents, the residents were making an argument similar to the FWWCP's: a community publication has to be controlled by the community. Indeed, it was out of this very concern that many initial FWWCP groups created their own "means of production" in which the writer and writing group controlled the content, design, and distribution of a publication. The Glassville residents had thus highlighted a fundamental fact about university/community publication projects: the audience for the community publishing is not simply our discipline. Rather, the audience must necessarily be defined as the community as well. Indeed, in "Whose History Is It? Selection and Representation in the Creation of a Text," Caroline B. Brettell writes:

> [T]he failure to communicate [with the community] emerges from the fact that we rarely define our respondents or informants as our primary readers. In our writings, we are, in general, addressing ourselves. . . . Until we fully address and explore the question of for whom we are writing, and how we write for whom we write, we will not resolve the problem of the misunderstanding generated when those we write about read what we write, hear what we have to say, or read some mediated version of what we have written or said. Nor do I think this problem has been eliminated by the production of experimental ethnographies . . . [which are often as] inaccessible to those whose voices they presumably represent, as are more conventional ethnographies. (1996, 101–2)

Within a community publishing context, then, the fundamental issue becomes more than just exchanging one text for another—-canonical for noncanonical—and more than choosing a multivocal narrative to speak to our colleagues, whether in anthropology or composition studies. Rather, we must bring together the insights of organizations such as the FWWCP and scholars such as Caroline Brettell to alter the means of production. (For a full study of community responses to ethnographic publications, see Brettell 1996.)

That is, we need to recognize a local community's right to have equal input with their scholarly partners into the publication itself (the formation of a community/university readership) and into subsequent curricular materials (the disciplinary formation of their identity within the university). For this reason, I argue that moments of curriculum reform that are designed to expand our students' education to "nontraditional" communities must be seen as part of a larger effort to form university/community partnerships.

That is, we need to explore how our inclusion of nontraditional voices might call for a general reworking of the current sponsorship networks existing within a university. (For a full discussion of the concept of sponsorship, see Brandt 2001.)

For these issues of control to become central, however, we must shift our attention away from the *exchange-value* of teaching one politically oriented text over another and toward the *use-value* of texts in general. Notably, some Marxist scholars have already argued for an increased focus on use-value. In "Scattered Speculations on the Question of Value," Gayatri Spivak reminds us that use-value is both inside and outside the network of exchange (1985, 87). For this reason, use-value can speak to both the labor relations from which the object emerges and the object's cultural and aesthetic value. Spivak's focus on use-value, then, demands that an instructor not mask larger narratives of economic exploitation when deciding to use nonstandard texts. A constant vigilance is required.

One can imagine a classroom practice for the *Glassville Memories* book based on this concept of use-value that highlights the ways in which the book developed within certain networks of economic exchange. That practice might do much of what this chapter has done. It would discuss the extent to which economic networks, in terms of who had the money to pay for the book's production, allowed the press to manipulate the images of the community—turning them into native informants of sorts. (The gesture of sharing profits from the book might thus be seen as an inadequate gesture at best.) It might also build off critiques of traditional ethnographic fieldwork and try to demonstrate that the writing program ultimately wanted to determine the way the community voices would be discussed and analyzed within the college course. To some extent, it might also talk about how the Glassville case is an example of a generalized pattern for university/community partnerships, where the community is the object upon which the university, as subject, acts. And indeed, as I discuss later, these conversations became part of the basic-writing course where the book was eventually featured.

Constant vigilance as a classroom practice, however, is an incomplete answer. Although it enunciates the teacher's responsibilities within the classroom, it does not enunciate the community's right to help define that classroom. A student's becoming aware of how a text is used (and framed) does not change the institution's actual working practices or its relationship to the communities being studied. Being aware of how text is used (and framed) within a class does not change the actual working relationship or practices of the institution to the communities being studied. Nor does it model to the student how such academic study can be connected to the actual work of building egalitarian university/community partnerships.

For this reason, we need to imagine how a focus on use-value might actually interrupt our current practices with community and neighborhood organizations. At this point, it is helpful to consider how political philosopher G. A. Cohen reframes use-value. Whereas Spivak ultimately accepts Marx's conception of surplus labor as a conceptual tool to explain exploitation, Cohen argues that we can shift our attention away from the laborer who creates value to the product that has value. For Cohen, Marx was wrong both in believing that labor power was transferred to the produced object and in believing such a viewpoint was necessary to talk about exploitation (1988, 207–38). Instead, Cohen argues that exploitation occurs through how the value of a product is appropriated—in other words, to what uses and ends it is put. It is irrelevant whether the worker has embedded her labor power in an object; the point is that she helped to create the object and should have a role in how the product is used.

Cohen's argument highlights the ways in which concepts of private property limit the right of the worker, either as an individual or as a collective, to determine how the product she created will be used. Under Cohen's scheme, private property allows the capitalist instead of the worker to control the uses to which a product's value is put. For that reason, economic exploitation cannot be solved by shortening the working day (limiting the extraction of surplus value) or simply by sharing profits (as in the case of the Glassville project); rather, it must be addressed by creating a system in which workers gain control over how an object is used: "[T]he crucial question for exploitation concerns the justice of the distribution of the means of production" (Cohen 1988, 234).

I argued earlier that nontraditional texts were being introduced into classrooms to make the canon more "representative." Within the limited scope of English studies, however, Cohen's argument demonstrates the inadequacy of such a move because the inclusion of marginal voices within traditional networks of production—curricula, required courses, textbooks, and publishers—simply reproduces the current networks of sponsorship and power. This is certainly one of the lessons of the Glassville project; the neighborhood was represented, but without being accorded its rights of self-representation. What is needed is a new model of aesthetic and cultural production that provides not only alternative cultural products for use inside and outside our classrooms, but also alternative systems of production for our students and community partners.

For all these reasons, I have come to believe that cultural and educational institutions should understand part of their work to be socializing the means of cultural and aesthetic production—an argument that I recognize goes against the current privatizing of university resources (see Soley 1999; White and Hauck 2000). Or, as Guillory argues, aesthetic and cultural production must be reintroduced as a right of every citizen and must become an aspect of everyday ordinary life: "The point is not to make judgment disappear but to reform the conditions of its practice. If there is no way out of the game of culture, then, even when cultural capital is the only kind of capital, there may be another kind of game, with less dire consequences for the losers, an aesthetic game. Socializing the means of production and consumption would be the condition of an aestheticism unbound, not its overcoming. But of course, this is only a thought experiment" (1993, 340). Guillory's "aestheticism unbound" is an argument for communities' right to create their own aesthetic self-definitions; it is an instantiation of Cohen's view that exploitation can be overcome only by expanding access to the means of production.

Rather than see its work strictly in terms of canon (re)formation, then, English studies should imagine itself as a field engaged in fostering new local public writing spaces. It should demonstrate to its students how the binary concepts of in/out and canonical/noncanonical are the result of negotiated literacy acts and practices. Ultimately, English studies can push against a literal view of language, where language is seen as a reflection of a community's reality, and toward a metaphoric view of language (à la Seitz), where different language communities bring themselves together for greater explanatory (and political) power—thus replacing the literal text with a catachretical text. I would even go so far as to argue that for students undertaking such collaborative work as part of their general education, this work would dem-onstrate the true *use-value* of the writing process.

It should be recognized, however, that the effort of socializing the means of literary and literacy production would necessarily demand a dif-ferent relationship between English studies and a local community. One of the ways to read the initial formulation of the Glassville project is as a tacti-cal intervention into a local community. As noted in the previous chapter, Certeau defines a tactic as "a calculated action determined by the absence of a proper locus. . . . The space of the tactic is the space of the other. Thus, it must play on and with a terrain imposed on it and organized by the law of a foreign power" (1988, 36–37). Within Certeau's logic, the Temple writing program wanted to become a tactical ally, marshaling resources for a "quick strike" against a larger public dismissal of Glassville (although as noted, the program actually operated as a foreign power). Within the writing program as well, the *Glassville Memories* publication acted as a tactical intervention into the first-year writing program, moving it toward greater inclusion of locally marginalized community voices. However, when the tactical project fell apart, the partnership could have just drifted away, the book simply put in storage and eventually forgotten, and individual faculty could have drifted off to other projects. In fact, for many *failed* university/community projects, the individual (read *tactical*) nature of the work allows the department or university to be unaffected. In this way, a tactical approach represents a lim-ited ethical and practical commitment to connecting a field's disciplinary work to a local community.

For this reason, as English studies moves toward socializing the means of production, a strategic sense of value must become dominant in the pro-cess. As noted in the previous chapter, according to Certeau, a strategy is "the calculation (or manipulation) of power relations that becomes possible as soon as a subject with will or power (a business, an army, a city, a scien-tific institution) can be isolated. It postulates a place that can be delimited as its own and serve as a base from which relations with an exteriority composed of targets or threats (customers or competitors, enemies . . .) can be managed" (1988, 35–36). Within Temple University, New City Writing and its press had become a strategic space whose very existence depended on community-based partnerships. By definition, it was a university/

community collaborative. For this reason, the "failure" of the Glassville project called into question the integrity of New City's borders, creating a scenario where "foreign powers" (deans, department heads, grant agencies, and other community partners) might use the moment to reclaim New City's space and resources for other initiatives. It was the development of this strategic space that necessitated institutional responsibility and recognition of the necessity of correcting the project. It was simply not possible to allow the project to fade away. Doing so would have affected not only the community, but the English department and the writing program as well. For this reason, I would argue that the *hope* of long-term success of such community-based work can be realized only by the creation of strategic university spaces that bring with them a collective ethical and institutional commitment to the numerous literacy populations that make up a neighborhood, city, or state.

In this sense, my definition of *hope* differs slightly from Mathieu's "tactics of hope," an important argument invoked in the opening chapters of this book. Although Mathieu's work represents a powerful argument for the power of individual teachers, she is, perhaps, less optimistic than I am regarding institutions' ability to change their policies to meet a community's actual needs. She writes, "When institutional priorities intersect with community needs, people can get hurt. Projects can lead to bitterness and disillusionment" (2005, 123). In the final chapter of her book *Tactics of Hope,* in fact, Mathieu reports an "academic horror story" of a community publication gone wrong—the faculty member failed to consult with the community, published their work without adequate input from them, and failed to address community concerns. Although this story is very similar to that of the *Glassville Memories* project, Mathieu draws the lesson that such stories indicate institutions' inability to change. She follows this story with case studies of three scholars whose work, in an individual sense, does align with community needs but does not require institutional support or change.

Although I recognize the difficulty of creating institutional change (and have more to say on this subject in the final chapter), I believe Mathieu would agree that there is a moral responsibility to create within the institutional resources of universities some "strategic spaces" that implicate colleges, departments, and faculty in meeting a local community's needs.

Without such a strategic commitment, in part, individual faculty can behave as Mathieu's colleague behaved, with little or no consequence. More important, without the creation of strategic spaces, the financial and intellectual resources of what are usually the most powerful nonprofits in a region are relieved of their local responsibilities. At a time when economic and political trends are drawing resources away from distressed and underresourced neighborhoods, I believe that mechanisms must be created that force universities to become more engaged and better community partners. "Socializing the means of production," then, also represents a moral obligation by faculty to undertake the difficult work of drawing resources into a common strategic institutional space and channeling those resources outward toward the community.

Returning to the connections among English studies, value, and community publishing, I want to reiterate my argument that the history of English studies has involved the slow inclusion of vernacular or marginalized voices—a limited definition of value. English studies now resides in a space, however, from which it can take on a strategic role in alliance with marginalized populations not only to produce community-based publications, but also to ensure that the emerging commitment to publishing the words and voices of our local communities is enacted in an ethical and institutionally responsible manner. In doing so, English studies will further articulate its own traditions and develop a framework that will enrich the work of students, community members, and faculty. For this reason, English studies programs should become part of the effort to socialize the means of literary and literacy production by becoming active in community publishing networks within their local communities or by establishing their own small or low-level community publishing efforts.

Such are the "common values" that can unite community publishing and English studies.

Common Ground

So how does the story of the Glassville project end? How did this revised sense of value shape my response to the controversy? To answer these questions, I would like to focus on two particular elements of the response: the use of the book in our composition classroom and the production of the second edition.

In the aftermath of the controversy, we were still faced with the commitment to use the book in our first-year writing courses; there were two thousand copies of the book in our storeroom. Recognizing the need to coordinate with the community over the inclusion of the book in our curriculum, I decided to discuss with the neighborhood association how the book would be used in university classrooms. In doing so, I explicitly promised the association president that when we used the book, we would not hide the project's mistakes or the community's anger. In fact, it was decided to use the book's history as a way to frame the difficulties and possibilities of a neighborhood/university partnership. The flawed product and the history of its production offered an interesting text for students in our introductory writing courses to study how universities and neighborhoods create *value*. (This is not to say the course abandoned its traditional goals or that judgments based on composition research were ignored. Rather, these disciplinary judgments were placed in dialogue with the community's insights. As Guillory argues, the point is not to make value judgments disappear, but to reform the conditions of their practice.)

The particular theme of this first-year writing course grew out of a community member's comment that "I sound like the village idiot." After she made this remark to me when she saw her interview for the first time, I spent more than an hour talking to the association president, arguing that I thought everyone in the book did in fact sound like an intellectual. I offered alternative ways to understand what it might mean to sound like an intellectual, citing such cultural studies luminaries as Antonio Gramsci and Raymond Williams. None of these academic readings of the community voices seemed to have much traction, however. As we talked, I realized I was arguing from an incredibly privileged space, ignoring the situation of those who don't have the university standing behind their intellect. This realization led me to ask, who is really allowed to exist within such broad and alternative definitions of the intellectual? Who has the power to decide he or she can afford such a definition? This conversation sparked a debate among those creating the course on what it meant to "sound like" or to be an *intellectual*. Or, as the question was posed to students, How do we understand the relationship between intellectuals sponsored by a community and those sponsored by the academy? How should these different intellectuals relate? In a sense, the idea of the intellectual became a metaphor for the class to examine how university and neighborhood organizations might interact in the production of knowledge.

Throughout the course, then, students were asked to inquire into how the book represented the working relationship between students and residents. They were not asked to read the text as an authentic and literal expression of a marginalized voice, but for how the text represented a negotiation among different intellectuals on the concept of community. It was also hoped that by being engaged in this process, students would come to learn the tentative and ever-changing character of community. In this way, the course moved *Glassville Memories* from a commodified product into an ongoing social practice in which they could participate.

Indeed, the students were aware that they were taking part in an ongoing debate about the publication and, in effect, were part of the material practices shaping its future. Perhaps because of this fact, they picked up on the tensions within the book. In particular, a significant number of students felt the interviews were disrespectful of the residents, both by showing a lack of knowledge about the community and by the brevity of the actual questions. Students pointed out how the interviewers' questions were predominantly personal and rarely asked the residents to offer systemic or theoretical analyses of why the community had managed to remain harmonious in the midst of economic change. In this way, the interviewers' behavior reaffirmed research demonstrating that working-class individuals are often asked questions that imply they lack the authority and knowledge to supply extended information, thus leading to short answers and no opportunity to represent their worldview fully.

Within this context, the students also developed an argument that the book itself failed to accord the residents the space to publish materials that would demonstrate their collective intellectual vision. There were few economic facts in the book, either as addenda or graphs, to affirm the residents' personal insights. No information was given on documents produced by the neighborhood association or on any plan being developed by the community to address the economic concerns presented in the book. Although calling for such texts might be seen as an attempt to make the book academic, it is also the case that such work would have highlighted the association's political goals as well as the residents' personal experiences. In the end, the Glassville book allowed the university students to see how a failure to imagine the community residents as intellectuals had determined both the scope and the limitations of the project.

Student readers did not, however, romanticize the Glassville residents. They consistently pointed out that many elderly residents appeared uninterested in modern culture. The residents, as represented in the book, seemed more interested in reproducing their past than in creating a different type of community that might intersect with the economic and multicultural terrain of modern Philadelphia. Whereas residents saw the world and their network of friendships in black and white, our students inhabited a multicultural world with a variety of languages and ethnicities. These issues were framed around the book's cover. Students believed the cover images accurately represented the book's emphasis on personal stories and historical nostalgia, one of their critiques of the book. In agreement with the community, they also faulted the placement of the black family images on the back of the book. Notably, they also faulted the book for failing to represent the new Asian population in the neighborhood on either the cover or in its content.

The *Glassville Memories* book, then, allowed students to see how a focus on personal relationships had failed to imagine the residents as community intellectuals or to challenge the residents' vision of a "race-free" community. In so doing, it demonstrated to the students the ways in which the seemingly literal language of community was actually the result of a metaphoric act of bringing disparate voices and interests together as if they were unified, even if that unity was actually exclusionary. As a final project in the course that used *Glassville Memories,* students were asked to rewrite the book by imagining what else the residents might have said, to recategorize the book's structure, to invent oppositional voices to critique the questioners, and to develop new cover and image montages. These moves allowed the students to move beyond simple critique toward a type of metaphorical writing practice.

Even prior to the publication of a second edition, then, the book was a curricular success for the writing program. The book did more than "exchange" one text for another. It reframed the students' relationship to their writing about community as well as the writing program's relationship to community. Through the Glassville book, the disciplinary interests of English studies were placed in a material dialogue with the immediate context in which issues of urban literacy and community development occurred. The book also demonstrated how students' work could not be seen as separate from the area surrounding the campus. For this reason, *Glassville Memories* began to model how a curriculum might be seen as the result of more than just strictly disciplinary interests. It demonstrated how a curriculum can interact with a community, and it articulated the responsibilities of students who work in that community.

But what about Glassville itself? How were the community concerns addressed?

Soon after the community protest meeting, discussions began on how to produce a second edition of the book. This process was not easy or contention free because many community members simply would not believe such a big institution could change its pattern of behavior. Throughout the book project (and the plans for the second edition), the residents had talked about the example of Federal Express. Prior to our collaboration, the company had agreed to build a plant right next to the neighborhood and hire residents to work there. The residents saw it as an opportunity to revitalize the neighborhood. For reasons that are still hotly debated, Federal Express hired individuals primarily from outside the community. Residents constantly invoked this incident as a precedent for the press's complicated relationship with the community.

The process of talking to residents while developing the composition course, however, began to create some trust between the neighborhood association and New City Community Press. In talking to the association president and other community members, I was able to invoke student work to show how, despite the controversy, the book was still a useful tool to teach students about race and community/university partnerships. Particularly important in this process was the students' critique of the university's behavior in the production of the first edition. This approach in the course that used *Glassville Memories* demonstrated that the community concerns were being heard and validated. As a result, a belief in the collective ownership of the revision process gained some traction, especially as it led to discussions about equalizing power and sharing among partners. In this context, a new model emerged that placed all participants on a common plane for decision making and mandated common access to the *means of production*. And although a full consideration of the category "intellectual" is not possible here, it is useful to note Gramsci's insight: "All men are intellectuals, one could therefore say: but not all men have in society the function of intellectuals" (1985, 9). As the parties moved forward in the revision process, each began to take on intellectual responsibilities formerly accorded to just the university students and faculty.

Sharing decisions and opening up the means of production initially meant a new focus on revising the aesthetic and framing aspects of the publication (the cover, the introduction, and so on). For instance, the neighborhood association, the involved professors, and I agreed that the second edition should be jointly designed and approved by community representatives and university participants. In response, new covers were designed featuring a neighborhood scene on the front and a picture of an interracial friendship on the back. Individual pages were also redesigned and organized to meet the residents' vision. The title page was changed to include the neighborhood association as one of the primary editors, and an introduction by the association president was added.

As discussions continued and deepened, however, it became clear that all conversations were inflected by race. As noted at the outset of this chapter, the Glassville residents imagined themselves to be a community in which race was not an issue. To a great extent, this assumption turned out to be true. Among the neighbors, longstanding friendships had overcome many of the racist or class-based attitudes that marked surrounding neighborhoods. Although we were new to the neighborhood, we assumed we had also entered this network of friendship. (It should be added that one professor involved in the project had actually become part of the network through a longer and more extended relationship with the community.) Despite the fact that all members of the press were white, we imagined we had transcended race.

Yet the project clearly had not transcended race. The controversy over the first cover demonstrated this fact. As we moved forward, we had to consider how our elision of issues of race had damaged our partnership and the book, for by ignoring race, those of us associated with the university had also ignored the extent to which our personal and professional positions were based on discriminatory sponsorship networks—networks that intentionally left behind citizens who lived and worked in neighborhoods such as Glassville. The discourse on friendship masked over the racial and class components in our assumption that we would control the process and production of the book. For those of us at the press, strong lessons needed to be learned.

We were not the only ones learning from the process, however. I have come to believe that those active in the book's revision also learned the difficulty of presenting their community as having solved the issue of race in strictly "personal terms." Because the broader worldview out of which the residents' friendships grew was not highlighted, a discourse or rhetoric to claim rights or power from a large institution was not put in place. To some extent, I like to believe the process of completing the second edition of the book allowed those involved to develop a stronger argument about the rights of a community when involved in university or corporate partnerships. (However, to be honest, not everyone agrees with this reading, and it is unclear whether any major corporation would cede power to such a small community group no matter what arguments were deployed.)

As the second edition emerged, then, arguments declaring that racism could be overcome by personal friendships or by offering to publish a book addressing this fact were no longer viable. This change resulted in an interesting mix of "old and new." Residents ultimately changed very little in their interviews. The disagreements concerning race relations within the interviews remained and in some cases were highlighted, although some residents went back to the interviews to clarify their statements about neighborhood history or neighborhood institutions. Some residents appeared more open to representing race as an ongoing issue in their community and to allowing the tensions in their neighborhood to serve as a case study of negotiation. That is, the "harmonious" new cover and introductory materials were now to be seen in dialogue with the voices of residents trying to achieve that goal.

In some senses, the residents began to think of the book less as a literal representation of their community and more as a document that expressed one particular working-through of the issue, a discussion piece for use in their neighborhood. This new view was evident in their decision not to include more demographic or research materials in the book. In part, residents felt that the editorial changes to their interviews cumulatively expressed their worldview. In part, they felt the university courses were providing this perspective for students. The second edition thus resulted in academic and vernacular culture being metaphorically conjoined to produce a dialogue about the nature of language and community as well as about the intersection of race and class. Therefore, in this second edition the Glassville neighborhood association did not have a perfect publication, one that expressed a utopian vision of their community, but they did have a publication they felt comfortable sharing at community events, giving to new residents, and using to advocate for community rights.

I do not want to leave the impression that all issues were permanently solved. That is not how collaboration works. Despite the attempt to reframe the discussion of race, the second edition failed to represent the full diversity of the community; new immigrants as well as some long-time residents of the community are not represented in the book. (In fact, as the book was heading to press, a resident in the community refused to allow a group photo featuring her grandmother to appear in the book because her family had not been interviewed. This act rekindled old feuds.) Although it is true that the book was used in the composition program for two years, neither *Glassville Memories* nor any other New City Community Press publication is currently being used in Temple University's first-year composition curriculum. Finally, personal divisions still exist among faculty, community, and program leaders about the history of the project and its *value*.

Despite such moments, what has succeeded, however, is the strategic space supporting the goals of community publishing. Since the production of *Glassville Memories,* the press has worked collaboratively to publish oral histories of Mexican farmworkers, the photography and writing of displaced union members, the poetry of urban school children, and community dialogues on slavery and freedom. In each case, teams of community, university, and student participants collaboratively produced and designed the publication. Each book found a home both within the participating community as well as within literature and composition classes; in fact, their adoption across the curriculum (not just for first-year writing) can serve as a sign of the long-term success of such projects at drawing together opposing aspects of an English studies department in support of community-based organizing.

In addition, a collaboratively developed curriculum for each of these community publications has helped them to be integrated into high schools, community organizations, and government agencies in the immediate local context of their production as well as literally across the country and around the world. In that way, the crisis of Glassville has created a strategic intervention into the work of the department and college, which has enabled a vision of English studies as an active participant in the creation of not only a community-based literature, but also a community-based curriculum at all levels of literary and composition instruction nationwide.

Hard Conversations

A shift in the meaning of value can bridge some of the divisions between English studies and composition/rhetoric. As we have seen, when value is framed strictly in terms of exchange-value (exchanging one text for another), a certain set of expectations and practices seems to be put into place. The principle agents become the professors and students; the principle site of activity is the university. However, with the introduction of use-value as a guiding metaphor, a different set of interests becomes part of the equation, forcing a different set of responsibilities onto the institution. It becomes possible to imagine each partner (the university and the community) as providing value to the project and as being accorded the right to determine its use. Value production can be seen as a communal process, the aim of which is to produce a mutually reaffirming literacy product. Invoking the category of "use-value" as an organizing principle, then, demands that a common (if contentious) space of negotiation and production be created.

It is for this reason that I believe curriculum reform must be more than the simple inclusion of texts that represent "alternative values"; it must mean more than providing diverse texts for students to judge by some moral standard or to use in learning academic discourse. The latter is important work, but it is only one piece. One of the goals of English studies and of composition/rhetoric programs in particular is to help students understand the connections between language and cultural power. To do so most effectively,

English studies must create a path for students that is based in both traditional course offerings (which teach the history of literary texts, cultural theory, key concepts in rhetoric, ethnography, and linguistics) and courses that engage their students in the informed production of use-value. That is, in addition to traditional courses, students must participate in both the creation of the aesthetic written object and the economy of partnerships out of which the object emerges. The work of producing collaborative publications between the university and their local communities, of socializing and expanding the aesthetic means of production, should ultimately become a key element of our pedagogical and professional work. Community publishing projects are a primary vehicle for such work.

English studies should also be about embedding our classrooms in a process that allows students to realize that the seemingly most literal language is metaphoric and the result of intense negotiation, of bringing disparate worldviews together. This vision of language will enable them to be active participants in local, regional, and national public spheres. For instance, in "Rogue Cops and Health Care," Susan Wells takes the prison visiting room as a metaphor for engaging our students in public writing:

> The image of the visiting room suggests that our work establishes a point of exchange between the private, the domain of production, and some approximation of the public sphere. It is not directed at the political opinions of students, however progressive or retrograde, but toward the production and reading of texts that move between the public (the political, abstract, the discussable) and the private. . . . The realignment of rhetorical pedagogy to the public I advocate is not, therefore, a prescription or proscription of a genre of writing. Personal essays are not intrinsically "private"; technical discourse is not necessarily "public." Rather, publicity is constructed as a relation of readers to writers, including notions of rationality and accountability that are continually open to contest. (1996, 335)

Reform is less about assigning a variety of writing modes than about a particular vision of language, a particular enactment of language politics. The work of producing collaborative university/community publications in partnership with our surrounding neighbors, of socializing and expanding the aesthetic means of production, can thus ultimately become a key element in casting pedagogical and professional work outward to the culture as a whole. This work should become our common value.

Clearly, such an undertaking will take significant work and hard conversations. Yet if we want to ensure that the production of value within an academic program is not seen as simply the circulation of texts, but the creation of venues through which all participants begin to recognize and regard the ownership of such texts and the education of students as a communal responsibility, it is just this set of hard conversations that we must undertake. The story of Glassville, then, is not that our institute or department succeeded in permanently socializing the aesthetic means of production. Glassville did not lead to a moment of epiphany, but to a contentious and difficult process. As I once heard a university president state, "One of the great contributions of higher education is to show people how to deliberate over contentious issues together." By taking on use-value as a guiding principle of our work, I believe we can contribute to that great tradition.

4

Writing Within and Beyond
the Curriculum

No Restraints, *Community Publishing, and the Contact Zone*

> Since all men are "political beings," all are also legislators. . . . Every
> man, in as much as he is active, i.e., living, contributes to modifying
> the social environment in which he develops (to modifying certain of
> its characteristics or preserving others); in other words, he tends to
> establish "norms," rules of living or behaviour. One's circle of activity
> may be greater or smaller, one's awareness of one's own perceptions may
> be greater or smaller; furthermore, the representation to power may
> be greater or smaller, and will be put into practice to a greater or lesser
> extent in its normative systemic expression by the "represented."
> —ANTONIO GRAMSCI, *Selections from the Prison Notebooks*

What about the Writing Student?

Each of the previous chapters focused on New City Writing's ability (or
inability) to establish productive partnerships with community and public-
school organizations. In doing so, each proceeded with the implicit sense
that students were gaining more than just insight into the machinations of
community-based literacy projects. They were also learning something about
the nature of writing—of language as a mechanism for generating social
change. In addition to community partnerships, New City Writing was thus
also attempting to create classrooms that demonstrated how writing can be
a tool for effective community advocacy. Particularly within the context of
Philadelphia, those of us associated with New City Writing hoped our classrooms might enable students to understand how their own emergent writing
abilities might connect with efforts to create a revitalized *new* city.

The nature and ability of community-connected courses to generate such insights for students, however, is open to debate. Often discussed under the terms *service learning* and *community-based learning,* such courses have been critiqued for failing to produce a collective vision for students and for instead reaffirming individualistic conceptions of social change (Herzberg 1994). Even when such efforts are done well, there is concern that the very nature of university mitigates against their producing actual change in "the streets" (Mathieu 2005). A more limited sense of change—personal or tentative—is often held as the barometer of success (Goldblatt 2007). Although acknowledging these potential limitations, I want to build on the previous chapter's argument for the value of community publishing to describe an alternative relationship among student, faculty, and community partners. In this alternative, the faculty and students are positioned within a local community's long-term struggle for political recognition, understanding that the university's work is only one element within this effort. In this relationship, the writing course and the student papers generated in it become one moment within a larger effort to produce a collective ethnographic document, a process that unites writing and political alliances for change.

In this chapter, then, I want to trace how the collective work of the student writers in our New City Writing classrooms developed from an initial intersection of a student paper with a community publication to the creation of a classroom aligned with local and international efforts for political recognition. In the process, the New City Writing classrooms emerged as spaces where students joined with urban populations in struggles for increased educational, cultural, and economic support. They enabled students to move from a personal engagement with the *contact zone* to a sense of collaborative action in the public sphere—action directed at producing a crisis in the current systems by which power is distributed. The creation of such classrooms represented a culminating moment in the history of New City Writing.

Student Writing and Community Publications

A central dilemma of composition's public turn has been the need to have students produce writing that fits both within and beyond the curriculum. Composition teachers, that is, have taken on the difficult task of both continuing to prepare students for academic discourse and accepting the new responsibilities of locating their pedagogical work in the community. As Paula Mathieu (2005) notes, this public turn has meant connecting existing scholarship focused on public writing, popular rhetorics, and political debates to community partnerships and service-learning initiatives. Students continue to write academic essays on Jürgen Habermas's concept of the public sphere, but now they do so in the context of producing a brochure for a community organization. The turn outward, then, implies not only a placement of faculty and students in the community, but also a reconsideration of existing scholarship for its utility in creating a community-based pedagogy.

Consequently, the old set of alignments that marked the field's relationship to process, cognitive, or academic discourse-based pedagogies is now orbiting around a different axis—community engagement. Debates about whether the process or expressivist movement depoliticized the writing classroom now carry less currency, for the writing classroom is no longer located simply within a university (and its curriculum), but within a network in which personal, political, academic, and scholarly voices interact with local residents in the production of collaborative writing focused on immediate needs. One example of such a public turn in previously situated scholarship might be seen in the work of Linda Flower (2002, 2008). Flower's original emphasis on the cognitive processes of writing has been translated into community-based projects focused on intercultural rhetoric and dialogue, categories she specifically marks as having primarily local significance, intentionally limiting their utility to other sites or as a replicable model. In her work and in the field in general, the central question has become which alignment of writing strategies at the local level (academic, expressivist, and so on) produces a productive partnership for both the university and the community.

It was within this emphasis on the local that the traditional discussion of voice, marked by the Bartholomae/Elbow dialogue, needed to be recast within New City Writing. Rather than understand the debate as a binary moment, where we must choose for or against the personal as a means to teach university writing, we now had to see the personal in its larger tactical significance within community-based politics: How can personal narratives by students intersect with community voices to create a common understanding of literacy as a social and political practice? How can this understanding impact both public-school and university curricula? To address these questions, New City Writing had to work within the hybrid nature of voice (personal and collective) both within and beyond the curriculum.

Whereas Flower used *intercultural* as her organizing term for community-based work, New City Writing used *writing beyond the curriculum* as the initial articulation of the public turn in the local context of Philadelphia. Cultural studies scholarship, particularly that of the Birmingham School, had previously been rearticulated for the specific context of Temple University and Philadelphia. As discussed earlier, however, this original framing did not adequately position New City Writing either as a partner with community organizations that were seeking a collective recognition of their political rights or as an agent to engage with the political state. Within the local context of the city, partnerships had to be constructed that would create a process to allow potential collective identities to emerge and formalize a political position. The public turn in composition, at least in Philadelphia, required a reformulation of scholarship and pedagogy that would bring new voices into the public sphere and reformulate public policy.

For although there had been both tactical and strategic successes, New City Writing's sense of collective action had not yet been translated into an effective form of collective student and community writing—as witnessed by the initial results of the service-learning courses connected to the Glassville and *Urban Rhythms* projects. If writing *beyond* the curriculum had come to stand for an alliance of university and community activists focused on expanding literacy options for both students and community members, it was still unclear what this alliance might mean for writing *within* the curriculum. How could the personal and the academic, the essay and the research paper, intersect in community-based activist projects? How could the model of "opening up the cultural means of production," à la Guillory, via community publishing impact the daily workings of a writing classroom?

An answer to this pedagogical and political dilemma began to emerge through a partnership with Gil Ott of Liberty Resources, an advocacy organization focused on the civil rights of Philadelphia's disabled residents. Around 2001, Ott contacted our community press about undertaking an anthology focused on disability culture in Philadelphia. Although disability rights had already attained national prominence, Ott felt that in the local terrain of Philadelphia, the disability community had not succeeded in gaining the same political influence as other identity-based populations. The proposed volume, eventually titled *No Restraints: An Anthology of Disability Culture in Philadelphia* (Ott 2002a), would be an attempt to capture the myriad personal experiences, organized efforts, and situated knowledges existing within Philadelphia's disability community.[1] The goal was to use the publication to create a vehicle for sustained discussion on a new collective disability. As the project progressed, it intersected with a writing course taught by my colleague Eli Goldblatt and the work of one of his students, Tameka Blackwell.

Student writing wasn't initially considered part of this particular community publication. Ott had created an editorial board for the project, consisting of artists, writers, and activists from the disability community, and he sought the input of other disability organizations, such as the Institute for Disability Culture and Artists for Recovery. No students were involved. The editorial board's role was to find existing work within the community as well as to ask individuals to create new pieces for the anthology that would capture the experience of being disabled in Philadelphia. As the work began to be submitted, it became clear that beneath any social or institutional identification that might be applied to an individual, a deeper exploration of the individual's public identity was occurring. As with the writing produced by the FWWCP, personal experience became a vehicle through which to imagine a common collective experience. That is, the artists' personal experience of interacting with a broad political and economic framework structured around "temporarily abled bodies" provided the starting point through which to imagine an alternative identity for the disabled community. In *No*

1. Throughout this book, I have been discussing a variety of projects that grew out of the immediate context of New City Writing. *No Restraints,* however, was the longtime ambition of Gil Ott, the anthology's editor. A poet, publisher, and disability rights activist, Ott was a primary influence on the development of New City Community Press and a formative influence on how writing beyond the curriculum was practiced in the press's community partnerships. His untimely death in 2004 was a personal tragedy for his friends and a political tragedy for the causes for which he stood. This chapter, which would not be possible without his efforts, is dedicated to his memory.

Restraints, then, personal experience, as framed around the management of the disabled body, became the central site through which to indicate the need for the partnering organizations to collaborate for political change across a set of legislative domains—educational, cultural, public, and political.

This merging of the body and the body politic (of individual and system) allows for a particularly literal vision of a community's organic intellectual to emerge. Referring to the organic intellectual, Gramsci writes,

> The problem of creating a new stratum of intellectuals consists therefore in the critical elaboration of the intellectual activity that exists in everyone at a certain degree of development, modifying its relationship with the muscular-nervous effort towards a new equilibrium, and ensuring that the muscular-nervous effort itself, in so far as it is an element of a general practical activity, which is perpetually innovating the physical and social world, become the foundation of a new and integral conception of the world. (1985, 9)

The "muscular-nervous effort," for Gramsci, is the way in which the worker's labor is related to social production. In a reading of this "body" through the lens of disability culture, it becomes clear that the work of an organic intellectual within the community necessitates the constant focus on how the very architecture designed to facilitate the productive worker-citizen, in the broadest sense, must be altered to allow greater civic participation and rights. It is this alternative definition of "muscular-nervous effort" that can also be used to reframe the goals of "general practical activity."

Indeed, *No Restraints* begins by documenting the variety of bodily experiences from which the emergent collective political identity emerges. One of the opening personal narratives concerns Reverend Nellie Greene and her struggle to succeed at a college where the physical space did not allow her free movement. Unable to see and physically challenged by the school's architecture, she details the difficulties her body encountered in interacting with "normal" campus facilities. Speaking in the third person, Greene writes, "She was too proud to use a wheelchair, or other assisting device, so when she stumbled on the ice while on her way to the dining commons or to class, she got on her knees and crawled, until she reached where she was headed. Usually, though, there were plenty of other students around to help her reach her various destinations separately" (2002, 39). Later pieces in the collection focus on how psychological or neurological issues are managed by mental health hospitals. Although there is recognition in the anthology that mental health drugs can be a valuable tool, David Kime uses individuals' experiences within the mental health community to create a zine, *Transcendent Visions*, that demonstrates the ways in which the personal experience of mental illness becomes institutionalized and managed within society. Dan Neubauer's cartoon "Malory Will" depicts the "adventures" of a mental patient who consistently comes up against the mental health system's bureaucracy.

1. Dan Neubauer, "Malory Will," in *No Restraints: An Anthology of Disability Culture in Philadelphia,* edited by Gil Ott (Philadelphia: New City Community Press, 2002), 85.

At no point do these authors claim that their experience speaks to the situation of any other disabled individual or community, however. There is recognition that deaf communities have a trajectory different from visually impaired communities. What these artifacts do begin to establish, across individual experiences, is a generalized map of how disabled bodies are configured in the Philadelphia region. In that sense, their different experiences are not required to fit into the same category—an essentialized experience of the disabled—as much as to present the larger patterns that organize that individual experience. In addition, although each artist recognizes the kindness of individuals, such as the students who helped Greene, the collective experience ultimately demonstrates how a neoconservative public sphere of individual benevolence is inadequate to the collective need for a different physical and political architecture. For many activists in the book, then, *disability community* is a catachretical term signifying a conscious choice to develop out of a unique and diffuse set of personal and historical experiences a broad political identity that will impact political and economic policies. In his introduction to the book, Ott writes: "It is this active self-identification that transforms a benign social category into a political and cultural force, a community" (2002b, 9). (For an extended excerpt from Ott's introduction, see chapter 5.)

As represented in *No Restraints,* it is a community that actively attempts to negate the existing rhetoric being used to define disability within Philadelphia in terms of pity, helplessness, and shame. Instead, the strategy is to claim the difference as productive, strong. In his essay "What Is Disability?" Erik von Schmetterling writes, "We are different and some of us are proud of that difference. Disability pride is an attitude few non-disabled people can fathom; it makes people very uncomfortable to think someone could be grateful—or even happy and proud—to have a disability" (2002, 16). To establish the collective work needed within Philadelphia to redefine disability, the book provides examples of how this personal experience embedded itself within collective efforts across disabilities to gain more political and economic power.

Each example, although local, significantly draws from existing tactics or national campaigns. The tactics do not develop spontaneously, but as the rearticulation of existing social and political narratives. For instance, the collective effort by Philadelphia activist organizations to redefine "indepen-dence," a classic trope within mainstream U.S. culture (and in Philadelphia, in particular) is featured. It should be remembered that during the time of the book's production, the turn of the millennium, a dominant conservative culture critiqued concepts of government support ("handouts") or interfer-ence in the economy ("socialism"). As represented in *No Restraints*, the very aim for independence, however, is linked to calls for government legislation for equal access and equal rights. Organizations such as Disabled in Action and legislative initiatives such as MiCassa (an independent housing initiative) were portrayed as calls for citizens to be relieved of "state interference" and "support." Here the call to reduce the size of government is actually a call to strengthen the role of government.

The 1950s and 1960s civil rights movement is similarly invoked in the book. Indeed, many of the writers in the collection highlight how their per-sonal experience resonates with the early civil rights movement. Von Schmet-terling writes, "For years, civil rights organizers have seen the importance of equality in terms of being able to ride mass transit. This is the essence of what inspired the Montgomery Bus Boycott—restricting where certain people could sit on the bus affected their abilities to [get to] work on time. A people's outrage and anger became the Civil [Rights] Movement. Not being able to ride buses, subways or other elements of a system's fixed route angers People with Disabilities, too" (2002, 20). Photos included in the book attempt to capture images of citizens being denied access to buses or housing—linking their bodies to the bodies of African Americans in the 1960s. In each case, these interventions' ability to create a crisis in existing public representations and policies are detailed in the success or failure to enact and enforce new social, political, and economic standards.

Indeed, the collective work of the Philadelphia disabled community as represented in *No Restraints* can be described as the effort to make that com-munity's new collective belief—that disability can be a positive attribute—the city's new legislative framework by recasting or reshaping existing narratives. Gramsci provides a road map for how to understand this process:

> Perhaps it is useful to make a "practical" distinction between philosophy and common sense in order to indicate more clearly the passage from one

moment to the other. In philosophy, the features of individual elaboration of thought are most salient: in common sense, on the other hand, it is the diffuse, uncoordinated features of a generic form of thought common to a particular period and a particular popular environment. But every philosophy has a tendency to become the common sense of a fairly limited environment (that of all the intellectuals). It is a matter therefore of starting with a philosophy which already enjoys, or could enjoy, a certain diffusion, because it is connected to and implicit in practical life, and elaborating it so that it becomes a renewed common sense possessing the coherence and the sinew of individual philosophies. But this can only happen if the demands of cultural contact with the "simple" are continually felt. (1985, 330)

For Gramsci, then, the emergent collective political framework must be embedded within a traditionally accepted philosophy and used as a means to expand this framework throughout the different domains in which common sense is determinant, which will allow a new common sense to emerge.

At its best, *No Restraints* demonstrates the ways in which a collectively organized set of personal experiences attempted to twist the currently accepted ideologies of the mainstream culture toward the creation of a new common sense. "Less government" meant "government intervention." "Civil rights" meant "disability rights." Or, as Lukacs would see it, by creating a crisis within the system through rhetorical and political action, *No Restraints* attempted to reconfigure the current network of partial narratives structuring the category "disabled" into a new and more progressive alignment. As a political strategy in a particular time and location, then, *No Restraints* was the articulation point in a network of progressive work in Philadelphia—foundations, activist groups, national coalitions, and legislative efforts—out of which new efforts and campaigns could begin. In this way, it represented the insights about the need for New City Writing to develop political alliances, as in the Philadelphia Writing Centers Project, and the insights about the need to create a crisis, as in the *Urban Rhythms* project.

Student Tameka Blackwell's essay was originally not intended for *No Restraints*. As noted at the outset, *No Restraints* was not seen as related to New City Writing's pedagogical or curricular work. Instead, Blackwell's essay grew out of an assignment in a personal writing course whose original audience was imagined to be the professor (Eli Goldblatt) and Tameka's fellow classmates. Eli felt her essay meshed nicely with the proposed collection, so we sent it on to Gil Ott, who helped her prepare it for publication in the anthology. The seemingly simple inclusion of her work, however, altered our sense of the New City Writing classroom and the potential alignment of writing classes with community politics.

Once placed within the confines of *No Restraints,* Blackwell's articulation of and intersection with the collection's themes became evident. Her essay concerns a visit to a doctor's office and how others observe the body of a quadriplegic in a wheelchair. From almost the beginning of the paper, for instance, Blackwell begins to position herself within the architecture of the building—both admiring its possibilities and recognizing how it exists within a cultural framework that would deny her access. She writes:

> I love the sunlight that shines in on Thomas Jefferson Hospital's glass enclosed bridge.
>
> The bridge has the appearance of hovering over Sansom Street. It was built as an extension for connecting Chestnut Street side of Jefferson Hospital to the Walnut Street side. They once operated as two separate buildings. The Walnut Street side was built many years before the Chestnut Street side. Thomas Jefferson Hospital has become the premier hospital in the Northeast that handles spinal cord injuries. Anyhow, I'm glad it exists.
>
> The elevators are full, as usual. Well, I'll have to wait for the next one, as usual. How dare these people delay my mission to the ninth floor, the purple floor, where my spot in the sun awaits me?
>
> Purple is the color scheme of the floor—room numbers, nurse's stations, and the large number that greets you when the elevator doors open. The other floors have color schemes, too. The fifth floor is yellow, third floor is green, and the eighth floor is red.
>
> Where are all these people coming from?
>
> All right, I am forced to jock for position. 5 . . . 4 . . . it's on its way down . . . 3 . . . 2 . . . you fools better move out of my way . . . 1 here I go—zoom. I love it.
>
> Don't leave on my account.
>
> Once I'm on the elevator people don't like to ride with me. They usually jump out to get in another elevator. Maybe I frighten them by moving so quickly? Well, if I didn't, people would never let me on. So fine, don't get on with me—fewer stops. (Blackwell 2002, 105)

What follows is a series of encounters between Blackwell, other individuals, and building structures at the hospital. At each encounter, she highlights how the culture is constructing her identity and her attempt to actively push against it. At one point, she informs the doctor not to infantilize her by calling her "sweetie"; later, she stares down a woman who will not stop looking at her. Throughout the narrative, she plays with her identity as a paraplegic and how it is read by others.

Her awareness of how she is read by others is most evident when she describes the accident that led to her being a quadriplegic. Here she attempts to form an alternative to the representations that would cast her as a victim of North Philadelphia urban crime. When asked by an elderly woman how she was hurt, Blackwell responds:

"No, my injury wasn't gang related. Actually, it didn't happen 'out there' in North Philly."

"Oh! Where did it occur?"

How did I know you were going to ask that?

"I was on the boardwalk with some friends."

"The boardwalk? The Atlantic City Boardwalk."

Look, lady, will you let me tell you the story?

"No. It was the Ocean City Boardwalk . . ."

"Were you vacationing, school trip, just visiting?"

What?

Man, Agatha Christie. Sit back on the edge of the bench and let me finish.

"Just visiting. And I was on the boardwalk and this man came over to me when I was laughing—I forget about what.   "Anyhow, he said, 'You know, you remind me of my wife.' Then as I began to leave and walk away, he shot me."

"My heavens! You poor dear. Well, did you look like his wife?"

Here comes the kicker.

"No, not at all. His wife was a thin women with honey-blonde hair."

"What? What do you mean honey-blonde hair? You mean his wife was white?"

"Yup."

"Was he white too?"

"Uh, huh."

"Well, how did he think . . ."

"I don't know. I doubt if there were any similarities. Maybe it was my laugh. My mother used to tell me my laugh would get me into trouble."

Especially when I was in Catholic School.

"What happened to him?"

"It is said that he went three blocks and blew his brains out."

"Oh, no."

"Yup. No trial, no sentencing and no punishment."

"Where did he get the gun?"

"Oh, a small arsenal was later found in his home." (2002, 115)

The truth of Blackwell's injury, that she was shot by a police officer's stray bullet while he was chasing a purse thief, is recoded to issues of domestic violence and gun control. The location is changed from "gang-related" North Philly to the seemingly safe Ocean City. In effect, by telling this story, she is critiquing readers who would have less sympathy for an urban crime victim. Only later in the story does the reader learn the truth. In this way, Blackwell is consciously attempting to disrupt the commonsense images that would frame her injury and to recast how the reader will ultimately understand her neighborhood and culture.

As a piece of writing for a college course, this essay has much to admire. Blackwell demonstrates the ability to create a strong narrative voice as well as to build drama—witness the story about how she was shot. She also uses humor to highlight the absurdity with which she is perceived. This particular student essay also represents the ability to "shuttle" between existing public narratives and personal experience, described by Kurt Spellmeyer in "Foucault and the Freshman Writer" (1989)—a movement that allows the writer to show the instability of any relationship she might create with any "collective" public identity. Indeed, both Blackwell's particular piece and the general framework of *No Restraints* attempt to show the complexity of forming a collective—a collective that is at once unified, always tentative, and often the result of personal commitments. As such, Blackwell's piece speaks to the type of work that might inform elements of a writing course concerned with issues of *public writing* and *community partnerships*. In fact, one can imagine the piece, à la Spellmeyer, continuing to be developed along the lines of an emergent identity's complicated relationship to the public sphere.

(In invoking Spellmeyer's concept of the essay to discuss Blackwell's paper, however, I do not want to be seen as endorsing his entire conceptual model. In part, as John Trimbur [1994] points out, Spellmeyer's work has a tendency to imply a free zone from which students can invoke personal experience without concerns of institutional formation—a framework that would collide with my formulation of the contact zone. In addition, Spellmeyer's generalized critique of theory, as discussed in "After Theory" [1996], does not account for theory as a tool by which to reformulate traditional models of benevolence on which many community partnerships have been based. That is, I argue that theory provides an important framework through which to imagine locally specific, community-based partnerships. Indeed, Marx's theory of value, which Spellmeyer alludes to as benefitting only Marx, was the lynchpin in resolving the *Glassville Memories* project.)

When considered within the goals of *No Restraints,* however, Blackwell's narrative takes on a different hue, for although the narrative voice is quite strong, it remains a singular voice. There is a sense that language is socially constructing Blackwell's reality, but there is no equivalent sense, beyond word play, that it is possible to intervene in changing her reality—the daily physical and political architecture. The protest remains at the level of the personal (staring at others, word play, and so on). The essay reveals only one-half of the power of language—to construct common sense—and not the other-half—to revise the language of common sense through collective action. (In this way, the project enacted only one-half of the voice politics articulated in chapter 1.) Nor, by itself, does the paper ask the student (or the class) to imagine a role in the formation of a larger disability community.

With the inclusion of Blackwell's paper in *No Restraints,* these issues came to the forefront of discussion. New questions emerged:

• What would it mean to imagine this paper as part of the collective disability rights effort occurring in Philadelphia? How might its rhetoric position the writer?

• How does the rhetorical position of the individual narrator interact with the collective identity being constructed within the disability rights movement?

• How does a classroom that values such a narrator imagine its space as public? How does such a paper confirm or disrupt the traditional role of the writing classroom within a larger literacy network?

The value of Blackwell's paper within a writing classroom rests in the complicated relationship it might have to these questions. It would be too easy, for instance, to say that her paper has no relationship to the collective disability rights movement. Many of the rhetorical gestures she employs are clearly echoed in the other work discussed earlier. The absence of direct reference to the political struggles, such as equal access, can be read as a sign of the relatively poor public profile of these movements in Philadelphia. The gesture to remove the cause of her disability from North Philadelphia, a predominantly African American part of the city, might even be read as a comment on how race and class are understood within the disability movement. The reader might ask, "How does the disability movement interact with issues of inner-city poverty and violence? Can Blackwell even see herself in local activists work?" In fact, as these questions begin to be answered, the essay's relationship to the idea of the collective becomes problematic. Of which collective does Blackwell imagine herself a member—the classroom audience, the university, the neighborhood, the disability community? All of the above?

Blackwell's paper and its appearance in *No Restraints* raised strong questions about how the New City Writing classroom would interact with collective movements for social change—how it might enable students to move from seeing writing as a means to record personal experience to understanding it as a means for engaging in collective action. It posed the question of how a classroom might continually attempt to position itself (and its students) as one node among a network of emergent collectivities and publics—a classroom in constant contact and negotiation with larger movements for social change. After *No Restraints,* it became clear that New City Writing classes should engage students in both aspects of writing—the power to construct *and* revise common sense. Its classrooms should be about the work of inviting student writers to write themselves into collective action. Such work would provide opportunities to participate in the creation of new urban collectives that would demonstrate the richest sense of language use and allow the strongest sense of the collective writer to emerge.

The question became how to turn this singular moment into a programmatic practice.

Positioning Student Writing in the Contact Zone

When New City Writing began many of its school and community partnerships, I found myself continually returning to Mary Louise Pratt's concept
of a contact zone: a space "where cultures meet, and grapple with each other,
often in contexts of highly asymmetrical relations of power, such as colonialism, slavery, or their aftermaths as they are lived out in many parts of the
world today" ([1991] 2005, 519). In part, the phrase "asymmetrical relations
of power" was a reminder to recognize the alternating strength the university might carry in any particular partnership. In the case of the Philadelphia
Writing Centers Project, for instance, New City Writing had too little power;
in the case of the Glassville project, it had too much. The concept of the
contact zone also became a way to frame university/community partnerships for students in a writing classroom. Rather than being a place where
only standard English or academic discourse was studied and practiced, the
New City Writing classrooms were marked from the outset by the variety
and scope of the discourses deployed. Indeed, in almost every classroom
described thus far, students were asked to read fiction, nonfiction, vernacular
texts, political treatises, academic prose, and community publications. Further, the ultimate goal was not only to adopt the possibilities of *contact* as
a central metaphor for gaining knowledge in the class, but through related
community partnerships to allow students to interrogate how unofficial and
official discourses collide in the actual production of knowledge.

At the outset, New City Writing student and community discourses
were often positioned as outside of the academic or political mainstream.
To slightly reframe Pratt through Certeau, the projects discussed so far in
this book imagined the student and community writers at the edge of an
established discourse, working to find a means by which both would be
heard and neither would need to abandon the values of their home community. The initial results were often similar to Pratt's primary examples, her
son and Guaman Poma. Writing was produced that failed to be read by its
intended audience or, if read, failed to be understood as a coherent example
of knowledge production because it seemed to fall outside the political crite-
ria of acceptable discourse. In response to students' descriptions of the harsh
reality of their lives, for instance, teachers in the *Urban Rhythms* project

consistently encouraged them to alter their writing to make it more "acceptable" and "positive." The Philadelphia Writing Centers Project produced a variety of texts that created new knowledge about a student's home community and its educational system. The main school district office, however, did not understand the discourse in which this knowledge was presented—vernacular and poetic—and so the program was dramatically reduced. Even the Glassville project is an example of this failed readership because the first set of interview texts produced by students were not seen as sufficiently representative of the community to be acceptable. Each of these failed writing partnerships, however, offered a rich area of study for students in New City Writing classes.

Indeed, Pratt argues that the contours and machinations of such rhetorical production should be at the center of a literacy classroom. By studying the conflicts that emerge when individuals attempt to negotiate rhetorical and language patterns across the contact zone, writers can gain a better sense of how community works. The very study of such literacy practices becomes a means through which to understand the political and social possibilities of different subject positions. In this way, Pratt is imagining a safe space where students not only can begin to understand different subject positions, but also can come to recognize how if that understanding is adopted within a particular community, it might collectively alter the dynamics between literacy and power. By allowing students to engage with different identities without consequence (because the class dynamic suppresses real-life community consequences), Pratt's imagined classroom models an idyllic form of democratic debate. (Blackwell's essay might be seen as an outstanding student paper in such a classroom because of its play and engagement with multiple public identities.) In such a class's strongest articulation, students gain a sophisticated sense of language and culture that they then act upon in their daily lives.

Pratt's argument is compelling. It offers a way to imagine our students' work as intimately connected with political debate and change. Nevertheless, based on my experience at New City Writing, I would like to suggest that despite the power of this argument to reinvigorate the content of the multicultural classroom, what the metaphor of contact has not done is change the parameters of the actual classroom—the nature of the contact with actual voices from outside. The voices of the contact-zone classroom are still primarily textual more than actual (to return to my argument concerning value and the Glassville project). Mark Hall and Mary Rosner have argued that the very word *contact* seems ultimately to work against Pratt's own vision: "[C]ontact suggests a state of benign or even genial relationship, not a violent battle. Contact denotes a state of being in or coming into close association or connection. Contact also suggests touching or unity. This interpretation is just the opposite of the breach, break, rupture, or split that results from the clashing and grappling that Pratt imagines" (2004, 106). They argue that it is just this soft version of contact that Patricia Bizzell adopts in her defense of contact-zone multicultural pedagogy (see Bizzell 1994, 2002). Nontraditional texts are brought into the classroom, but they are sufficiently acceptable so as not to spark actual conflict and negotiation among a variety of communities. Yet, as I had come to learn through my experiences, community partnerships often spark actual conflict, protest, and struggle. To understand rhetoric and composition, students have to experience this struggle as well.

A similar critique can be made about the term *arts*, with its focus on the individual who is able to finesse and negotiate language rather than on the collective struggle to alter social and political patterns. In this sense, it is important that both of Pratt's primary examples, her son and Guaman Poma, do not seem to be acting as part of a group or general movement. Their *arts* are representative because they are acting as individuals. This individual focus also seems to be replicated in Pratt's classroom. Based on her essay, it does not appear that student texts are connected to collective movements for change on the national or local level. In this way, the "arts of the contact zone" do not refer to the robust engagement imagined by use-value, where communities are collectively brought in to share power, but to the more limited exchange-value of curriculum reform, where individual voices are invited into the classroom as objects of study. The classroom becomes a safe house, whose internal workings are discretely separated from the surrounding neighborhood's collective legislative struggles. Although Gramsci would clearly recognize Pratt and Bizzell's work as legislative in its limited effort to reform English studies, I would argue that it too easily accepts the limits of disciplinary boundaries instead of exploring the larger network in which language and power interact.

At this point, it is useful to go back to the example of Guaman Poma and consider an alternative framing of his work and its application to the writing classroom. According to Pratt, Felipe Guaman Poma de Ayala was most likely "an indigenous Andean who claimed noble Inca descent," "who had adopted (at least in some sense) Christianity, and [who] may have worked for the Spanish Colonial Administration" ([1991] 2005, 519). Although this situation is clearly complex, it is important to note the set of legitimate discourses Guaman Poma attempted to draw upon—Andean royal heritage, Christianity, and an official government position. Each discourse is placed in opposition to the other in the colonial context, but they all are legitimate in their respective domains. Without essentializing the position of the subaltern or denying the complexity of the situation, it is clear that Guaman Poma does not represent those who are merely described (and not agents) within these official discourses. His twelve-hundred-page "letter" to the king of Spain is more a negotiation between historically legitimate discourses than an intervention that would speak to the needs of the unrepresented mass of the Inca (or the Spanish, for that matter). In this sense, it is important to note that as represented by Pratt, Guaman Poma's letter does not imagine a call for an independence movement based on collective struggle. Instead, it recommends a partnership among elites. Even in the more recent example of her son, Pratt does not use this moment as a way to organize parents to expand the contours of what is acceptable prose; she ultimately represents her son's writing as an individual moment.

An alternative way to frame Poma's letter, then, would be to imagine how it might have been occurring within a terrain where other individuals and groups were arguing for a third alternative—a different sense of power that worked against both Andean and Spanish royalty. Arjuna Parakrama's study of the Sri Lankan "revolt" of 1848 (he calls the term *revolt* into question) examines the status of a "pretender king" who exists within the context of active anticolonial struggle. In *Language and Rebellion* (1990), Parakrama cites numerous official documents by the British colonial authorities that discuss a "pretender" who is said to have initiated a rebellion against their rule. Through close reading, Parakrama argues that a focus on official documents cannot offer an accurate picture into "the rebellion":

It is, therefore, no surprise that my examination of the discourses on the rebellion have established that one of the reasons for the denial of peasant agency concerns the fact that peasant discourse is predicated on an alternate paradigm which cannot co-exist with any casual-rational-legal model which is the only one that has any explanatory power within elite historiography. Even when there is some accounting for the rebel voice within the discourses on the rebellion, such accounting has become possible only through an exclusion of the types of response that call into question this very model itself. . . .

In this view, if it is possible to formulate tentative statements that arguably present the underlying thesis/theses of the discourse, then one must re-examine the discourse itself for strands that have been left out or covered over. The proper object of study must then be one that defies its propositional representation. (68–69)

Pratt's reading of Guaman Poma's letter attempts to position it as a text that defies "propositional representation." I would argue that this is only partially true. Its failure to be "read" does demonstrate the elite Spanish authorities' inability to understand a mixture of elite discourses, and in that way it does defy propositional representation. Her reading does not, however, attempt to highlight or recognize those nonelite rhetorical models and actions that defy propositional representation within either set of elite discourses—the voices of those outside of administrative, religious, or mainstream power structures à la Certeau and suppressed by colonialism. Such rhetorical models, as discussed in previous chapters, rest upon the edge of discourse—the unarticulated collection of experiential, fragmentary, and emergent understandings of collective subject positions. Beyond Guaman Poma and Spanish colonial authorities are the voices and struggles of everyday people; beyond Guaman Poma, that is, lies the possibility of the formation and production of an oppositional vernacular culture.

For this possibility to become reality, however, processes must be created that can permeate this diffuse terrain and articulate a common sensibility among a set of individuals. Prior to this moment of articulation, fragmented and partial knowledges rest adjacent but not connected to each other. The culture is latent and not actualized. In this sense, vernacular culture is the successful production of an oppositional collective subject position drawn from a community's personal experiences and knowledges. It is the result of contentious active negotiation and organization. However flawed, *Urban Rhythms*, the Glassville project, the Philadelphia Writing Centers Project, and *No Restraints* represent prototypes of the process necessary to create new vernacular cultures within the specific field of educational politics. It is this process, I believe, that most accurately represents the true work of the contact zone.

A writing class focused on the connections between the production of writing and the production of a vernacular politics would recast Pratt's focus on autoethnographic texts. Pratt appears to define autoethnographic texts as only rhetorically connected to larger struggles concerning issues of political power or collective politics. She does not frame them as *part of* larger social struggles. She writes:

> Guaman Poma's New Chronicle is an instance of what I have proposed to call an autoethnographic text, by which I mean a text in which people undertake to describe themselves in ways that engage with representations others have made of them. Thus if ethnographic texts are those in which European metropolitan subjects represent to themselves their others (usually their conquered others), autoethnographic texts are representations that the so-defined others construct in response to or in dialogue with those texts. Autoethnographic texts are not, then, what are usually thought of as autochthonous forms of expression or self-expression (as the Andean quipus were). Rather they involve a selective collaboration with and appropriation of idioms of the metropolis or the conqueror. These are merged or infiltrated to varying degrees with indigenous idioms to create self-representations intended to intervene in metropolitan modes of understanding. Autoethnographic works are often addressed to both metropolitan audiences and the speaker's own community. Their reception is thus highly indeterminate. ([1991] 2005, 519–20)

In making her argument, Pratt is attempting to respond to some of the difficulties ethnographers encounter as they attempt to record culture—the historical pattern to frame the voice of "the other" within westernized forms of knowledge and understanding. She is suggesting a collage or multivocal strategy to capture the complex relationship of an ethnographer (or any individual student) to the interrelated discourses and power relationships existing at that moment (see chapter 3). To some extent, she repositions Guaman Poma's letter as a form of informed anthropological scholarship designed to recast debate by producing a well-sourced persuasive essay. Although such rhetorical strategies are important, it is unclear how they intersect with collective movements to redefine—in a concrete legislative (political, economic, social) fashion—the actual political terrain. That is, it seems odd to base a practice on a strategy that fails to produce actual results.

For that reason, my emphasis on autoethnographic works would be to stress how concepts of "own community" are the results of collective struggle. I think autoethnographic texts should also be read as part of a general movement to create new communities and thus alter the normative patterns in which debates occurred. Reading the texts in this context demands greater attention to how they are surrounded by other voices collaboratively creating a new subject position from which to speak. Rather than in *auto*-ethnographic texts, singular, my interests lie in *collective* ethnographic texts, such as *No Restraints,* that not only attempt to alter the representational logic in which a population exists, but are also part of a collective political and legislative struggle as well. Moreover, as discussed in previous chapters, the goal of such texts is to produce a community-based readership; that is, the audience is not "scholars," but community members, scholars, and politicians who might model a potential collective identity. Thus, although it is certainly necessary to imagine the writing classroom as engaging with texts representing different subject positions, doing so is not sufficient if the goal is to provide students with a model to understand how writing is a legislative act in the larger sense—a collective writing and rhetorical project designed to gain social status as a recognized community that can then argue for legal and political rights. Such texts must also engage in the process of creating a readership, a community of commonly identified individuals committed to a concrete agenda.

This was the lesson of *No Restraints.*

For all these reasons, the New City Writing classroom became focused on how individuals work to form collectives so that the larger public can hear and respond to their "voice." That is, New City Writing positioned itself as aligned with Elbow's focus on the personal as one strategy through which to build a writers community (although here the community was imagined as both students and local residents), and it accepted Bartholomae's vision that writing needs to be seen within a tradition of discussion and insights by experts, although here the students and residents were drawing forth that local tradition of thought through their writing and research with community experts. As such, this positioning respected the hybrid nature of voice while recognizing the need for the university to serve a strategic role in the locally determined struggle for a community's right for self-representation.

The particular focus of a New City Writing classroom *within the curriculum* would thus be to have students study how certain discourses gain the collective status to represent a community and how this community works to expand its legitimacy by embedding its members' voices in a variety of existing institutions. The goal would be to supply the theoretical and academic models that would enable the students to move into advanced and disciplinary-based courses. In addition, however, they would work *beyond the curriculum* in that the course would also provide community-based venues in which students would actively work on the *edge of discourse,* understanding their research and writing in the context of identities that do not yet have full social standing and of discourses that have not yet gained dominant social power. It is only through actively studying and engaging in such work that students can begin to see the full terrain upon which language operates and upon which Pratt's contact zone is based.

Yet if contact-zone pedagogy demands a writing classroom focused around issues of emergent communities and implies writing in relationship to those communities, then the conception of the classroom as a public space must also be adjusted. In either the multicultural or safe-house classroom, the public sphere is held in opposition to the work of the classroom, which itself becomes disconnected from the outside world. The classroom, however, should be seen as only one moment or element in a network of literacy and language production—central within some aspects of the network, marginal in others. The work of the writing class should be both to highlight the situatedness of its particular writing domain and to demonstrate how its work operates and can participate in establishing new collective nodes that rearticulate existing literacy and political pathways. Instead of a safe house, a writing classroom should be a space of constant border crossing and engagement with individuals and groups outside the classroom who are attempting to redefine the legislative context. Here the term *contact* implies the constant need to engage with emergent collective identities as political and social forces that shape the contours of public interaction—from the personal to the political. In this way, the work of a writing classroom is not so much mixing multicultural texts as coming into *contact* with the voices from the *edge* that are trying to reshape public debate through writing.

It is important to recognize, however, that there are many different publics. The current generation of students has grown up in a world where neoconservative visions of public engagement have been dominant. In such a worldview, the public is marked by the individual citizens who volunteer time to maintain the public sphere's sense of justice or "the good." Basing community engagement on such individual participation, however, leaves out alternative ways in which members of the public organize themselves *collectively* (see Welch 2008). As Nancy Fraser (1990) argues, there is a long history of voluntary nonliberal sites of organization or protest—with the term *liberal* used here as shorthand for "bourgeoisie male-dominated discursive practices." These "weak publics" might not have the same legislative authority as "strong publics," such as state entities, but they can have social and political impact. An important element of New City Writing's work, then, was its engagement with a variety of publics—public schools, arts organizations, community rights groups, and so on—all of which offered alternative models for organizing and framing the public sphere. For students in our classrooms, the goal became to create partnerships that allowed them to imagine a variety of subject positions and writing/rhetorical strategies from which to alter the normative patterns of their communities—to become collective legislators within their neighborhoods. Through New City Writing courses, students came to recognize how the classroom is simultaneously a weak public in its history of formulating opinion and a potential ally to those engaged in altering the strong publics that structure individual and collective lives.

Connecting the classroom to the community, to the public, is not enacting a neoconservative vision of service. Rather, it is the necessary step to ensure that our students understand the ways in which one public (students and the university) is currently structured in relationship to other aspects of the collective public (community rights organizations, state and federal agencies, and so on). More to the point, the writing that occurs in the classroom should ideally operate so that the question of the responsibilities and rights of collective identities are not just debated, but become imbricated in the very nature of the writing done for class. This does not mean that all writing has to be public—as in published outside of class—but that all writing must understand its actions as either participating in the formation of a new collective identity or attempting to suture itself within current rhetorical and political possibilities. The student paper, then, should be read for how its rhetoric positions the writer within educational, social, and political networks; it should be read for how it imagines the role of the student-citizen-writer as a participant within multiple public spheres. That is, because our classroom is inherently public (part of a network of literacy and political institutions), we must teach our students to understand that all writing is a negotiation of voice participating in the publicly negotiated civic culture.

I believe that through such work, the student writer begins to develop a set of tools to better negotiate the demands of citizenship. Here I align myself with Gwen Gorzelsky, whose *Language of Experience* (2005) argues that the rhetorical language patterns used by individuals are key determinants in how they structure their lives. By engaging individuals within a process that offers alternative rhetorical strategies, the possibility exists for individuals to alter how they see themselves interacting with the world. For Gorzelsky, it is only through an internal altering of how an individual makes rhetorical contact with the world that changes in behavior will actually occur. To this extent, she is also critiquing a pedagogical methodology that works from the assumption that learning the abstract theories on social change will result in political change. Her focus asks us to consider how the rhetorical patterns a person shifts through within a classroom allows different types of affective and political personalities to emerge.

Indeed, Gorzelsky's model can reframe New City Writing's work with different communities as moments in which a connection was fostered between the personal development of those involved and the collective writing activities of a particular project for the purpose of creating a more inclusive and progressive public sphere. In chapter 1, a student's personal and political growth was seen as stunted by a curriculum divorced from community traditions of collective responsibility *(Urban Rhythms)*. Next, chapter 2 considered students and teachers' ability to use writing as a framework to develop a new educational community aligned with progressive politics (Philadelphia Writing Centers Project). Finally, chapter 3 looked closely at a model wherein students' academic writing was put in dialogue with a community struggle for greater economic and political rights (Glassville). In each case, the implicit aim was to examine how expanding an individual's rhetorical and conceptual strategies connected with larger collective or community goals. The overt goal was to use the university classroom as a site to produce writers whose language practices are intimately connected to struggles for a community's collective recognition.

By asking students to participate in alternative rhetorical and literacy practices—practices that are intimately connected to collective movements for political and social rights—the New City Writing classroom was attempting to participate in the production of a new progressive definition of "citizen" and "legislative action." It was this vision that my colleagues and I developed for our classrooms after the *No Restraints* experience. It was the vision we would ultimately implement into our work as teachers and administrators.

Writing Within (and Beyond) the Curriculum in Action

After *No Restraints* and in the midst of the Glassville crisis, FWWCP coordinator Tim Diggles visited New City Writing. His visit in 2003 was prearranged and designed to occur as students across multiple sections were reading *Glassville Memories* in relationship to *The Republic of Letters* (Maguire et al. [1982] 2010), the FWWCP's manifesto about the value of community-based writing, and *Once I Was a Washing Machine* (FWWCP 1989), an anthology of FWWCP's previously published work. *The Republic of Letters* situates the FWWCP's commitment to expansive writing practices within the larger political goals of working-class rights. At Temple University, which at the time was still admitting a large cross-section of the urban working class, this message resonated with the students. In my experience, they seemed to grasp intuitively the connections between literacy and power—between who produces knowledge and who benefits from it. What also resonated with the students was the absence of such an organization in their own neighborhoods. Indeed, many of them reflected on the value of such an organization as they struggled to define the connections among intellectual work, community rights, and literacy practices. In writing classrooms dominated by the Glassville crisis, the FWWCP offered students an alternative model of community organization—a model that would have had Glassville residents organizing to write their own history as opposed to being recorded by university students, a model where they would have produced their own book as opposed to having their experiences and community filtered through the university.

There was another component to the FWWCP's involvement in the New City Writing classroom, however. For the FWWCP, our writing classroom represented an opportunity to support the next stage of its continued battle for recognition. Despite more than twenty years of publishing, Diggles believed the FWWCP was still trying to legitimate as *intellectually* valid the writing its members produced. That is, there continued to be a struggle to define the writing produced by "everyday folk" as worthy of funding from arts and private foundations. As Diggles headed back to England, he suggested that the student writers' could support FWWCP's efforts. Up to that point, there had been little academic validation of FWWCP's work; few colleges assigned FWWCP texts in the United Kingdom or the United States. Diggles felt it would be an important intellectual and cultural argument for British foundations that FWWCP writers' work was the object of study at a major U.S. university.

Within classrooms already actively debating the process and imagined product of a revised Glassville publication, a new possibility to connect their writing to public debates appeared. Diggles suggested that the FWWCP's *Federation Magazine* sponsor an issue entitled *Liberating the Literary World* (2003) that would feature a collection of writing by Temple students. As stated in the "Feditorial," the magazine's opening statement:

> From within a group like the Fed it is often difficult to gauge the impact its work has in the wider world. The Fed works mainly through volunteers, and its funding, although increasing, is relatively small compared to that of the other arts projects. Often because it is a voluntary activity, what we

do seems like a way of life. There are people around who always seem to have been involved in community publishing and working class writing. It is valuable to us, because in this context we have invested a lot of time and energy, but is it important to anyone else?

This issue deals with questions of how our writing and publishing is represented. The testimony of Temple University students, for example, shows that our message is getting across, that there is an important role for the Fed and its members in showing people how they can own and facilitate their own cultural representation, rather than conceding the presentation of the community to other interpreters. This is the message conveyed by the homeless Speakout recipes organized by Groundswell, and permeating this issue's Broadsheet.

If we don't Speakout [*sic*] then more credence will be given to the bowdlerised, sexed-up and sentimentalized versions of community life offered in popular culture than to the reality of our own experience. We'd not know ourselves if we saw ourselves coming down Coronation Street or down the market at Walford. Our diversity cannot be confined to a convenient box in the corner of the cultural living room, we have much more to offer, much more to engage with through active participation. You can't maintain a passive recipient role in the Fed. (Pollard 2003, 3)

The resonances of the "Feditorial" with the work of New City Writing are evident. In the call for self-representation, the *Urban Rhythms* students' voices intersect with the FWWCP's goals. In the call for communities not to cede their representation to "outside interpreters," the tumultuous history of the Glassville project is evident. There is even a connection to the "use-value" of literature in the claim that FWWCP writing cannot be "confined to a convenient box in the corner of the cultural living room." It should not be surprising, then, that the New City Writing students, engaged in a classroom where the FWWCP and many of these New City projects were discussed, were able to articulate the value of the FWWCP across community and academic boundaries:

Meredith B. Lindemon:
[The FWWCP offers] written accounts of their lives and personal experiences. Like all scholars, they provide knowledge on a subject that has

previously been neglected or little known, and incite a response from their audience. . . .

The boundaries of intellectual thought and scholarship are beginning to shift. Through the publication of works such as *The Republic of Letters* and others, readers may be able to recognize and identify with the "intellectuals" in their own communities. This alone will give people the power to start viewing themselves as scholars in their own right. Writing today has become a lost art, quite possibly due to the fact that mainstream literature has become a dump bin of works which do not inspire the readers to react in any way. If groups like the FWWCP continue in the backing of talented young writers, and make the dream of publication a reality, then perhaps these boundaries will make a more rapid shift.

Christine Rosato:

From a political standpoint, the FWWCP is fighting for literary equality; they believe that stories should not have to embody stereotypical "classic novel" characteristics in order to be published. The reader should be the ultimate judge of a particular writing.

This is shown through the FWWCP's statement, "we have come to believe within the federation that it is vital that we should develop alternative values and other contexts by which to celebrate the achievement of writing, in order that new writers may feel that there is proper recognition of all efforts and very hard work required to produce a manuscript."

Having autobiographical tales from Philadelphia would be a great way to show how much culture the city has. In *The Republic of Letters* the FWWCP states, "language has been for many centuries one of the main forms in which class and cultural differences have been expressed"[;] some writings may be about stress of being a high quality lawyer at city hall, while others may deal with the embarrassment and frustration of begging for change near the subway. These writings could give Philadelphians "power"[;] by writing and reading these works citizens may gain a better understanding of each other. City problems such as poverty, welfare, pollution, and job-related issues may be brought to the attention of the reader that could better the situation for many of the venting writers.

Marta Gershman:

The Federation addresses the systems of those with power versus those without power and the rights that each group receives. This may be just the first step in breaking the class systems that create glass ceilings for so many people. This new found inspiration can motivate those who are used to pressing their faces up against that glass ceiling to grab a hammer and break that glass. The FWWCP is telling us all that we don't have to be born into royalty or be extremely rich to fit into any of those stereotypes that come with being a good writer or a good anything. It seems that it is time that all our voices are heard.

Sherley Legerme:

When people submit their work to the FWWCP, it is obvious that their approach to their writing and even their actual dialect is very different than what some people might be accustomed to. For example, the piece entitled "Once I was a Washing Machine," written by Olive Rogers, shows how language varies depending on the individual. When first read by us as a class, this particular piece of writing had to be analyzed, this was not necessarily an easy task to perform. The style of writing was not familiar to the class, nor was the use of metaphors. This proves that language isn't universal or neutral, because this particular poem was not as easy to understand as it might have been for someone else. Someone that might have come from the same environment, or has dealt with the same issues as the person in the poem, would probably have been able to understand the author's writing style and dialect much more clearly. However, a contrast in language doesn't mean one's work is turned away from the Federation's magazines and books. After all, "Language isn't neutral." Throughout the world, everyone has a different way of speaking. . . . Language will not be the same in every part of the world, but yet people find ways to accept the various ways of speaking, and somehow incorporate this new dialect into their own. Consider an example that can be found right outside your front door. The concept of slang has been floating around the United States for centuries now. At first, it was not accepted into our society because it was considered improper to speak in such a manner. The proper English language was the only language recognized in the United States, but who is to say what should be considered proper? The word "gonna" has been used so often that many don't even recognize it anymore as a slang term. This just proves that throughout the years, pieces of other languages are incorporated into our own. Different ways of speaking often require different forms of language that one might not be familiar with. Language is never going to be the same, no matter where one might go. The beauty of it all is that these different forms of language allow various kinds of writing to be published. This is what the FWWCP is trying to say, that "different work, reflecting popular experience; different writers, whom you may know and can certainly meet; different distribution, through local centres and face-to-face contacts—all these have created a new reading public" *(Republic of Letters)*.

Renee Bowe:

Many ideas portrayed by the Federation should be taken into account here in our community and in the United States. I believe that to produce a variety of literature, educational facilities should open their department up to more literature options. "There is a struggle which goes on inside the university literature departments, as well as outside; there is a consistent resistant to the inclusion of modern works of study." (all excerpts from *Liberating the Literary World* 2003, 10–15)

What is important to note about these excerpts is how the students intentionally expand the definition of the terms *intellectual* and *scholarship* to include the FWWCP's work. As important, they do so while consciously critiquing concepts of the intellectual that are based on elitist categories— traditional literature, for instance—and they do so in essays that themselves enact a form of academic scholarship. The writers quote from numerous sources, offer different types of evidence, and take a position based on facts, not emotion. In this way, the students are demonstrating their own argument—that such voices deserve to be actively studied by current and future scholars. At such moments, these writers were moving beyond the category of "students" to become "cultural critics" who wrote not only on behalf of a set of community beliefs, but in support of organizations that enact those beliefs. In doing so, they recalibrated the classroom's relationship with the public sphere, shifting its location in the network of literacy education from a required course in the traditions of academic writing to an advocacy site for community-based writing both locally and internationally.

In this sense, the students were collectively developing a different rhetorical relationship between their education and public debates over literacy and education. Instead of seeing academic writing as the domain of an ivory-towered elite or a required passport to higher education, the students were using those very academic tools to argue for a different relationship between the university and the public sphere. They were coming to realize that the tools of academic writing itself—critical analysis, close reading, and so on—could be turned to important cultural and political debates concerning education and literacy. À la Gramsci, they were recasting the common sense of the academy along a new political trajectory. In line with Gorzelsky's argument, they were beginning to use their new rhetorical skills to reshape their relationship to the public sphere. They had moved from student writers to legislators, from writing required papers to requiring a new sense of writing from others.

In this moment, the student voices took on a public role within a current debate concerning the definition of literacy and the importance of economic support. They were addressing both local writing requirements (the goals of a required writing course) and definitions of public writing (the FWWCP newsletter). They were doing so both as critics (studying the mistakes of the Glassville project) and as advocates (endorsing the FWWCP). They were able to use their emergent academic knowledge to participate in a variety of collective activist projects designed to foster alternative vernacular cultures. Most important, they were doing so collectively, as a community of scholars working across neighborhood, institutional, and national boundaries, engaged in addressing real questions of literacy, access, and community power. They were helping to create a *crisis* in partnership with a variety of community and international organizations across systems in the hope that new alignments of power and representation might be made.

This was the work of students enrolled in New City Writing classrooms. Moving beyond static notions of inhabiting existing subject positions or artfully playing among established discourses, our students stood on the edge of a precipice—the precipice upon which knowledge is created and valued, an edge where a disparate collection of individuals and knowledges come into contact to create a collective enterprise and alternative future. Located in a classroom in North Philadelphia, they were active partners in the process of creating a new city—one that would exchange an individualist common sense for a collectivist communal sense, one that was based on a larger sense of justice than the profit motive, and one that would speak to a deeper sense of humanity than currently exists in our public debates.

Such writers represent a culminating moment in the history New City Writing.

5

The Insights of Everyday Scholars

New City Community Press

> Our mission is to provide opportunities for local communities to repre-
> sent themselves by telling their stories in their own words. We document
> stories of local communities because we believe their voices matter in
> addressing issues of national and global significance. We value these
> stories as a way for communities to reflect upon and analyze their own
> experience through literacy and oral performance. We are committed to
> working with communities, writers, editors and translators to develop
> strategies that assure these stories will be heard in the larger world.
> —New City Community Press mission statement

NEW CITY WRITING was premised on the concept "writing beyond the curriculum." Whereas previous chapters focused on New City's internal efforts
to support community-based writing, our goal was always to have the writing
produced circulate across the neighborhoods in which it emerged and through
the city, region, and nation in which it exists. Our vehicle for this public mission was New City Community Press. Through the press, publications such as
Glassville Memories have been used in classrooms in the suburbs of Philadelphia and at universities in Indiana; and *Espejos y Ventanas* has become part of
Mexican consulate and embassy education programs in Texas, the Carolinas,
and Michigan. All told, more than twelve thousand copies of New City publications have been sold and distributed across the United States.

These publications represent a sustained argument about who is an *intellectual*. For although the academy has certainly broadened its most restric-
tive definitions of this category, it is still the case that the store owner across
the street or the electrician fixing a plug in a faculty member's office is not

innately understood as an intellectual with a voice that carries wisdom and importance. In this way, to invoke Guillory (1993), New City Community Press has argued that if the university were to open up the means of aesthetic production, we would discover a formally marginalized set of working-class voices—across ages, ethnicities, and sexualities—from which we can learn about our world as it is and as it should become.

In this chapter, then, I step back from being the single narrator and provide a partial representation of the collective voices that have been a vital part of our successes. The excerpts are taken from the following New City Community Press publications:

Chinatown Live(s): Oral Histories from Philadelphia's Chinatown, edited by Lena Sze and published in 2004. Through twenty-two interviews, the varied and complex nature of Philadelphia's Chinatown is discussed.

Espejos y Ventanas / Mirrors and Windows: Oral Histories of Mexican Farmworkers and Their Families, edited by Mark Lyons and Leticia Roa Nixon, with an afterword by Jimmy Santiago Baca, and published in 2004. This collection details the individual stories of the Mexican community of Kennett Square, a community of three generations who have migrated to work in the world's largest mushroom industry, and relates their personal and political aspirations.

Glassville Memories, published in 2002.[1] This ethnographic project focuses on an urban neighborhood and its ability to achieve a richly realized sense of cultural diversity.

Free! Great Escapes from Slavery on the Underground Railroad, published in 2006. Lorene Cary uses William Still's Underground Railroad to capture the bravery exhibited by Africans as they escaped northward.

No Restraints: An Anthology of Disability Culture in Philadelphia, edited by Gil Ott and published in 2002. This collection of poetry, memoir, and photography documents the personal and political struggles of disabled citizens in Philadelphia.

OPEN City: A Journal of Community Arts and Culture, published in 2001. This publication brings together professional writers, community

1. As noted in chapter 3, *Glassville Memories* is a pseudotitle.

activists, school children, and artists to consider key terms such as *community* and *hunger*.

Soul Talk: Urban Youth Poetry, edited by M. Kristina Montero and published in 2007. Sixth- and seventh-grade students respond to the work of Luis J. Rodriguez, using it as a way to explore the nature of their education in an urban environment.

Urban Rhythms: A Journal on Music and Culture, published from 1997 to 1999. This online writing project for students, faculty, and community members includes work that discusses the value and complexity of urban identity.

Working: An Anthology of Writing and Photography, edited by Greg Hart, Mary Ellen Mangino, Zoeanne Murphy, and Ann Marie Taliercio and published in 2008. Workers in Syracuse, New York, share their stories of confronting the challenges of a new global economy and the valuable role unions have played in helping them survive such a difficult economic transition.

In their words and deeds, the individuals whose work is included in these volumes truly represent the goals of writing beyond the curriculum.

OPEN City: A Journal of Community Arts and Culture

Mama Frasier

YOLANDA PALACIO

Out of the house and up the sidewalk to the corner of 43rd and Chestnut Streets, we argued. The steeple of the ancient church across the street seemed to scold us for our pettiness but we kept on. On our way to 30th Street Station to catch the R5 to North Wales to see my mother, we hoped to catch a bus or cab at the corner. I was carrying an out of tune child's guitar; a gift for my sister. Already late, about to miss our train and pissed at one another, we stood in our frowns on either side of the bus stop sign with our thumbs out. The world was moving in slow motion. Out of the hot air, out of the heat waves of the summer, out of nowhere, an old woman with a face decorated with pockmarks and blackheads made her way with a cane across the street to us. As if she knew us, she started commenting on the downfall of young girls in clothes tighter than their friendships. She told us about the man she loved.

"You know how me and my husband made it through? We sang to each other. It make everything easy."

I kept looking for a bus, waiting for her to ask for change or hand us a religious pamphlet. I didn't know she would have us singing to each other on a hot day in July, late for our train with a huge riff between us. She reached for us, put our hands together as folks walked by on their way to and from the supermarket, the Rite-Aid on the next block. Her hands were swollen and rough, soft on the insides like dough. "Go 'head," she instructed. He sang an El DeBarge song to me, our hands gently rocking, "Someone just like me . . ." I hesitated, to have my voice all out in the open—I was embarrassed for myself, my lack of playing skills, my trembling alto. She said, "Honey, play that instrument in your hand and sing to this man. Look in his eyes." With her hand cradling my elbow, I sang the only song I could think of to the man I loved. Have you ever sung to your beloved? That day was a first for me. The words seemed to fly out of my mouth like confetti from a window and blow through the corridor of Chestnut Street. "*No* words to say . . ."

"See?" We smiled at each other, easily. The day was a fresh lily and this woman's face was a sun. Her pockmarks glittered. I pictured her man rinsed in her rough songs, his head thrown back, catching the jewelry of her voice around his neck.

"Where y'all going?" she asked. I told her we were going to 30th Street and she hailed a cab for us in less than three minutes. Told the driver where we were headed and held open the door as we got in. I asked what her name was; I wanted to write a poem 'bout her. She said, "Mom Frasier. I've been living here for years. This my neighborhood." She closed the cab door. Turned and walked away with the help of the cane. We made our train with one minute to spare. The woman had powers, the woman was love, and I didn't expect to see her again.

At the Crossroads: An Interview with Johnny Irizarry

YOLANDA PALACIO

Johnny Irizarry is an artist whose opus is his community. For over 20 years he has been at the forefront of creating program, curriculums, and goals for the Puerto Rican community and other communities of color in Philadelphia. But his work as Executive Director at Taller Puertoriqueno Inc., an organization which promotes Puerto Rican arts and culture, and his educational work in Puerto Rican, Latin American, and Latino Studies and multiculturalism came to a crossroads when he took on the challenge of running a school in the heart of the neighborhood. He is now the principal of the Eugenio Maria de Hostos Community Bilingual Charter School at 5th and Bristol Streets in North Philadelphia, which was founded to "promote excellence by providing middle level students a bilingual, bicultural academically enriched curriculum that draws from the social historical experience of Puerto Rico and Puerto Ricans living in the United States."

Getting past the obligatory protocol of description, I sat down to a warm chat with Johnny at Hostos Charter School amid cheerful student interruptions and visits to classes bustling with laughter and energy. I was afraid before getting off the bus that this man who had done so much for his community would be too busy to be approachable. But he was like an uncle who had seen a lot of the world in a little bit of time. He talked for hours about his students. It felt as though we talked about every student in the school. They felt like his own kids, the way he gleamed when he talked about them. We met in Johnny's office, a pleasant, light-filled room. I left feeling that Johnny gives his heart to the school in his attempts to bring reading, writing, art, and social issues together for one big masterpiece every day.

Open City: I want to start out with your beginnings and your experience with art and writing as a youth in the context of your family, school and community.

Johnny Irizarry: I didn't do a lot of reading actually because my parents weren't readers. My dad, I think, went to third grade and my mom went to eighth grade. They both spoke Spanish so they both worked in factories. My dad washed dishes and sold peanuts on 34th Street. So basically, there wasn't a lot of reading. I read a lot of church stuff, Bible stuff, and I actually used to hate reading.

But then my refuge became the library. I grew up in Harlem, West Harlem. And that library on 125th Street was there when I just couldn't take it anymore. It was a really weird place because it was huge with a lot of books. And I would go in there and there'd be a lot of people in there all the time. It was so different from where we lived because it was in the middle of the projects, this library. I had a cousin that had drug issues, but he read all the time. He was constantly telling me, "you got to read, you got to read." So that started my interest. When I moved to Puerto Rico, my uncles there were great readers of politics, and they got me into reading again.

OC: I'm interested in what motivated your decision to move from building and working with Taller Puertoriqueno to being the principal at Hostos.

JI: At Taller I burned myself out, I tell you. I took things too seriously. I wasn't burned out about working hard. I wasn't burned out about working with the community. I was burned out with bureaucracy, although our organization was not bureaucratic at all. We ran it, you know. But the bureaucracy forced it to be a certain way, you know, and so I sort of got burned out and thought that I couldn't do that work any more, right? But then I went to the school district for almost three years and had a pretty good position in Latino Studies. We wrote curriculum and did workshops, and I realized that before I had displaced myself even when centered in the culture. I had displaced myself from what I really believed in and where I thought I could really work. So when the charter school opportunity opened up, since I had been part of the original group of people that helped write the Curriculum, I jumped back. I really wanted it because it brings together two lives. Brings together arts and culture. Brings my educational experience into my work. It's the perfect opportunity. It's community controlled and very focused. We've taken on 200 kids. And with that comes another 500 individuals and probably trickles into another community based on what we do or how we perform. Everybody will be measuring us as people, right? So it's a big mission, but it's real. [The students] are here with us more than they are with their families.

OC: How do you see the university, the schools, and the community being interrelated? What kinds of possibilities do you see coming out of that kind of alliance?

JI: That's a deep question . . . we could be here all year! Well, there will always be great possibilities. The thing is that a lot of what's done at the University (now that I've been there a little bit), scholars and the assumptions that they make, the work that they've written about us, the biased research they've done about [us]—all that builds a resentment in people like me. People that live by Practice, you know. I don't have the doctorates to write it and it gets delegitimized when I say it. At the school district it happened to me all the time. I would go in there and do a whole workshop about exclusion and biases, how we're taught to hate ourselves and how they're all part of it, and just show examples and examples of our brilliance too. And afterwards people would always come up and go, "So where's your degree from?" knowing that I would have to say, "Oh no, I don't actually have a doctorate": And I'm thinking, Well, I'm *so* glad you graduated from the University of Columbia into all the "have you read so and so?" [Folks from the university] come with this assumption that because they read many books they know our reality and they know us and they can solve our problems for us. So they don't come in joining, they come in leading us, and the last thing we need is somebody else to tell us what to do.

A perfect example, at one of our morning assemblies [here at Hostos], I just came in and asked the kids, "Why does our neighborhood look like this?" And a bunch of kids said, "That's because we're pigs, that's 'cause we throw trash, 'cause we don't care, 'cause we're poor. . . ." And I said. "Look at this. I didn't ask you why our neighborhood looked dirty. I didn't ask you why our neighborhood looks torn down, I asked you why does our neighborhood look *like this*. You could have assumed I was asking why are our beautiful people walking down the streets. Why is it that there are a bunch of bustling little businesses all over the place? Why is it we have so much traffic? You could have said all this other stuff." But the kids didn't even see it that way—they are so taught to internalize their negativity.

Working with universities was really frustrating because it was a lot of patronizing relationships. There are people and departments who are a real good breath of fresh air. But there's always this assumption that they know better when they sit at a table with us. And I know that a lot of times it's our own fear to deal with intellectuals and confront them. Before I used to come in and be intimidated by them. You know, like "Oh man, he has a doctorate from Harvard or a doctorate from Yale. There's no way I can compete with that."

I used to do that, but now I don't do it—I don't care. So I would always fear when people would come from the university and tell us, "we want to work with your kids" or "we want to research" or "we want to do this research project" because it always became very exploitive. A lot of interns did really literally just come in and use us. On the other hand, a lot of interns came in and really gave, too. You can't shut the doors because for the student body I think it's critical. [Interns] can come to a neighborhood organization like this, and their knowledge blows up because all that theory they throw them [in the university] suddenly becomes a reality in their hands.

OC: How did the community assemblies with the kids begin here at Hostos?

JI: Actually, the principal before me started it and then she stopped because it "became a little overwhelming." I can see why because you've got to create dialogue. I create it in two sections. One is a learning opportunity and the other is a planning opportunity. So the assemblies are an opportunity to announce what's coming up and an opportunity to address serious issues. So for February, instead of just studying African-American heroes and focusing on the contributions of people of African descent, we focus more on the concept of anti-racism. So we talked about what is an anti-racist, how do you become an anti-racist, can we be a racist, can people who are victims of racism be racist, can you live as an anti-racist, what does it look like, what does it reflect, right? The assemblies concentrate a lot on this dialogue around bias, racism, prejudice and what are the differences between those terms. There was a lot of good conversation around that.

This month—March—we started Women's Heritage Month, with Women's International Day. I gave all the girls a tag day [a privilege which allows a student to attend school in street clothes] so they didn't have to wear their uniform, right? So the boys went crazy. And I have this bad habit of always saying, "Yo guys, come on, cool it, be quiet." We had just started getting into how gender bias works so one day I was doing the assembly, and I said, "Yo guys, come on," you know, and then the kids tell me that "guys" is a gender bias word. So I said, "All right, we'll switch the assembly. Every time we refer to the full group, we will say, 'Yo girls,' first." So we all started, "Yo

girls" even to the boys, right? And all the guys started squirming in their
seats, saying "No, no. It's not fair." And I said, "Why was it fair when it was
'guys' and everybody was fine with it? Even the girls weren't complaining."
So we created signs and we would choose four students every assembly to
raise the sign every time a gender bias word would come up. So they trained
me not to use "guys."

Today we went to the word "patriarch" and what is it to be patriarchal.
And we talked about machismo and what does that mean to our culture.
And that was a great conversation. We had them do debates—we would ask
them a bunch of questions about what can a man do and what can a woman
do and whose main responsibility is it to care for a child if a young lady gets
pregnant? And we started a conversation. It was pretty mixed—the girls'
feeling was that it was the girl's responsibility to care for a child and there
were girls that felt that it had to be a shared thing. There were boys that felt
it should be the girl's responsibility and boys that felt the opposite. And that
day was amazing. And they took it on, you know. Then it got more serious
with students saying, "Actually my dad does the wash," and "My mom won't
tolerate things like that." Their families are struggling with these issues that
the system assumes we don't even know about.

OC: Does any writing come out of these assemblies?

JI: For Valentine's Day, because they were all in love, we took these
paper hearts and I asked them to write a commitment to themselves and to
their classmates that didn't have anything to do with how cute they were.
And then we posted them all over the auditorium for about three weeks.
They didn't have to sign it but they looked really pretty because there were
all these hearts all over the room. I'm trying to use that concept of them
writing, reflecting, and seeing it again and being reminded of it. That is
good pedagogically because they'll turn around and forget what they told
you two minutes ago, you know.

OC: How have the kids responded to the assemblies and topics?

JI: A few of them have been coming and telling me it's boring so I want
to be fair to them. You've got to model democracy. What they told me was
that I bring up too many issues over and over again. So I told them, "All
right, it's boring. So what can we do?" I put up two sheets of paper, and I

just wrote the question "What can we do for assemblies?" It stayed empty. Every day I would come back and they would say "We can play games." And I would say "You know better than to put playing games into our assembly. You mean educational games?" And they said, "Yeah, yeah. Like you know, we guess things. That's good." And I told them, "Somebody create the game and I'm not going to sit here and play *Jeopardy* with you." Still nothing goes on the paper. I tell them that they have got to be dedicated to figuring out what other things to do. Finally, they said, they wanted a chance to show their own talents. And we've been doing it, and it's been a lot of fun. They've been great audiences. Some of the kids have actually gotten up there. Yesterday, one young man got up and read two short stories he wrote. I've got four other students registered to do dances and stuff. Some of the girls said they wanted to do it outside, so when the kids come in tomorrow I'm going to tell them to move their chairs outside and we're going to do this assembly. Yeah, that'll be a nice change.

OC: You mentioned that you really need programs here to nurture these kinds of talents in your student body. What kinds of programs are you looking to develop?

JI: The programs have to involve people with conscience, people that know how to motivate the students to write. They love to read, they love to read. We created one program that they can get a tag day if they read an extra book that's not assigned. These papers right here are from the first two weeks of kids. What they do is take this form and they put their name on it and their parent signs. I tell them they need to write three paragraphs on the book. If they can't do that, I tell them, "Write what you can."

OC: Just to hear everything you are doing with your kids is amazing. When I was a child, I lived through the experience of reading and writing . . . and listening to music. When you look back, those things were really important to you as a kid—even more so than how we related to school and success. It's really how we kept our sanity when things were going real—

JI: Yeah. That oral tradition of storytelling. Our grandfathers would remember. In Puerto Rico, my grandfather was illiterate but he would remember a poem that was at least ten pages long. And that's what they would do. They would memorize the books because there were no books.

Diary of a Scrapple Advocate

KEN FINKEL

Scrapple[2] is an underachiever. When sliced down and fried, a brick of scrapple yields smells, sounds, and tastes appreciated unchanged for more than three centuries. Scrapple is a classic, albeit an unsophisticated one. From pigs scrapple gets everything but the oink. From people, it gets everything but respect.

Surely this says something about Philadelphia.

Scrapple the food, as well as scrapple the idea, began eating at me in the mid-1970s. This culinary diamond in the rough has a transparent name, a shameless hue, and a pretensionless price. Its ancient roots give way to associations very unfoodlike: Quaker plainness and Pennsylvania German thrift. With little more than a nudge and a twist, scrapple could be re-purposed as a metaphor for Philadelphia.

Little by little, I was moved from notion, to realization, and finally to action. My period of scrapple advocacy lasted, in fits and starts, for many years. The following is a chronicle of those times, before advocacy retreated to dormancy.

Fall 1975: The Bicentennial is coming. Millions of hungry visitors are expected. The primary street vendor food—the hotdog—has no association to this historic place. Concerned by the inconsistency, I sketch a Scrapple and Pepper Pot Soup Stand and share it with a few friends. They think I am joking. I am, although not entirely.

Summer 1976: History seems as dry and tasteless as the crack in the Liberty Bell. I remain faithful to the Scrapple Stand idea. After all, the pedigree of the ingredients in the hot dog is no better, and worse when you consider all the dyes and preservatives.

Fall 1980: I learn about haggis, the ancient Scottish dish made with oats and sheep innards. Haggis has earned a ritualistic, symbolic, and perhaps

---

2. Scrapple is a loaf-shaped cornmeal mush mixed with pork scraps and onions, served in fried slices.

even an ironic following. I am jealous when I learn that some say haggis tastes the way bagpipes sound. Why is there no voice for scrapple?

January 1, 1981: Does scrapple taste like the Mummers sound?

October 1982: It is Philadelphia's 300th birthday. Let's rename scrapple Philadelphia Pâté.

Winter 1984: I discover a newspaper column, circa 1900, by Louis N. Megargee. He asks "all Philadelphians good and true to raise their voices in behalf of succulent scrapple." Megargee is responding to a push in Boston for the baked bean. Finally, a comrade! But Megargee is long dead.

Summer 1985: So is William Bunn. In his 1908 collection of after dinner speeches, Bunn berates Philadelphia as "Scrappletown" for accepting poor quality water. But then again, he adds, "Scrappletown takes her scrapple on trust." Are my sentiments eight decades out of date? Or are Megargee and Bunn visionaries? I wonder.

Fall 1985: I locate a version of the story about a British Royal's visit to America. When asked what he did in Philadelphia, the Royal answers. "I met a lot of scrapple and ate a lot of Biddle." I conclude that this anecdote, if true, is not about scrapple.

Spring 1986: Full press toward a broader acceptance of scrapple. I show a cookbook from 1935 suggesting scrapple croquettes with pineapple to the executive chef at the Commissary Restaurant. Inspired, he experiments. He tosses fried bits into salads and devises appetizers with scrapple squares, goat cheese and sun-dried tomatoes. But scrapple never makes the menu: I am dejected.

Summer 1986: A Port Richmond pizza shop indulges my request for a scrapple topping. Failure. Then ridicule. It dawns on me that scrapple may be a culinary cul-de-sac. But too late. My chef friend and I have already committed to a lecture and a tasting.

Fall 1986: Some fifty people attend an evening with scrapple at the Historical Society of Pennsylvania. The *Philadelphia Inquirer* reports my plan to rename scrapple "Philadelphia Pâté." No letters to the editor; no follow-up editorial. I am now convinced that my campaign is overly focused on scrapple as food.

Spring 1987: I look up at the PSFS [Philadelphia Savings Fund Society] building's 27-foot red letters on the skyline and imagine it as an acronym for

"Philadelphians Savor Fried Scrapple." I share this with friends, who urge me to "Let it go." I reflect upon their advice. Scrapple's revival, I realize, must not be caloric, but entirely metaphoric. It's all in the mind. Perhaps it is only in the mind. And having long since come to terms with my own platonic embrace of scrapple, I . . . let it go.

Fall 1987: At the celebration of the Bicentennial of the United States Constitution, I contemplate (for a moment) whether its signers knew and ate scrapple.

I let it go.

No Restraints: An Anthology of Disability Culture in Philadelphia

What It Is: An Introduction

GIL OTT

Like any identifier, "Disability" is something a person must accept, must in fact reinvent for oneself in order to join its determined community. This self-nominating process is more pronounced for those of us with hidden disabilities, since it is the visual signifiers of disability which activate the social stereotypes which make, for those with visible disabilities, self-nomination moot. But even for those so stigmatized, membership is not a given; consider Christopher Reeve, who insists that he will not accept, but will overcome his paralysis.

In society, stigma's operation tends to isolate. In the case of disability, isolation is doubly reinforced; the non-disabled do not know how to transcend their reactive fears and charitable impulses, and the Person with a Disability is locked within the particularities of his or her own condition. Given these pervasive disincentives, it is truly wonderful that more and more individuals are declaring their disabled status as participants, both in the broader American community, and in that specific to their "otherness."

It is this active self-identification which transforms a benign social category into a political and cultural force, a community. If the Twentieth Century in America has been the Century of Civil Rights, it is not surprising that Disability Pride should follow Black Power, Women's Rights, Gay Pride and other collective bids for empowerment and integration. What characterizes every one of these movements is their proposal of a mechanism to resolve alienation through acceptance and redefinition of what had been a stigma, and which then becomes a criterion for membership in the group. In every case, advocates have dismissed stereotypes of moral or physical weakness attributed to their group, and have demonstrated that those very characteristics that had been considered weak are, in fact, sources of great individual and collective strength.

These communities are called "movements" for a good reason. Once they have declared their alignment, their members must continue to move, that is, to demonstrate and re-demonstrate that alignment for a majority society which would prefer to remain ignorant, idle, and entrenched. The record of such demonstration, performed individually or collectively, becomes available to all members of the group. It forms the basis of a distinct subculture.

The form of such demonstration can be as diverse as the group's membership. It is specific to, and, in a way, antithetical to, the very identifiers which determine the group, and it bears that contradiction forward like a banner. For some, an aggressive ownership of this contradiction is itself an emblem of distinction, one forbidden to those outside the group. In the case of the community of People with Disabilities, terms like "crip" or "gimp" signify membership beyond the reach of the able-bodied world.

Of the several Civil Rights movements active in America today, the Disability Rights movement is perhaps the most complex. The very coherence of "disability" as a broad category is often challenged both from within and without the community. The Deaf and Blind communities, for instance, have their own distinct histories and institutions, as do several chronic conditions, such as muscular dystrophy and multiple sclerosis. Other groups, such as People Living with AIDS/HIV, have only recently realized their status as People with Disabilities. In fact, the tendency continues for disability-specific groups to organize outside of the rubric of Disability, to present their particular cases to the American public. What is it, then, which unifies the entire field of Disability?

This question is at the root of this Anthology. By defining Disability as "any condition which limits a major life function," the Americans with Disabilities Act (ADA) drew a very wide and inclusive border around the community of People with Disabilities, a border so broad that no one has yet found it. In effect, this ADA definition has left the defining up to subsequent social and political refinement. Litigation is only the most tangible course of this refining process; of far greater importance is the cultural process, the multitude of ways in which individuals and small groups declare and assert their membership and belief in the community of People with Disabilities.

In gathering material for this Anthology, the operative definition of culture has been the broader, social and political one, and not exclusively the narrower, artistic one. What these definitions have in common, however, is their reliance on creative solutions to problems of identity and communication. Viewed in this way, protest becomes art, and art, so far as it participates in the values common to the group, becomes political statement.

Culture can be interpreted to include virtually every arena of human endeavor, as can Disability Culture. Athletics, fashion, business, spirituality, psychology and all forms of social interaction, all are particularly nuanced within the community of People with Disabilities. Viewed critically, Disability Culture becomes an evolving system of codes lacing together the difficult fabric of integration and specific identity.

In assembling this Anthology, there has been no attempt to be comprehensive. Since New City Press and Liberty Resources are located in Philadelphia, Philadelphia became a geographic determinant. Philadelphia's perspective on Disability Culture has its own flavor, determined by the issues specific to our city, and by the personalities and organizations unique to it. Furthermore, Liberty Resources is an advocacy-centered organization, so recruitment of writers and artists has proceeded through the network of activists and community members, and not academics or other professionals. What may be lost in objectivity is far compensated by the open-ended urgency of community-building and culture-making at the speed of life.

What has resulted is a snapshot of a dynamic culture in motion. Because a culture is both a collective and an individual thing, there has been no attempt to square divergent viewpoints. At all points, *No Restraints,* which takes its name from the struggle for humane treatment of psychiatric patients, has opted for individual representation over unified group portrayal. Some contributors address Disability as subject matter, while others are simply

Artists with Disabilities. Also, there are noticeable gaps in these contents; Philadelphia is a national leader in Disability Rights, and has produced a varied contribution to its culture. One anticipates that *No Restraints* is only a first compilation of its type, both locally and nationally.

The publication of *No Restraints* takes advantage of a fortuitous convergence of individuals and organizations, some of whom I would like to acknowledge here. Steve Parks, August Tarrier, and Nicole Meyenberg make up the staff of New City Press, which is founded on the vision that Philadelphia's community groups, given the means to produce their own books, will create a new, truly transformative literature. At Liberty Resources, President Fern Moskowitz and Deputy Assistant Director Linda Richman, as well as Erik von Schmetterling and other members of the Board of Directors, recognized early on the importance of this project, and gave it their backing. Also, Carol Wisker, Director of Accessible Programs at the Philadelphia Museum of Art, supported the Anthology from its inception through its publication launch.

Compilation of *No Restraints* began with discussions among an Editorial Committee, which included, along with myself, Leslie Fredericks, Barbara Gregson, Jessie Jane Lewis, and Joanne Marinelli. Many others contributed in many ways, including Steven Brown (Institute for Disability Culture), Joyce Burd (ArtReach), Jennifer Burnett, Eli Goldblatt, Cassie James, Solomon Jones, Bethany Meadows, Connie Schuster (Artists for Recovery), and Deborah Scoblionkov. The true "community" that put this Anthology together, however, is the group of artists, activists, and writers who have contributed their work and their time to make sure that this collection truly represents Disability Culture today.

It is a tribute to the strength of the idea of Civil Rights in America that the Movement for Disability Rights has emerged. Here is a movement that cuts across the accustomed boundaries of prejudice, the very determinants of movements based on skin color, gender, or sexual orientation. To a great extent, this Movement is new, and its membership daily reinvents itself. Its various parts work continually to find how they might fit together. It is in this fertile growing stage that shared values, expressed as elements of a nascent culture, are of great importance. In *No Restraints,* we are here, together, at the beginning of Disability Culture.

And the Sun Still Shines

TAMEKA BLACKWELL

I love the sunlight that shines in on Thomas Jefferson Hospital's glass enclosed bridge.

The bridge has the appearance of hovering over Sansom Street. It was built as an extension for connecting the Chestnut Street side of Jefferson Hospital to the Walnut Street side. They once operated as two separate buildings. The Walnut Street side was built many years before the Chestnut Street side. Thomas Jefferson Hospital has become the premier hospital in the Northeast that handles spinal cord injuries. Anyhow, I'm glad it exists.

The elevators are full, as usual. Well, I'll have to wait for the next one, as usual. How dare these people delay my mission to the ninth floor, the purple floor, where my spot in the sun awaits me?

Purple is the color scheme of the floor—room numbers, nurses' stations, and the large number that greets you when the elevator doors open. The other floors have color schemes, too. The fifth floor is yellow, third floor is green, and the eighth floor is red.

Where are all these people coming from?

All right, I am forced to jock for position. 5 . . . 4 . . . it's on its way down . . . 3 . . . 2 . . . you fools better move out my way . . . 1 here I go—zoom. I love it.

Don't leave on my account.

Once I'm on the elevator people don't like to ride with me. They usually jump out to get in another elevator. Maybe I frighten them by moving so quickly? Well, if I didn't, people would never let me on. So fine, don't get on with me—fewer stops.

Mom pushes the number nine and away we go. Man, she looks so tired.

"Mom, I got a plan."

"Yeah. What?"

"I'm a start my story for Eli's class when I get on the bridge."

"Yeah. You said that for the past two weeks."

"I know. But today is the day."

"Uh huh."

"Listen. My appointment is not until . . . what, another hour or so? I can start writing now. Right?"

"Right . . . turn around straight. So you can get off without hitting the arm of that chair."

"I got it."

"Yeah."

Man, she sounds tired. Bing!

The Ninth floor, sunshine here I come. Great, no one else is on the bridge. My three favorite elements for writing—and sleeping—sunshine and peace and quiet. Just as I like it.

"You need all three of your pillows?"

"Yes' um."

"Yes' um?"

"Thanks mom."

"Yes' um. I am going to sit in the lounge and it's about 11:00 o'clock. So come around about quarter of . . . 12."

"How am I supposed to know that?"

It's funny, after so many years she still forgets about my inabilities.

"Oh, that's right. I'll come back at twenty of."

"OK."

"Don't fall asleep or daydream with all this sun."

"You know me too well."

She even walks tired.

All right, Let the Story Writing Begin. Or, Let My Story Begin. Yeah, that sounds better as a title. This sun feels so good. I like to just turn my face up to it.

The flashing red lights on that ambulance are so red. It's pulling into the Emergency and Trauma Unit on Tenth Street. That wasn't here, at Jefferson, when I was brought to this hospital. I wonder if the person inside's body is packed in ice for stabilization? As mine was. I wonder if they even do that anymore, after a person's been pronounced DOA? As I was. I wonder if they need a tube inserted in their trachea so they can breathe? As I needed. I wonder if the person is being transferred here from another hospital because of the severity of their illness? As I was transferred here from another hospital that wasn't capable of handling a person with my level of spinal injury. Whew! What a ride, from then to now. Thank you, Jesus, for my Life.

"Hey, Tameka. Right?"

"Hi, Dr. Dittuno." A Spinal Cord Specialist and my doctor during my seven-month stay here.

I cannot believe this man is still here. Still wearing his glasses on the tip of his nose. Let me peek at the feet. Yup, the brown Stacey Adams turned up at the toes.

"How are you, sweetie? You look wonderful. Here for a tune-up?"

I frown at the word "sweetie." I know I was young when I came here, but I am well past the sweetie stage. And I'm still processing the "tune-up" remark. I left my house this morning promising myself not to become "Super Woman: The Crusader for all Causes." But, I can't help it.

"Sweetie, doc?"

"Oh yeah, how old are you now?"

"Too old for sweetie."

An awkward silence falls between us while he rocks back and forth on the worn heels of his shoes. Should I release him now, or let him squirm a little more? Oh, I'll dismiss him, only because he looks so uncomfortable and I have work to do. Besides, I can't hold in my laughter any longer and he's blocking my sun.

"Yup, here for a routine checkup."

"OK then, see you later. Keep up the good work."

Laughter.

It amazes me how little common sense some of these doctors have. (Smile.)

I guess many people don't expect the things that come out of my face. Man, this sun feels nice. I'm glad that cloud is gone. I don't want any clouds on this beautiful sunny day. All right, back to my story.

Why is Mom coming now? It can't be 11:45 already. I only have drawings of sunny smiley faces on my page. I wanted to have at least three or four pages written before she came for me or I get back home. Watch she asks me how much I've written.

"How much did you write?"

"Aren't you early?"

"No, it's quarter of. That's all you did was draw pictures of smiley faces?"

"I'm still thinking."

"Yeah, OK. Do you want all this stuff put away?"

"No. But, listen. My brain juices are just getting started."

She smiles. "Yeah, all right. Get started around to the doctor's office."

Laughter.

I love her one-liners, and her smile. She doesn't look as worn out when she got a smile on her face.

I hate this office. I always have to skillfully maneuver my way around the Ikea-looking doctor's office furniture in order to find a corner to squeeze into while I wait my turn. There is a spot, between two cheaply framed chairs. It's about twenty-two inches wide. Thank goodness I'm twenty-one inches wide.

Then I only have to go through the same ritual to get out of the spot where I wedged myself in.

Not bad. I whipped myself right in here. You go BIG GIRL.

"The lady said Dr. Chinkins is running around thirty minutes late."

"OK. That'll give me time to write at least a page or two."

"Yeah, alright. Put everything back on you?"

"Mm, hm. Thanks."

"Mm hm."

Back to my empty page with the sunshine faces on it. Better yet, I'll start on a clean slate or clean page.

"You have an audience." Despite my mother leaning over to tell me this—she cannot whisper. I'm sure everyone in this matchbox of an office heard her.

I nod, in agreement, before she loudly whispers something else.

Yes mommy, I'm aware of the woman across from me whose skin and attire look as if she just flew in from Florida. I know it's nice today, but sandals and puddle-pushers? Oh, excuse me, capris. Aren't you aware it's still March? I saw her when she came in. Try to ignore her and write. I have two pages of thoughts down. Don't stop the flow and do not look up again to meet her eyes—too late. No. Please don't stare. I do not feel like playing the staring game with you. I have work to do. And trust me, I am much better at it than you are. Just smile then.

Smile.

All right, the soft smile I gave you was a hint that you're being rude. It must've not worked because your eyes are still on me. I'm forced to give you the eye treatment. OK. What shall I focus on? Maybe your black roots that need a blonde touch up. Or maybe your thin red painted lips. No, not the lips. I'll wind up laughing before I'm finished treating you with my eyes. Found it. That blotchy sunburned forehead with its four deep creases has my full attention.

She looks and I look. She looks and I look. She looks and I look. She looks and I look. Has anyone ever told this intelligent woman how rude it is to stare?

The woman with the gold hoop earrings and the blue raincoat, a London Fog like my grandmother used to wear, sitting next to my sunburned friend, appears to understand the purpose of my eye treatment. She shakes her head in disgust. Raincoat lady got the message. She probably was taught the same lesson I was privileged to learn. "DO NOT STARE, it's rude and impolite."

She looks and I look. She looks and I look. She looks and I look. She looks and I look. Oh, great. You call my name now. I am just getting relaxed. Do I turn away now? NEVER!

"Come on Mekey." This is my affectionate family name given to me by my niece when she was two. She couldn't pronounce my name Tameka properly.

She looks and I look. She looks and I look. She looks and I look. I don't feel like being Super Woman and teaching this woman some manners.

"Come on, your chair is on." My mom's voice tells me she's fed up with this lady's rudeness and my response to it.

I rest my head on my headrest, with my eyes locked on her forehead. My chair lunges forward. I take my head off the headrest, stopping the chair right in front of the rude woman's feet. She jumps, lifting her feet off the floor.

"I don't know if anyone has ever told you, but staring at people is very rude."

The woman blinks her eyes rapidly and looks at me as if she is amazed that I can speak.

All right, lady, I heard you call me the first time. Getting out this tight spot was a lot easier than I thought it would be. Maybe I feel as if I got something to prove. Or, I don't care whether I take a few of these cheap chairs with me, including the one Mrs. Florida is sitting in. Anyway, I got skills.

"Hi, Tameka?"

"No, she's Tameka."

"I'm Tameka Blackwell."

Where is Erica, who sat at this desk for the past five years? She knows who is who. I hate breaking in new people.

"Yes, Ms. Blackwell. Dr. Chinkins will not be able to see you today and apologizes for any inconvenience."

Silence.

Where is Erica? This woman sounds like a recording. BEEP, please hold. BEEP, press one.

"Are you having any problems with your toes? Are you diabetic?"

"No, no problems. Nor am I diabetic."

"Because you could see Dr. Freed."

Dr. Freed? Not hardly. He's the same quack that don't believe it's essential for a person with a spinal cord injury to have their nails cut regularly and properly.

"No, that's quite all right."

"Would you like to make an appointment for next week?"

"No, I'll just call. Thanks."

"Let's go Bo." This is the affectionate name I gave my mom after I turned twenty-five, in order to keep from calling her "Mommy" in public.

It is warm enough to sit outside. I'll start to write when I get back home. Well, I get to enjoy the sun a little more. Finally, I don't have to fight to get on the elevator. Man, everyone is out today. You can always tell when it's lunchtime and when it is getting warm. The sun feels so warm.

"I am going to sit over here."

"OK. I'm going to sit over there, where the sun is."

"Keep watch for your ride."

"All right."

Well, if I'm not going to write, I still can think, while I'm sitting here. I'm still not sure about how to put my story on paper and make it interesting. I am not a very exciting person. I don't do much of anything.

No, please don't sit over here. I am in a corner minding my business. Besides, my eyeballs are tired of staring. Also, this wooden and stone bench next to me doesn't look very comfortable. Great, just what I don't want.

"Hi, honey." At least this little osteoporosistic white haired lady has the decency to speak. But that usually means there will be a slew of questions that will usually follow the gesture of politeness.

"Hi."

"Sun feels good, huh."

"Yup."

"I bet it feels really good to *your* body?"

You bet right, lady.

"Yup."

No, don't move any closer. Can't you tell by my short answers that I don't want to talk? Please, lady, that's close enough. If I move back I won't be in the sun.

"Where do you live, honey?"

I knew you had questions. It didn't take you long, sister. I know you didn't come sit over here for the sake of sitting.

"North Philly."

"Oh, yeah, I heard about that place. A lot of dangerous things happening out there."

Now, before I come to the rescue of North Philly and scare the living daylights out this lady, let me process her idea of North Philly being somewhere afar or "out there."

"Were you born like that? Did something happen to you out there?"

Slow down, granny. I knew you were full of questions, but dag.

"I was shot."

I love to see people's facial response when I say that.

"Oh, my word."

Whew, I didn't know she had such beady little blue eyes behind all that hanging skin.

Silence.

I feel my mom's eyes on me. I'm not going to look in her direction.

I feel her eyes on me, just like those days when I was in church and talking with friends when I shouldn't have been. I would turn around to see her eyes chastising me.

Oh, I can't help it. Yup, she's looking at me. Smile.

"Was it gang related?"

Oh, God, this woman watches too much TV. Her favorite is probably detective shows because she is one hell of an interrogator. But let me give her a dose of reality.

Super Woman to the rescue!

"No, my injury wasn't gang related. Actually, it didn't happen 'out there' in North Philly."

"Oh! Where did it occur?"

How did I know you were going to ask that?

"I was on the Boardwalk with some friends."

"The boardwalk? The Atlantic City Boardwalk?"

Look, lady, will you let me tell this story?

"No. It was the Ocean City Boardwalk . . ."

"Were you vacationing, school trip, just visiting? What?"

Man, Agatha Christie. Sit back on the edge of the bench and let me finish.

"Just visiting. And I was on the boardwalk and this man came over to me when I was laughing—I forget about what. Anyhow, he said, 'You know, you remind me of my wife.' Then as I began to leave or walk away, he shot me."

"My heavens! You poor dear. Well, did you look like his wife?"

Here comes the kicker.

"No, not at all. His wife was a thin woman with honey-blonde hair."

"What? What do you mean honey-blonde hair? You mean his wife was white?"

"Yup."

"Was he white too?"

"Uh, huh."

"Well, how did he think . . ."

"I don't know. I doubt if there were any similarities. Maybe it was my laugh. My mother used to tell me my laugh was going to get me in trouble."

Especially when I was in Catholic School.

"What happened to him?"

"It is said that he went three blocks and blew his brains out."

"Oh, no."

"Yup. No trial, no sentencing and no punishment."

"Where did he get the gun?"

"Oh, a small arsenal was later found in his home."

Silence.

Thank goodness someone is calling. This lady is full of questions.

She shakes her head and pats my arm. Then she stands, while still shaking her head. She walks slowly toward a woman holding open a car door. The woman at the car has hair as gray as the inquisitive old lady, but her skin is considerably younger.

"Hey, Bo."

"What are you doing?"

"Why is it that you think I'm doing something?"

"Don't answer a question with a question. Besides, I know you."

"I wasn't doing anything but chitchatting."

"What did you say to that woman for her to go away shaking her head like that?"

"I told her what she wanted to know."

"What was that? What happened to you?"

"Yup, what else?"

"What did you say?"

"I told her all about my trip to Ocean City."

"Why you tell her that? You know that is not how you got injured."

"Because if I had told her that I was actually injured by a stray bullet from a police officer's gun who was running down my block and shooting at the back of a purse-snatching thief, she would not have felt the same despair about gun violence as she did hearing about my friend Eileen's shooting on the boardwalk. Or the story of Sharon's father shooting her because he thought she was a burglar. All my story does is confirm every stereotype about violence in North Philadelphia. And I'm sure my friends don't mind me sharing or borrowing their stories to make a point about the unexpectedness of gun violence."

"Maybe. But let people think what they want. What happened to you was no fault of yours. So who cares what they think? You are not the saving grace of North Philly."

"I know, but I can't help it sometimes."

"Well, when someone asks you what happened to you, just say . . ."

"Ask me no questions and I'll tell you no lies."

"Yeah, that's good. Or tell them you'd rather not discuss it."

"I like mine better."

"Somehow I knew you would. I'm going inside to call and see why paratransit is late."

"All right."

When I get home on my porch I'll start my paper, for sure. Right after the double episode of *This Old House* goes off. I missed it last week when I was sitting in the sun and beginning my paper. Man, this sun is awesome.

"Hi."

"Hi. What is your name?"

"Thomas."

"My name is Tameka. How old are you?"

"6." He holds up six fingers. "Why are you sitting there?"

Super Woman to the rescue! I can't pass up an opportunity to teach little Thomas here about the dangers of guns. I better hurry up before my mother gets back.

"Well, my cousin was playing with a. . . ."

Free! Great Escapes from Slavery on the Underground Railroad

Woman Escaping in a Box

LORENE CARY

We don't know her name, but we do know that in 1857, a young woman who was pregnant with her first child determined to get away from the wealthy household in Baltimore where she was enslaved to work as a ladies' maid and seamstress. Babies born of mothers in bondage would be slaves, too. So the young woman determined to get herself and her unborn child out of Baltimore so that the child could be born free. She and a young man named Thomas Shipley made a plan; then she watched for just the right chance to put it into action. It came on the day of the Grand Opening Ball at the Academy of Music, and everyone in the household was aflutter with preparations. They sent the young woman to buy a few last minute articles.

She kept on going.

When they realized she was missing, the young woman's owners questioned a free African-American woman whom they paid to wash their clothes. Because she could not—or would not—tell them where the young woman had gone, they fired her. They also offered a reward to anyone who could help them find the runaway. But no one said anything.

Meanwhile, the young woman met Thomas Shipley at a secret location.

Shipley was a wealthy young man who had already begun giving his money to help others. In this case, he became involved more directly. The two had come up with a plan to mail the young woman north as if she were a regular package of dry goods. Shipley had a large wooden box ready. He lined the bottom with clean straw. The young woman got in with her knees bent under her. Then he gave her a pair of scissors for her to use if she needed to make a hole to breathe.

No one has recorded what they said at that moment, if anything. So we do not know the nature of his fear or hers, or his encouragement. We do know that they went ahead with the plan. Shipley tucked more straw around her sides and over her head. Then, very carefully, he nailed the lid, drove the box to the Baltimore depot, and mailed the young woman care of the General Delivery in Philadelphia.

Once the box was paid for, Shipley traveled to Philadelphia, in order to arrive early and find someone who would pick it up the next day. Nice and regular. That was the point. It had to look like a normal business delivery.

The box was dark inside. No light. The air inside was choked with chaff from the straw. When packers came through to load the freight onto the railroad cars, they turned the young woman's box upside down more than once, throwing her onto her head and her side. When they went away, she worked to dig a tiny hole with the scissors Shipley had given her. Still, very little fresh air came in. She dared not cough or sneeze, and she hadn't drunk any water so that she would not have to urinate. She became thirsty and stiff. It was hard to breathe, hard to stay conscious, and so very dark and alone.

In Philadelphia Thomas Shipley hired a man named George Custus to fetch the box. Custus was a deliveryman who owned a one-horse cart, called a dray, to take packages back and forth along the port, the railroad depot and businesses in the city. Shipley also arranged with an elderly lady, Mrs. Myers, to accept delivery.

Meanwhile, early in the morning, the young woman's box moved north with the rest of the mail on the railroad cars. She arrived in Philadelphia at 10 A.M. Although it was bright morning now, and she was in a free state, inside the box she remained imprisoned in the dark.

George Custus did not know what was in the box, but he judged from Shipley's worried face that whatever it was mattered a great deal. So Custus met the railroad car when it pulled into town. Before the train could be unloaded, Custus asked the conductor if he could go right into the railroad freight car and take out the box he'd been sent for. The conductor balked. He didn't like the idea of anyone taking mail out before it had been properly unloaded and inventoried, but Custus convinced him. He told the conductor that he needed to get this one to its destination immediately. And he reminded the conductor that he'd been coming to the depot every day for years. "You know me," he said. "I'll be responsible for the box."

"Take it," the conductor said, "and go ahead with it."

With great effort, Custus loaded the heavy box onto his dray and drove it to Mrs. Myers' house.

She had been waiting, and she thought she was ready. Once the package was delivered to the rowhouse at 412 South Seventh Street, however, once it sat in her house, silent and unmoving, the old lady got nervous. She hurried up the street to the house of her friend, Mrs. Ash, an undertaker. Mrs. Ash was used to dealing with dead bodies. Myers hoped that the person in the box was alive, but she couldn't be sure.

Together they pried off the lid and saw the bulge of a human head and dark hair poking through the straw. The two women hesitated. One of them ventured a few words: "Get up, my child."

The woman in the box made a weak, tiny movement, just enough to rustle the surface of the straw. The two older women strained to help her straighten her body and climb stiffly out of the box. Then they led her upstairs to lie in a soft, clean bed.

All she could say was: "I feel so deadly weak."

In an hour or so, the women convinced her to drink some tea. Then she fell asleep. She slept that day and straight through the night. The next day she was able to talk a little more, but still with difficulty. On the third day she was able to sit up and talk. Soon after, the Vigilance Committee sent her on to freedom in Canada.

Before she left, the young woman tried to describe how afraid she'd been in the box, how alone, how real and suddenly close dying seemed. She couldn't explain, but maybe the wise old women understood, that once the box was tossed onto the platform, she was no longer a person, but a piece of mail, a box that could be dropped, left in the corner of a depot or a railroad car, knocked onto the rails, crushed under the weight of other freight loaded on top. She could not find words to say that that one night of imprisonment reflected her life of enslavement like a deadly magnifying glass: that all her life she'd been boxed in, really, moved around like an object, unable to draw a free breath on free soil, or bear children in the sunlight of liberty. What she did say they remembered and wrote down—that of all her fears the worst was that she'd be discovered and sent back to slavery.

Espejeos y Ventanas / Mirrors and Windows: Oral Histories of Mexican Farmworkers and Their Families

Jesús Villicaña López

Jesús Villicaña López is from La Ordeña, a village near Moroleón, in the state of Guanajuato. He was 16 years old when he did this interview, 6 months after coming to the United States.

I made the decision [to come north] on my own because I wanted to find a new way of life or a future for myself. I wanted to be self-reliant and also to help my family—my mom and my brothers. I have four siblings, all younger than I: my sister is 8 years old and I have one brother who is 14 and another who is 12. Because I am the oldest, I have a great responsibility to be with them, to protect them and my mom. It's my duty to give them the best, to create opportunities for them so that they can get ahead. I am responsible for showing them how to live life.

In Mexico, I lived in a stone house patched with clay that had a dirt floor—it was tiny, with only one room for the entire family. We made our living growing corn and beans to eat—this is a staple food of the region. . . . My mother insisted that I go to school. . . . I know that school is very useful, but I didn't have the resources to continue my studies and neither did my mom or my grandparents. So I decided to leave school and come up here. I believe that by doing this work here in the US, I can help my brothers and sister get ahead in life and provide them with a better education, a career, so that they won't have to make the same sacrifice that I made when I came here for them. I send my family four or five times as much as they used to earn each month. Every three or four weeks I send around $1,000 to Mexico.

I left Moroleón for the North at daybreak, with great sadness. I was with a group—my uncle and some friends of his, all older. I was the only young person in the group. The night before I left I tried and tried to get to sleep so that I could leave easily in the morning, but I couldn't sleep the whole night. I stayed up all night with my mom and then it was time for me to prepare to leave. My uncle came to the house and said that they had come for us. I left with my suitcase and then, with the blessing of my mother, I climbed into the car and we left. Crying, with great sadness, we left our families and the village where we lived behind. We left focused on our future, with the intention of finding a new way of life and confronting new problems. But, then, at the same time, it was a risky and very dangerous adventure.

I am one of the younger people in the camp. When I first came here the truth is that I felt an enormous fear inside of me, since I didn't know where I was and I knew no one except my uncle, who came with me. At night I felt this profound loneliness because I was in such a big place without knowing anybody.

Actually, I was very surprised at the conditions here in the camp. When I left Mexico, I thought that I was coming to a place where we were going to be, well, free, with a big living space. But when I got here, I realized that it wasn't that way—it was a small place where many of us were cramped together. At times we really have to make an effort to get along, since there are so many of us—we are 16 now, and in the summer there will be 20. The camp is one long room, an open dormitory, without separate bedrooms. Each of us has our own space where we sleep, but there is no real private space. We make sure to respect each other's things, though. With so many people living together, there are bound to be conflicts sometimes, but we know that we have to try to avoid them.

I get up faithfully at daybreak, at 2:00 in the morning. Before I leave for work I eat a little. If I want to, I can rest one or two days a week, but since I'm not that tired, I figure I should put more energy into work. So I work seven days a week, 12 or 13 hours a day. . . . It's piecework—they pay me by the box—so if I want to make more money, I have to force myself to try to harvest more mushrooms. They ask you to pick an average of six boxes an hour—they pay $1.00 a box. Each box holds ten pounds of mushrooms. There are times when I fill eight or ten boxes an hour—so I pick 80 to 100 pounds of mushrooms each hour.

I would like to say something to all the people who might think that being here in the United States is easy. I want them to know it isn't that way because you don't necessarily know what you're up against. You think you will come here and find happiness, a new world full of marvels—but it isn't that way. You will face tremendous loneliness with a great many problems, large and small. And you have to be responsible for yourself instead of expecting to rely on others.

I would advise all who are thinking of coming here to think carefully about things. First, think about what you will do when you are here, who might accompany you on your trip, and if you are mentally and physically prepared, if you are strong enough to face your personal and social problems. Because if you are not prepared to face life, to face new challenges, it will weigh very heavily on you over time. Often it is misfortune that makes us unable to bear this burden and that gets us into trouble. And everything that you hoped for when you came here can turn out quite differently than you planned. You can succumb to temptation, like alcohol or drug addiction, and all the desires and dreams that you came here with can so quickly disappear into oblivion. If a person comes with desire, with interest, and if he knows why he's coming, what he's coming to and what he intends to accomplish here, then, yes—it's worth it.

[A few months after this interview, Jesús's father died. Jesús was not able to return to Mexico for his burial. In the Spring his mother, two brothers and sister moved into their new three-room house in La Ordeña—paid for with the $10,000 that Jesús had sent home.]

Jesús Villicaña López (en Español)

Jesús Villicaña López es de La Ordeña, un rancho cerca de Moroleón, en el estado de Guanajuato. Vino a Kennett Square cuando tenía 16 años—6 meses antes de hacer esta entrevista.

Yo decidí venir [a el Norte] por mí mismo, por querer buscar una nueva forma de vida o un futuro para mí mismo. Por querer realizar mi vida dependiente de mí mismo y ayudar a mi familia—a mi mamá y a mis hermanos. Tengo cuatro hermanos, todos son menores que yo. Tengo una hermana que tiene ocho años y un hermano que sigue enseguida de mí de catorce años y el menor de doce años. Por ser el hijo mayor tengo la mayor responsabilidad de estar junto de éllos, de protegerlos a ellos y a mi mamá. Tengo la obligación de darles lo mejor, de tratar de abrirles más las posibilidades de que se superen, a vivir la vida.

En México, vivíamos en una casita de piedras pegadas con tierra y con un piso de tierra, con solo un cuarto para toda la familia. Nuestro sustento y alimentación era el cultivo de maíz y de fríjol—el cual se alimentaban la mayoría de los habitantes de mi región. [Mi madre] insistía en que la escuela sería la forma para superarme. . . . Yo sé que la escuela sí es de mucha utilidad, pero como yo no contaba con los suficientes recursos para seguir estudiando, ni mi madre ni mis abuelos. Pues, tuve que venirme para acá y decidí dejar la escuela. Yo en mis pensamientos creo que a través de mi trabajo que estoy realizando aquí en los Estados Unidos puedo sacar a mis hermanos adelante, brindándoles un mejor estudio, una carrera para que no tengan que hacer el mismo sacrifico que yo estoy haciendo aquí por ellos. Yo les mando a mi familia cuatro o cinco veces de lo que ganan en México al mes. Ya pasan tres o cuatro semanas ya junto mil dólares y los mando para México.

Salí de Moroleón a el Norte por la madrugada, muy triste. Estuve con un grupo—mi tío y alguno de sus amigos, todos mayores. La noche antes de salir yo traté y traté de dormir bien para en la mañana salir bien, pero no pude dormir toda la noche. La pasé en vela junto con mi mamá y entonces se llegó la hora en que yo tuve que prepararme para salir. Mi tío llegó a la casa y dijo que ya habían llegado por nosotros. Salí con mi maleta y, pues, con la bendición de mi madre, subí al carro y salimos. Todos tristes, llorando, dejamos las familias y nuestro rancho atrás. Íbamos mirando siempre hacia adelante con el fin de encontrar una nueva forma de vida y enfrentando distintos problemas. Pero, pues, a la vez, era una aventura riesgosa y muy peligrosa.

Yo soy uno de los jóvenes en el campamento. Cuando al principio venía aquí, pues la verdad es que yo me sentía con un miedo enorme dentro de mí, puesto que yo no sabía dónde estaba ni conocía a ninguna otra persona, sólo a mi tío que me estaba acompañando. De noche a mí se me hacía una profunda soledad de estar en un lugar tan grande y sin conocer a nadie.

Pues la verdad, yo me sorprendí mucho las condiciones dentro del campamento. Cuando salí desde México yo pensé que iba a llegar a un lugar donde íbamos a estar, pues, libres, con un espacio grande para vivir. Pero al llegar aquí me dí cuenta de que no era así—era un lugar pequeño donde estábamos agrupados muchos. A veces cuesta trabajo entendernos unos a los otros, puesto que somos muchos—somos 16 personas hasta ahorita, pero en el verano serán 20. El campamento es un largo cuarto, un espacio abierto, sin dormitorios separados. Cada quien tiene su propio lugar en donde descansar, pero no hay ningún sitio privado. Pero todos los que están allí respetamos las cosas de los demás. Al estar viviendo muchas personas juntos, sí a veces se llega a haber muchos conflictos, pero nosotros sabemos que debemos de evitar eso.

Yo constantemente me levanto por la madrugada, a las dos de la mañana. Antes de ir al trabajo desayuno un poquito. Si yo quiero, puedo descansar un día o dos días a la semana, pero ahora que no estoy cansado, pues es cuando debo de echarle más ganas al trabajo. Así, trabajo siete días a la semana, algunos días trabajo 12 o 13 horas. Me pagan por caja, yo ando por contrato—si quiero obtener más dinero, yo tengo que esforzarme más por tratar de pizcar más hongo. Le piden a uno que pizque de promedio de seis cajas cada hora—le pagan $1.00 por caja. Cada caja contiene diez libras de hongos. Hay veces que lleno ocho o diez cajas cada hora—o sea, pizco 80–100 libras de hongos cada hora.

Me gustaría decir algo a todas las personas que piensan que estar aquí en los Estados Unidos es algo fácil. Quiero que sepan que no es así porque uno no sabe a lo que se va a enfrentar. Piensa que va a venir aquí encontrando la felicidad, un mundo nuevo lleno de maravillas—pero no es así. Va a enfrentar una soledad tremenda, con una inmensidad de problemas grandes y chicos. Se tiene que hacer responsable para sí mismo sin ayuda de los demás.

Yo le aconsejaría a quien piensa en venir acá que pensara bien en las cosas. Primero, se pusiera a pensar en qué va hacer al estar acá, con quién se va a venir en ese viaje, y si está preparado físicamente y mentalmente para enfrentarse a sus problemas personales y sociales. Porque al no estar preparado para enfrentarse a la vida, enfrentarse a nuevos retos, es algo que con el tiempo se le va a hacer a uno un peso enorme. Muchas veces puede ser por la desgracia que uno no puede llevar ese peso, y llega a andar en malos pasos. Y todo lo que esperaba de venir acá va a estar en otros pasos que no deseaba. Puede recaer en diversos vicios, en el alcohol o en la drogadicción, y las ganas que les traía acá, a trabajar y superarse, se van a quedar en el olvido. Pues, si la persona viene con ganas, con interés, y sabe por qué viene y a lo que viene, y qué es lo que va a realizar acá, pues sí—vale la pena.

[Unos pocos meses después de esta entrevista, el padre de Jesús falleció. Jesús no pudo regresar a México para asistir a su entierro. En la primavera del 2004 su madre, dos hermanos y hermana se mudaron a su nueva casa de tres cuartos en La Ordeña—pagada con los $10,000 que Jesús les había enviado.]

Margarita Rojas

Margarita Rojas is 32 years old. She grew up in the town of Zacapu, Michoacán, and came to the United States when she was 18 years old. This interview was completed one week before her final deportation order was to go into effect.

After I left high school, my dreams were always to be a kindergarten teacher, to have some money—which we didn't have at home. . . . But the economic situation didn't make my dreams possible and, afterwards, the man who came into my life—the father of my children—ended my plans. I discussed with him that I was going to continue studying, but tradition dictated otherwise. It was more like, "Women shouldn't study because eventually they get married and never practice their profession."

It was very difficult for me to bring myself here because I was leaving my heart there—my land, my family—but I knew that I had to struggle to make a better life. I thought that it was going to be better. For me, it was very difficult to change countries, to change customs, to change everything.

I remember that when I went to say goodbye to my parents, my house was very sad—it seemed as if somebody had died, everyone was crying. I had to hug my parents and tell them that I was going. My parents cried, but they didn't stop me—they always believed that we should make our own lives. But, I tell you, I left half my heart there.

All those five years [here in the United States with my first husband] were full of abuse, violence, mistreatment and daily insults. And all this time [my daughter] Adriana saw how we were living—she was frightened and crying. She was six years old and was very traumatized. She didn't love him. She would tell me that when she would see her dad, her stomach would hurt—she was scared of him because he also beat her, he abused her. Then, I remember it well—it was December 30, 1994—he beat me over and over, viciously, without feeling, without reason. He just went crazy. I thought, "The moment will come when God will grant me a chance to leave because today I am leaving." Then, throughout the early dawn hours I stayed up to make sure that he would be sleeping. I kept my children all dressed up, including their jackets. When I heard that he was snoring—that was about 5:00 in the morning—I took my Richie in my arms and I woke up Adriana and I told her, "Big girl, let's get out of here." She was suddenly happy and my daughter left quickly, like a little kangaroo, without making noise. And we got out, thank God.

I dedicated myself to working hard to help my children get ahead so that they would be able to have nice clothes and good shoes, and I was succeeding. In the morning I cleaned houses 'til 12:00 or 1:00 P.M. After cleaning houses, I took a bath and went out to do demonstrations, selling clothes, gold jewelry, beauty products and lingerie. I was the owner of three businesses; I had a chain, an enormous network, like you can't imagine, of people who depended on me—they were selling and they paid a percentage of the sales to me. I was popular. I was able to have an apartment for me and my children. It transformed me. My life changed after I started living alone and then I was happy. I wanted tranquility and peace. I wanted to help my children get ahead by myself, so that no one would tell me, "You and your children eat because of me" or "Because of me you all have a place to sleep and to live." That's why I had cried so much. I wanted to say, "I can do it by myself, I don't need anybody." I stopped crying then.

Finally, I started a very beautiful relationship [with a man called Pablo, who is Mexican and an American citizen]. . . . Pablo wasn't the typical *macho* that I had known. He gave me a lot of courage to be able to be free, to be able to make my own decisions, and he was never going to oppose them. In September 2000 we got married officially before the judge. I tell you, for me, all of this was very beautiful because now I felt protected, I felt loved, I felt very supported and respected. He wanted a family and I gave that to him. I wanted happiness, attention and support and he gave all that to me.

[I applied for a work permit at INS (Immigration and Naturalization Service), but] the only thing that they gave me was a deportation order. . . . I feel very bad, I feel like they have me tied up and I can't do anything—I feel like a criminal. I say it's unfair, after so much struggle, because I am married to an American citizen, with two children who are citizens and one who is a resident. I feel very frustrated because I think, "What will happen to my children, with their rights, the dreams that they have?" I feel worse for them, worse that they will lose everything that is their life here. Right now, I feel like they have me in a plastic bag and I can't breathe, like I am drowning. I wish they would let me breathe, let me be free.

My dreams are for my children to be able to go to college, to fulfill their lives as professionals, and not to have to depend on anyone the way their mother did. I wouldn't want them to have to do the kind of jobs that I did—I don't want my daughter cleaning houses or my son running all over the place looking for work. As I have said to Adriana, "I would be so happy to see you working, helping a lot of people, lending your hand to whomever needs it because you remember how we were in need and how we had many people who helped us."

I feel very bad because my husband and I finally found happiness and now a law is going to separate us. The only thing that I ask God is that when we go to Federal Court the judge turns out to be a just person. If I had the opportunity, I would tell the judge not to act as a judge, but rather as a normal human being with feelings. I would say to him, "I am not a criminal. I didn't murder anyone—why are you judging me this way? Think more about the welfare and rights of the children. Have compassion—we all have children. Don't pay so much attention to what I did by violating this law to re-enter the United States—millions and millions of people do it, almost every Mexican who is here has done it." I am a proud person and it's very hard for me to ask for forgiveness—it's like I am stooping down and humiliating myself, but I will do it for my children. I would tell the judge, "Maybe I don't show it, but my heart is broken. Now, I no longer cry—for a very long time I did cry, but I don't want to cry anymore. The only thing I ask of you is that you do not destroy my family."

[Margarita Rojas decided to fly to Mexico with her children on January 25—the day before she was to appear before INS and face deportation. However, at the last minute she chose to stay in the United States and appeal her deportation order one last time so that her daughter, Adriana, could receive the medical treatment she needed. On January 26th she said goodbye to her children and appeared before the Immigration Service, prepared to face detention in jail pending an appeal of her deportation order. Her deportation was postponed and she was allowed to return home to care for her children. Her case is still in the courts.]

Margarita Rojas (en Español)

Margarita Rojas tiene 32 años. Creció en Zacapu, Michoacán, y vino a los Estados Unidos cuando tenía 18 años. Esta entrevista se completó una semana antes de que su orden final de deportación fuera puesta en efecto.

Después de que yo salí de la secundaria mis sueños siempre eran ser maestra de *Kinder,* tener algún dinero—que no teníamos en la casa. Pero lo económico no facilitó mis sueños y, después, el hombre que llegó a mi vida—el padre de mis hijos—me quitó la intención. Yo le platicaba que yo iba a seguir estudiando—pero no se usaba mucho, en las tradiciones de ellos, que la mujer estudiara. Como que era más, "La mujer no debe de estudiar, ya al rato se casa y nunca va a ejercer la carrera."

Era muy difícil venirme acá, porque dejaba mi corazón allá, mi tierra, mi familia, pero yo sabía que tenía que luchar por hacer una vida mejor. Pensé que iba a estar mejor. Para mí era bien difícil cambiar de país, cambiar de costumbres, cambiar de todo. Yo recuerdo que cuando yo me fui a despedir de mis padres mi casa estaba muy triste—parecía que alguien se había muerto, todos estaban llorando. Yo tuve que abrazar a mis padres y decirles que me venía. Mis padres lloraron, pero no me detuvieron ellos—ellos creían siempre que nosotros deberíamos de hacer nuestra propia vida. Pero le digo, dejé la mitad de mi corazón ahí.

Todos esos cinco años [aquí en los Estados Unidos con mi primer esposo] fueron de abuso, violencia, de maltrato, insultos diarios. Y todo este tiempo [mi hija] Adriana vió como vivíamos—ella se asustaba y ella lloraba. Ella tenía como seis años, y estaba muy traumada. Ella no lo quería. Ella me decía que cuando veía a su papá le dolía el estómago—le tenía miedo, porque también a ella la golpeaba, la maltrataba. Entonces, bien recuerdo—fue el 30 de diciembre del 1994 cuando él me golpeó mucho, muy feo, sin sentido, sin razón—él estaba loco. Yo pensé, "Va a llegar el momento que Dios me va a permitir salir, porque hoy me voy." Entonces, en el transcurso de la madrugada, yo lo estuve velando que se durmiera. Dejé a mis hijos vestidos, inclusive con la chamarra. Cuando yo escuché que él estaba hasta roncando—eso fue como a las 5 de la mañana—yo tomé a mi Richie en brazos y desperté a Adriana y le dije, "Madrecita, vámonos de aquí." Ella se puso feliz y, rápida, mi hija salió, como cangurito sin hacer ruido. Y salimos, gracias a Dios.

Me dediqué a trabajar fuertemente para sacar a mis hijos adelante y que ellos pudieran tener una buena ropa, un buen calzado. Y lo estaba logrando. En la mañana limpiaba casas, desde las 12 hasta la 1 de la tarde. Yo, después de limpiar casas, me bañaba y me salía a hacer demostraciones, a vender ropa, joyería de oro, productos de belleza y ropa interior de mujer. Yo era dueña de tres negocios; yo tuve una cadena, una red enorme, como no se imagina, de gente que dependía de mí—ellos vendían y a mí me pagaban un porcentaje por las ventas. Tuve popularidad. Pude tener un apartamento para mí y mis hijos. Me transformaba. Mi vida cambió después de que yo me fui a vivir sola—estaba entonces feliz. Yo quería tranquilidad, quería paz. Yo quería sacar a mis hijos adelante, yo sola, y que nadie me dijera, "Por mí comes tú y tus hijos," o "Por mí tienen donde dormir, donde vivir." Por esa razón yo había llorado mucho. Yo quería decir, "Yo puedo, yo sola, no necesito de nadie." Yo dejé de llorar entonces.

Por fin empezé una relación bien bonita [con un hombre que se llama Pablo, un mexicano y ciudadano americano]. . . . Pablo no era el macho típico que yo había conocido. Él me estaba dando mucha confianza de poder ser libre, de poder tomar mis decisiones; y que él nunca se iba a oponer.

En septiembre del 2000 nos casamos oficialmente ante el juez. Le digo, todo esto para mí era lindísimo, porque ya me sentía protegida, ya me sentía amada, me sentía muy respaldada y respetada. Él quería una familia y yo se la dí. Yo quería felicidad, atención, apoyo, y él me la dió.

[Yo apliqué por un permiso para trabajar de la Inmigración, pero] lo único que me estaban entregando era una orden de deportación. . . . Yo me siento muy mal, me siento como si me tienen amarrada, que no puedo hacer nada, me siento como una criminal. Yo digo que es injusto después de tanta lucha, porque estoy casada con un ciudadano americano, con dos hijos ciudadanos y una residente. Me siento muy frustrada porque pienso, "¿Qué va a pasar con mis hijos, con los derechos de ellos, los sueños que tienen?" Me siento más mal por ellos, más mal que ellos van a perder todo lo que es su vida aquí. Ya me siento como que si me tuvieran en una bolsa de plástico, que no puedo respirar, me siento ahogándome. Quisiera que me dejaran respirar, me dejaran ser libre.

Mis sueños para mis hijos son que ellos puedan ir al colegio, que se puedan realizar como unos profesionales y que no tengan que estar dependiendo de nadie como lo hizo su madre. No me gustaría que ellos tuvieran que pasar los trabajos que yo pasé—no quiero que mi hija esté limpiando casas y ni que mi hijo esté buscando trabajos que lo corran de un lado, que lo corran de otro. Como yo le he dicho a Adriana, "Qué feliz fuera yo verte trabajando, ayudando a mucha gente, que extiendas tus manos al que lo necesita—porque recuerda cómo nosotros necesitamos y tuvimos mucha gente que nos ayudó."

Me siento muy mal porque al fin mi esposo y yo encontramos la felicidad, y una ley nos va a separar. Lo único que yo le pido a Dios es que cuando vamos a la Corte Federal, el juez sea una persona justa. Si yo tuviera la oportunidad, le diría al juez que no se pusiera como un juez, sino como un ser normal con sentimientos. Yo le diría, "Yo no soy una delincuente, yo no maté—¿por qué me estás juzgando así? Piensa más en el bienestar y derechos de los niños. Tenga compasión—todos tenemos hijos. No tome tanta atención en lo que yo hice, por haber violado esta ley y re-entrado—lo hacen millones y millones -casi cada mexicano que está aquí lo ha hecho." Yo soy orgullosa, y para mí es bien difícil el pedir perdón—es como estar doblegándome y humillándome; pero sí, por mis hijos, lo hago. Yo le diría al juez, "Yo quizás no lo demuestro, pero mi corazón está partido. Yo ya no lloro—por muchísimo tiempo lloré, y no quiero llorar más. Lo único que le pido es que no destruya mi familia."

[Margarita Rojas había decidido volar a México con sus hijos el 25 de enero—el día antes de su fecha de aparecer ante las autoridades de Inmigración, y enfrentar deportación. Pero, al último minuto, ella decidió quedarse en los Estados Unidos y apelar su orden de deportación una vez más, para que su hija, Adriana, pudiera recibir la atención médica que necesitaba. El 26 de enero ella les dijo adiós a sus hijos y apareció ante el Servicio de Inmigración, preparada para enfrentar detención en una cárcel, en espera de la apelación de su orden de deportación. Su deportación fue pospuesta, y a ella le dejaron regresar a casa para cuidar a sus hijos. Su caso todavía está en las cortes.]

Salvador García Baeza

Salvador García Baeza is 54 years old and is from the town of Moroleón, Mexico. He came to work in the mushroom industry in Kennett Square in 1979 and got his permanent residency card in 1986. He brought his sons to Pennsylvania in 1996 and his wife and daughter in 2000.

I think that our family survived the separation because above all there was communication through letters, when they were little ten-year-olds, twelve-year-olds, fourteen-year-olds. There were individual letters for each one, giving them advice. I think my wife has maybe 300 letters—all those that I sent during those 22 years, she has them all. Each month I sent one letter. There was a lot of communication by telephone, asking about everyone, talking with them for 10 or 15 minutes. I gave them advice. I felt happy after talking with my wife, with the children. I felt renewed energy to begin work another day.

Of course, it was difficult being separated from my children. I didn't see them grow up. Now I know how they are doing because I see them. Well, I can say that I feel proud of how they've behaved and also I'm proud of my wife, that she knew how to take charge when I was in the United States. There are families that aren't like that.

[In my present job] they pay me $7.20 an hour and I have worked there for eight years. Nowhere do they pay overtime. I've been working 13 hours a day for a month and a half—70 to 80 hours a week—and they still don't pay time-and-a-half. They say that they don't pay overtime because it's "agricultural work." I think that after 40 hours a week, you should be paid overtime, it doesn't matter what you call it—"agriculture" or whatever kind of work. I think the important thing is that we do our jobs.

Where I am, it's not easy to complain and band together because people have a horrible fear—they're very scared to defend themselves. They fear that they would be told, "No more work for you because you're a troublemaker." I think they're afraid because most of them don't have papers—maybe 10% have papers. Of the 80 Mexican employees where I work, 15 have work permits and proper papers and I think that 65 are illegal. . . . But, also, it's true that undocumented Mexicans aren't very afraid of being deported. Let's say that one day INS comes in and rounds up the 65 illegals. Suddenly the factory is left without people. The 15 of us that are left will not do the work of the other 65, isn't that right? [Laughs.]

Even though the bosses are very aware that it's against the law to hire illegals, they do it anyway—because they can pay them cheaper wages, right? It's a type of exploitation—they increase their profits by using illegal workers. The US government says that the illegal is a burden for the United States, but I don't think so. Because if the illegal makes $300 dollars a week and they take out income tax, they take out Social Security and local taxes, state taxes, then how is the illegal a burden? If the government is thinking about kicking out those illegal people, sending them back to Mexico or El Salvador or Guatemala or to Argentina, wherever, tell me, who will do the work? Who? Americans will not work for $6.50 an hour. The people who work in factory jobs or picking mushrooms or construction or who work in hotels or restaurants like McDonald's, Burger King, Wendy's or Chi Chi's—most of them are Mexican. I think the US government should do what they did with me and all of the Mexicans in 1986—give us amnesty and residency.

I remember the day I got my green card, in '86. I went to an Immigration office in a town called Lima. They asked me questions—if INS had caught me, if I had problems with the police. I told them no. Then they asked me if I was a Mexican, and I said yes. They said, "If you are a Mexican, sing us the song 'La Bamba.' How does it go? If you sing it and we see that indeed you know it, then you are a Mexican. If not, you are lying to us." So they had me singing "La Bamba" and there I was, showing them that I was indeed a Mexican.

> ♫ To dance "La Bamba"
> To dance "La Bamba"
> You need a little bit of
> A little bit of grace, for you, for you
> And get up, come on
> I am not a sailor
> For you I will be, for you I will be
> Bamba, Bamba
> And to get to heaven, you need
> A little bit of grace. . . . ♫

I feel great pride for having gotten [my green card]. This green card represents years of sacrifice—not being with my family, living and working with men only, suffering. It's hard.

When I die, I would like to be remembered with affection. I want people to remember what I gave them in my life—the little things. What I am most proud of is the people that I know—friends and neighbors, in Mexico and here. And coworkers I have lived and worked with. I am proud to have fulfilled my obligations to my family, my children. I always took care of my family when they were in Mexico and sent them money so they would have enough to eat. Even though I would drink a few beers, it was never more than six or so. And I didn't spend all of the money that I earned on myself. I always thought of my wife, of the children. I wanted to make sure that they had a place to live, clothes to wear, food to eat, and an education. I tell my wife, I tell her, "You got lucky when you married me."

Salvador García Baeza (en Español)

Salvador García Baeza tiene 54 años de edad, y es del pueblo de Moroleón, México. Vino para trabajar en la industria de los hongos en Kennett Square en

1979, y obtuvo su residencia permanente en 1986. Trajo a sus hijos a Pensilva-
nia en 1996, y su esposa e hija vinieron en 2000.

Yo pienso que nuestra familia sobrevivió la separación porque sobre todo
hubo comunicación por cartas, cuando eran pequeños de 10 años, de 12
años, de 14 años. Había cartas individuales, una para cada uno, dándole
consejos. Creo que mi esposa tiene unas 300 a la mejor, tiene todas las que
yo le mandé durante esos 21 o 22 años. Había una carta cada mes. Hubo
mucha comunicación por teléfono, preguntaba por todos, platicaba con ellos
10 minutos, 15 minutos. Les daba consejos. Yo sentía una alegría después
de hablar con la esposa, con los hijos. Me daba un ánimo muy grande para
empezar a trabajar otro día.

Sí, como no, era duro por estar separado de mis hijos. No los vi crecer.
Ahora sé cómo son porque los veo. Entonces digo para mí es un orgullo
por el comportamiento que tienen y también un orgullo con la esposa, que
los supo dirigir cuando yo estaba en los Estados Unidos. Hay familias que
no son así.

[Ahora donde trabajo] me pagan $7.20 cada hora, y he trabajado allá
por ocho años. En ninguna parte se paga tiempo y medio. Ahora estoy yo
trabajando un mes y medio trece horas diarias—70-80 horas semanales—y
no pagan tiempo y medio. Ellos dicen que no se paga tiempo y medio porque
es un trabajo que le nombran "agricultura". Yo pienso que pasando de 40
horas la semana se debe pagar tiempo y medio, no importa cómo se llame—
"agricultura", o cualquier clase de trabajo. Lo importante que pienso yo es
que uno trabaje.

Yo pienso que donde estoy, no es fácil de quejarse y formar un grupo porque allí le tienen un miedo horrible, espantoso a que uno vaya a defenderse.
Porque tienen miedo que les digan no más trabajo para ti por andar quejando.
Yo pienso que el miedo de ellos es que la mayoría no tienen papeles—10%,
no más, tienen sus papeles. De esos 80 empleados mexicanos donde trabajo,
quince tenemos permiso de trabajo y papeles buenos, y pienso que 65 son
ilegales . . . Pero es la verdad también que los mexicanos sin documentos no
tienen mucho miedo de ser deportados. Entonces, por decir, algún día la
inmigración entra, y hay una redada de los 65 ilegales. Automáticamente la

fábrica se queda sin gente. Entonces, los 15 que quedarán no vamos a hacer el trabajo de los otro 65, ¿verdad que no? [Se ríe]

Aunque los patrones saben bien que es ilegal agarrar ilegales, ellos lo hacen—porque pagan más barato ¿Si? Es un tipo de explotación—las ganancias de ellos son muy buenas con el ilegal. El gobierno de los Estados Unidos dice que el ilegal es una carga para los Estados Unidos, pero yo pienso que no. Porque si el ilegal gana $300 a la semana y a uno le rebajan *tax* sobre ingresos, a uno le rebajan Seguro Social, *taxes* locales, y *taxes* de estado, entonces ¿cómo es el ilegal una carga? Si el gobierno está pensando en echar esa gente ilegal para afuera, para México o para El Salvador, o para Guatemala, o Argentina donde sea, dime ¿quién va a trabajar? ¿Quién? Porque los americanos no van a trabajar por las $6.50 a la hora. La gente que trabajan en las fábricas, las hongueras, la construcción, muchos hoteles, los restaurantes, ¿no? Como *McDonald's*, o *Burger King*, o *Wendy's*—la mayoría son mexicanos. Yo pienso que el gobierno de los Estados Unidos debe hacer lo que hizo conmigo y con todos los mexicanos en1986—darnos la amnistía y la residencia.

Yo me acuerdo el día que recibí mi *green card,* en el 86. Fui a una oficina de migración que había en el pueblito que se llama Lima. Me hicieron preguntas, que si migración me había agarrado alguna vez, que si tenía problemas con la policía. Les dije que no. Entonces me dijeron que si era mexicano, les dije que sí. Me dijeron, "Si eres mexicano cántanos la canción de "La Bamba". ¿Cómo es que es? Si la cantas y vemos que sí tu la sabes, es que eres mexicano. Si no, es que nos está mintiendo". Ahí me tienen cantando "La Bamba", y yo allí demostrándoles que sí era mexicano, sí.

♫ Para bailar la Bamba
Para bailar la Bamba
Se necesita una poca de gracia
Una poca de gracia para ti, para ti
Y arriba y arriba
Yo no soy marinero
Por ti seré, por ti seré, por ti seré
Bamba, Bamba
Y para subir al cielo, se necesita
Una poca de gracia . . . ♫

Bueno, para mí significa un gran orgullo por haber obtenido mi *green card*. Este *green card* representa años de sacrificio—de no estar con la familia, de vivir y trabajar con puros hombres, de sufrir. Es duro.

Pues cuando me muera, me gustaría que me recuerden con cariño, que me recuerden por lo que yo les di en mi vida—cositas. El orgullo más grande que tengo es sobre la gente que yo conozco, de amigos, de vecinos, en México y aquí. Y compañeros de trabajo, que he vivido con ellos y he trabajado con ellos. Tengo orgullo de estar cumpliendo con mi familia, con mis hijos. Siempre estuve pendiendo en ellos cuando estuvieron en México, de mandarles dinero, que no les faltara para comer. Aunque aquí luego me tomaba unas cervezas, nunca fue más de seis, o así. No gastaba todo el dinero que ganaba sólo en mí. Siempre pensaba en la esposa, en los hijos. Que no les faltara en dónde vivir, y qué vestir, y qué comer, y su educación. Yo le digo a la esposa mía, le digo, "Tú corriste con suerte conmigo, en tu matrimonio conmigo."

Mayra Castillo Rangel

Mayra Castillo Rangel is 22 years old and came to the United States when she was 12. She is a graduate of Chestnut Hill College, where she majored in French and Communications. She now works at Arcadia University in the offices of admissions and financial aid and is also the Minority Recruitment Coordinator. Mayra is the teacher of the dance group Danza Tenochtli, of La Misión Santa María de Dios, in Avondale, Pa.

We arrived here on July 14th, I think, during the summer of 1993 right after I graduated from 6th grade, primary school, there. When I entered school here I entered an all-English school, although I had some bilingual teachers and classes. Before I started I remember my dad bought my brother and me a blackboard, chalk and an eraser and lent us his English books to start preparing for school. He said I had to learn all I could alone and at times he would help with what he knew, which I now realize wasn't a lot—but even though it was little, that and the encouragement all helped. He showed me the alphabet, the numbers and some basics. He also took us to a Puerto Rican friend of his at the mushroom plant where he worked so she could help us too. She read books for us and my first English book I read was by Dr. Seuss. I think it was something like *One Fish, Two Fish, Red Fish, Blue Fish*. I felt very proud because by the end I could read the whole book by myself, even if it was from memory. I could recognize some of the numbers and colors and other words and I could tell I had good pronunciation.

I think entering school was very difficult. I was very afraid. . . . I had to present myself at the main office to get my schedule and be advised on how classes were going to work. . . . I was so happy when I learned that [the principal], Mr. Carr, spoke some Spanish. That comforted me, but I still couldn't help but cry in front of him. . . . I was very, very nervous and afraid and couldn't help it. . . . [I felt] grief and shame and more fear and then I cried even more.

I think my family continues to be very ingrained in the Mexican traditions. I'm between the Mexican and so-called "American" traditions myself. I like that and work it to my advantage, to understand the two different worlds. Living in the US, I think I understand the culture and the language, but I try not to stray too far from my Mexican culture. I am still proud to say that I'm Mexican, but I'm happy to live in another country where I've had to adapt myself to the new culture. As a Mexican I love to dance the *cumbia*, a little *quebradita* and, of course, our folkloric traditional dances. I love the food and although I don't know how to cook the traditional dishes I still have my mom and I ask her from time to time to make me *un molito*, or *un pozolito* or maybe some *enchiladas* or even her own *gorditas*. Of course, I love my language, the Spanish that we speak at home. I forget some things from time to time since I don't speak it a lot. Since living in the US, I like the liberty, my freedom. I'm no longer a submissive Mexican woman, meant to be only a wife and a mother. That's what I've come to conclude about myself now that I live here.

I think that in part, my mom has been my role model, perhaps without wanting to be or without her realizing it. I have heard my mom talk and seen how hard she has worked all her life, sometimes at two or three jobs, plus she is also a mother and housewife, all at the same time. We Mexicans tend to believe or always say that the man is the head of the household, the one that contributes the money, the one that works more, yet my mom has shown me that I can go forward and I can do what I want because she has done it herself.

I just graduated [from Chestnut Hill College], where I studied French. That is what I chose as a career, although I haven't figured out what I'm going to do with it. People say I have a gift for languages, and maybe I do, but the toughest part is figuring out what to do with this gift. At times I have thought about being a school counselor because I had one in high school who really helped me when I was going through a tough time. I had two college professors who gave me a lot of support and believed I could do a lot with my life—they said I would go far in life. When they told me that, I believed it and little by little I got the courage to look for and ask for more in life. If anything, that is what I would like to do with the youth from our community and others—encourage them, make them see that we are in the land of opportunities and more possibilities than what our parents had in Mexico and that if they really want something, to go ahead and grab it. It is tough at times, but it can be done.

I wonder if my family has accomplished the American Dream—in part, yes, and in part, no. Our dream was to have a better life than we had in Mexico and we do have it, in a way. My parents have a home, a job, my dad has some benefits, we have food on our table and some other amenities that have come along the way, like cars—not luxury cars or even new cars—but what we need for transportation and to feel accomplished in one way or another. I have an education that I know I would never have had in Mexico. I have traveled to many places around the world—something I don't think I would have done if I had stayed in Mexico. I actually think I would be married with children now; there's nothing wrong with that, but I'm just happier where I am now, single. Yes, materially we are better off, but we have all suffered a lot. We have lost the comfort of feeling at home when we go back to Mexico because we have become *Norteños* [Northerners] and have lost part of our Mexican identity while gaining a new one in the US. We have all suffered racial discrimination in one way or another and felt inferior at times and that was definitely not part of our dream.

Mayra Castillo Rangel (en Español)

Mayra Castillo Rangel tiene 22 años de edad, y vino a los Estados Unidos cuando tenía 12 años. Ella es graduada de Chestnut Hill College, donde se especializó [sic] en el idioma francés y comunicaciones. Ahora ella trabaja en La Universidad de Arcadia, en las Oficinas de Ayuda Financiera y Admisiones; y también es la Coordinadora de Reclutamiento de Minorías. Mayra es la maestra del grupo de Danza Tenochtli de la Misión de Santa María Madre de Dios, en Avondale, Pa.

Llegamos aquí el 14 de julio, durante el verano de 1993, justo después de graduarme del 6to. grado de primaria allá. Cuando entré a la escuela aquí, fui a una escuela donde enseñaban solamente en inglés, aunque había algunos maestros y clases bilingües. Antes de empezar la escuela, recuerdo que mi papá compró un pizarrón, gis y borrador para mi hermano y para mí. También nos prestó sus libros de inglés para empezar a prepararnos para la escuela. Dijo que yo tenía que aprender lo que pudiera sola y que en ocasiones él me ayudaría con lo que sabía—ahora me doy cuenta que no era mucho—pero aunque era poco, eso y el alentarnos era una ayuda. Me enseñó el alfabeto, los números y cosas básicas. También nos llevó con una amiga suya puertorriqueña en la planta de los hongos donde trabajaba para que ella nos ayudara también. Ella nos leía libros y el primer libro en inglés que leí fue escrito por el Dr. Seuss. Creo que era algo como *Un Pez, Dos Peces, Pez Azul, Pez Rojo.* Al final de la lectura me sentí muy orgullosa porque pude leer todo el libro sola, aunque fuese de memoria. Podía reconocer algunos números y colores y otras palabras y podía darme cuenta de que tenía buena pronunciación.

Creo que entrar a la escuela fue muy difícil. Tenía mucho miedo . . . Me tenía que presentar yo sola en la oficina principal para obtener mi horario y para que me dijeran cómo funcionaban las clases. Estuve tan contenta cuando supe que el [principal], Sr. Carr hablaba algo de español. Eso me confortó, pero aún así no pude evitar llorar delante de él . . . Yo estaba muy, muy nerviosa y asustada y no podía evitarlo. Sentí tanta congoja y vergüenza y más miedo y entonces lloré aún más.

Creo que mi familia continúa muy apegada a las tradiciones mexicanas. Yo estoy entre las tradiciones mexicanas y las llamadas "americanas". Me gusta eso y creo que es ventajoso para mí entender dos mundos diferentes. Viviendo en los Estados Unidos, creo que entiendo la cultura y el idioma, pero trato de no apartarme mucho de mi cultura mexicana. Todavía me siento orgullosa de decir que soy mexicana, pero estoy contenta de vivir en otro país donde he tenido que adaptarme a una cultura nueva. Como mexicana me encanta la cumbia, un poco de quebradita y, claro, las danzas folklóricas tradicionales. Me encanta la comida y aunque no sé como cocinar los platillos tradicionales, de vez en cuando todavía le pido a mi mamá que me haga un molito, o un pozolito o quizás algunas enchiladas e incluso unas gorditas. Claro que me encanta mi idioma, el español que hablamos en casa. De vez en cuando se me olvidan algunas cosas ya que no hablo español todo el tiempo. Viviendo en los Estados Unidos, amo mi libertad. Ya no soy una abnegada mujer mexicana, destinada solamente a ser esposa y madre. Es a la conclusión que he llegado de mí misma ahora que vivo aquí.

Creo que en parte, mi mamá ha sido el ejemplo a seguir, quizás sin siquiera querer serlo o darse cuenta de ello. Yo he oído a mi mamá hablar y he visto cómo ha trabajado fuertemente toda su vida, agunas [sic] veces hasta con dos o tres trabajos, aparte de ser madre y ama de casa, todo al mismo tiempo. Los mexicanos tendemos a creer o siempre decir que el hombre es el jefe del hogar, el que contribuye con el dinero, el que más trabaja, sin embargo mi mamá me ha mostrado que yo puedo salir adelante y hacer lo que quiera, porque ella misma ha hecho lo mismo.

Me acabo de graduar de Chestnut Hill College, donde estudié francés. Eso es lo que escogí como carrera, aunque todavía no he planeado qué voy a hacer con esta carrera. La gente me dice que tengo el don de aprender idiomas, quizás sea así, pero la parte más difícil es descifrar qué hacer con ese don. A veces he pensado en ser consejera escolar porque tuve una en la escuela secundaria que realmente me ayudó cuando estaba pasando por una etapa difícil de mi vida. Tuve dos profesores universitarios que me apoyaron mucho y creyeron que podía hacer mucho con mi vida. Dijeron que lograría grandes cosas en la vida. Cuando me dijeron eso, les creí y poco a poco me hice valor para buscar y pedir más de la vida. Si hay algo que quisiera hacer para la juventud de mi comunidad y de otras, es alentarlos, hacerles ver que estamos en el país de las oportunidades y de más posibilidades que las que tuvieron nuestros padres en México y si quieren hacer realmente algo, sigan adelante y alcancen sus metas. Eso es difícil a veces, pero se puede lograr.

A veces me pregunto si mi familia ha logrado el "sueño americano", en parte sí y en parte no. Nuestro sueño era tener una mejor vida que en México y de alguna manera la tenemos. Mis padres tienen un hogar, un trabajo, mi papá tiene algunos beneficios, tenemos comida en la mesa y algunas otras diversiones que hemos logrado, un gran avance como son los carros—no carros lujosos o incluso carros nuevos—pero lo que necesitamos para transporte, y sentimos que hemos logrado algo de una manera u otra. Tengo una educación superior que yo sé no hubiera tenido en México. He viajado a muchos lugares del mundo, algo que no creo que hubiera podido hacer si me hubiese quedado en México. En realidad pienso que estaría ya casada y con hijos ahora; nada malo en eso, pero simplemente estoy mucho más contenta como estoy ahora: soltera. Sí, en el aspecto material estamos mejor, pero todos hemos sufrido mucho. Hemos perdido el confort de sentirnos en casa cuando regresamos a México porque nos hemos convertido en "Norteños" y hemos perdido una gran parte de nuestra identidad mexicana mientras que hemos ganado una nueva en los Estados Unidos. Todos hemos sufrido discriminación racial de una manera u otra y nos hemos sentido inferiores en ocasiones y eso definitivamente no era parte de nuestro sueño.

Working: An Anthology of Writing and Photography

What Can the Union Do for Me?

ANN MARIE TALIERCIO

In an effort to answer the question, "What can the Union do for me?" I many times answer: Joining a Union is like joining a health club. If all you do is pay your dues every month will you have a leaner, stronger body?

Well, it's the same with joining a Union. Once you join the Union, it's not just about paying Union dues every month; learn what the contract says, find out where the Union office is, ask, "Who is my Shop Steward?," "May I have the current contract?," "When and where are the Union meetings?," "When is the next contract being negotiated?," and "How do I get on the Committee Negotiating Committee?"

Joining a Union is like joining a health club; utilize the equipment that the Union provides. That's what paying monthly dues is all about.

The misfortune of having a late in life child befell Georgina when she had worked down in the hotel laundry for over twenty years. I use the term misfortune not because a twenty-one daughter [*sic*] was her only other child and Georgina thought that her maternal responsibilities were over, but because she gave birth this second time just before the start of an unusually harsh Syracuse winter.

Under the state laws of New York, maternity is considered a disability. When a working woman becomes pregnant she is required to work up to the point that her doctor declares that her disability, her pregnancy, is preventing her from performing her job. She then has to return to work as soon as her doctor certifies that the disability, her pregnancy, has gone away and that she is well enough to perform her duties again. The typical time frame for all of this to occur is between six and eight weeks after the baby is born.

Georgina's son was born by normal delivery in the autumn of that year and her six to eight weeks ran out by the end of December. In preparation for her return to work, Georgina looked for a day care center that accepted infants. She found one that was close to her job, located at the end of her walking route to work. With that important arrangement finalized, Georgina believed that she was returning to work with all of her problems solved.

However, despite the planning, by the end of January Georgina was being disciplined for taking too many days off from work because of her son. The baby was well, but it was the weather. In January, the thaw never came and the plowed snow accumulated so high that school-aged children were wearing poles with flags that extended upward from their waists so that cars could see them as they attempted to cross the city streets from behind the snowdrifts. It wasn't so much the daily record-breaking temperatures that prevented Georgina from getting to work each day, as it was the blustery arctic winds that convinced Georgina to call in sick for her 8 A.M. start time, rather than risk the possibly fatal consequences of carrying her three-month-old son to his day care.

As a single mother, Georgina certainly needed a full week's pay each week. But, she did not make enough money to own a car and the only form of affordable transportation from the Southside of the city was the bus. The bus did not have conveniently spaced stops on the Southside. The closest bus stop for Georgina was several blocks from her house and if she walked that far, she might as well walk a few more blocks into downtown and work.

Georgina's boss, Paula, the head housekeeper at the hotel, was formerly an hourly worker herself at the telephone company. She was not trained to manage and had been hired into the position by a personal friend, the owner of the hotel who believed that individuals from different industries could bring new and better ways of doing business to his landmark property. The owner, as well as Paula, came from a world where no one walked to work except if it was part of a prescription from his or her doctor for a healthy heart. The owner's thinking still might have brought success if he provided management training to her since regardless of one's business background, one can be trained to be a good manager. Good management is taught to respect and inspire each worker under its authority, to lead, and to definitely not ask each worker to leave his or her humanity outside the employee entrance.

Georgina had washed the hotel linen for more than twenty years, but with no end to the Syracuse freeze, by the end of January Georgina had accumulated enough days off to warrant a discipline. Knowing in her heart that she had called in sick for a good reason, Georgina felt this discipline was unjustified. Unjustified discipline is a funny thing. At first the worker thinks that it is petty and not important because they know it's not fair, but then a second and a third one accumulates for other petty and stupid reasons, and before you know it the individual finds themselves terminated. Having survived twenty years at the Hotel, Georgina knew to bring the write up to her Union Steward, Keri Langley. Miss Keri, as all at the Hotel respectfully referred her to, was a fellow laundry worker. Miss Keri was also the moral compass at the hotel and was called upon many times in her capacity as Chief Union Steward, to eloquently argue the right and wrong of a situation. Despite being well equipped to argue this grievance, even Keri Langley couldn't get their supervisor to understand why Georgina was having such a tough time getting to work each day.

Not receiving any satisfaction at the first step meeting, Keri called me, their business agent, asking me to take the grievance to the next step. Keri wanted to get this write up resolved and out of Georgina's file. When the three of us met to discuss the case, Georgina asked me, "Why doesn't Paula understand? It's only because of the cold weather and in this cold I'm not taking my baby outside for no one."

"I know Georgina, I don't blame you," I responded. "But the company has the right to expect that you come to work everyday and if you don't, they write you up." I went on to explain, "If you continually can't get to work, for any reason, even medical, the company has the right to continue disciplining you until they have enough against you to fire you. I know that it doesn't make sense but unfortunately in our industry our work can't be piled on the desk until tomorrow and in this country that is how the laws are written."

Understandably so, Georgina was discouraged.

"But Georgina," I responded to her frustration, "what we can do is have a meeting with Paula, go over why you are calling in sick and perhaps she'll take pity on you and remove the write-up from your file. After all she has two children of her own." Georgina shook her head; "Man, what if my baby was sick and I couldn't leave him at day care? What would I have to do, lose my job for that too?"

"I know," I sadly responded, shaking my head along with hers and Keri's. "That's one of the reasons I never went out of my way to have children myself. When you have to work and have no family to help you, how can you have children? They do get sick!

"Well, don't get discouraged Georgina, we'll figure out something. How about a later start time? Would it be easier to get here by 9 o'clock, when at least the sun is up?"

Keri said, "Yeah Georgina, that shouldn't be a problem. If I'm on, I can start the machines because Johnny doesn't get those washers started on time anyway. Perhaps Paula will let you come in at 9 a.m."

It took a few weeks, until almost the end of February to get the meeting with Paula, but at least we had a plan that gave Georgina some hope.

Keri, Georgina, and I met with the head housekeeper Paula. She came to the meeting with her two housekeeping supervisors.

Since the Union called the meeting I began: "Paula, we are here today on behalf of Georgina." Keri took notes as I explained to Paula why Georgina had accumulated so many days off in such a short period of time. "Her intent was not to fraud the company by calling in sick, but she needed the time off to take care of her son. Some days it is just too cold outside to walk an infant to day care . . ."

"Why can't she just take the bus? Can't anyone drive her? I don't understand," said the head housekeeper. "It's her responsibility to get here and to get here on time. She should have a back-up sitter. Why doesn't she have someone to watch him when it's too cold to take him to day care? Why . . . ? Why . . . ? Why . . . ? When I had my children my husband's mother would watch my kids, can't her mother?"

"Paula, everything you are saying is true but Georgina doesn't have anyone she can ask to watch her son on the exceptionally cold days. The bus stop is too far to walk to, no, she doesn't know anyone with a car, and it's almost spring. What's the difference? Just take the write-up out of her file, she is a good worker and has managed not to get fired in twenty years, so just work with us and give her a second chance. This issue will be gone with the bad weather.

" . . . Yes, I know Paula, it's only a first-step verbal, but it's still a write-up and a woman with twenty years of service doesn't want any write-ups in her file." Miss Keri then asked the head housekeeper, "Can you blame her Paula? Would you want a write-up in your file because it was too cold to walk your baby to day care?"

I then offered the solution of allowing Georgina the opportunity to start her workday at 9 A.M. Keri offered that Johnny doesn't always have the wash finished by 8 A.M. anyway. Paula immediately shook her head in unison with the two supervisors. "No, I can't do that, I need her here. We have laundry to press and fold and the maids need their linen by 10 A.M. otherwise we can't get the rooms done on time. If she doesn't want to work then she can quit. I pay her good money to work and I expect her to be here."

Almost an hour and a half passed with both sides arguing back and forth. The best we could walk away with was getting Paula to agree to take the write up out of Georgina's file in three months from the date of the write-up if Georgina didn't call out of work excessively over that period of time. I privately recommended that Georgina accept this resolution because I not only knew that the problem would go away with the bad weather but that Georgina would have a clean file again in the same time that it would surely take to go to mediation and then arbitration. With experience, you learn to pick your battles, and anyway, you never really know which way an arbitrator is going to rule. Of course, even after reaching this resolution, Paula kept insisting that Georgina had to find some way to get her infant son to his day care on cold mornings or find someone to take care of him at home. The three of us just nodded, "yeah, yeah, yeah," and walked out

knowing that there was no way that we were going to make Paula understand that the hotel would survive but that Georgina's baby might not.

Afterwards I said to Keri and Georgina, "I think that we did the best we
could. If we decided to go to arbitration on this one, the arbitrator would
most likely rule in the company's favor because in this country all of the
power is on the side of the management. You've both read Article 2: Management's Rights, in the contract. And for a first-step verbal, an arbitrator
would have probably said, 'Just get to work everyday, the company has the
right to expect you there to do your job.'"

I reassured Georgina, "Don't let it worry you Georgina, it's almost spring
and almost a month of the three months is up, it'll be out of your file before
you know it and if we have this same type of weather next year, your son will
be old enough to go out in cold weather." Georgina nodded, "I know."

Keri agreed and added, "What would she do if she was in Georgina's
place?"

"I don't know" I responded, and they both went back to work.

As I many times do, I went back inside to say goodbye to the manager. Paula looked at me apologetically and said, "I am sorry that it took
so long for me to get back to you about setting up this meeting." She then
stumbled and said, "My children; I mean I was sick and wasn't able to get to
work." I just nodded and said goodbye, because in that one sentence, Paula
has summarized the universal dispute between labor and management. It is
accepted and revered that any need of management or of the company always
outweighs the needs of the workers. In a society that considers pregnancy a
disability, it is not at all that surprising that the many who create the wealth,
the hourly workers, primarily women, are the ones who are asked to leave
their humanity on the other side of the door, each day, as they faithfully file
through the employee entrance.

The Tree of Thanks

VERA BEATON

My daughter came home for the Canadian Thanksgiving holiday, and we
had some very interesting family times together. Specifically, we talked about

family and times, in short bursts and in extended sessions. I have no clue about what prompted this, but part of it came from my reflections about a little boy who is currently in treatment at my place of work.

I don't usually discuss people at the hospital with family or friends—it usually seems like a violation of one kind or another. But this little boy had kind of hit me where I live, and I wanted to share this with someone that I knew would consider this from a loving perspective, rather than discount the story as a more eccentric blithering from the strange mind of Minerva Jones.

The little boy in question is a child who ended up in a group home following a time of chaos in his family. His parents were getting divorced, and he was caught in the crossfire of their battle. He became angry, and began to act out. His misbehavior took the form of writing long stories with violent themes. When he went to the group home, this activity did not stop. In fact, after some time in the group home, he started writing stories about the group home.

He was sent to the psychiatric hospital after a staff member found a seven-page story about his plan to kill his enemies at the group home by turning on the gas stove and letting the residence fill with gas. At the end of the story that he wrote, "everyone perished in the resulting explosion."

People are taking this sort of early warning very seriously these days. When this boy arrived on our doorstep, the lessons from the Columbine High School shooting came to the fore. Staff speculated about this boy's "sociopathy." Was he signaling some horrendous intention?

The Demon Seed. The boy seemed like a regular kid, but unusually intelligent. He is extraordinarily creative. He developed a daily newspaper on the ward, and he started a lottery by putting a winning symbol on a piece of paper in pencil, then coloring over it with a crayon. He'd pass these out to the other kids, and they would scratch off the crayon, revealing a winner. There were no prizes involved. Kids liked the idea of being winners, and he'd post the results on his bedroom door, with the daily winner acknowledged. He made a *Jeopardy*-type game. When I saw this, I asked for "Animals, $300."

The question: What animal has eyes bigger than its brain?

Answer: See below.

I started to tell my daughter about this kid because he had done a funny and interesting thing. The recreational therapist had made a construction paper tree for the unit, entitled *The Tree of Thanks*. The therapeutic task assigned to the children was to cut leaves from various colored paper, and then write something they were thankful for on each leaf. I saw the finished product when I came to work in the evening.

These kids were thankful for so many things—their moms, pets, grand-parents, toys. One kid was even thankful for me, which was nice. But buried in the leaves of this *Tree of Thanks* was a kid who was thankful for "[his] evilness." It was written in jagged purple crayon on a peaceful green background.

I had to laugh. "What a little beauty!" I thought.

I knew this had to be the work of my creative/sociopathic boy. So many people were telling him that he was having bad thoughts. In fact earlier in the week, during a treatment meeting, one of the social workers had gone on about his attempt to blow up his group home after I recommended that we test this boy's IQ. I had to remind the social worker that the boy had not tried to kill anyone; he had only written about it. He did not fight with his peers physically, but he did occasionally have disputes. For the most part, he adapted to his environment, and dealt with his episodic anger through written expression. For example, he became angry at a certain staff member when she wouldn't allow him to use the phone to call his mother. He wrote on the floor of his room "Mrs. S. is a mean bitch."

This seemed like a natural response to powerlessness, in my way of thinking.

He was congenial with his peers and had moments of generosity and compassion with them.

I told my daughter about this boy, in the same general terms as I have here—no names, no identifying details. No loss of confidentiality, no betrayal. But I wanted to tell someone how glad I was, after all the trials of this young boy's life—the break up of his family, and the involuntary com-mitments—how he was still able to retain a sense of himself and the integrity to be thankful for the "evilness" that allowed him to explore and display his anger without causing harm to anyone else.

I'm hoping one day we'll all catch up to this kid.

(Answer to the *Jeopardy* question: OSTRICH. My first instinctive response was people, but then I remembered that, generally, our brains are bigger than our eyes. This may not be a good thing.)

More Tree of Thanks Stuff. So after I discussed the young boy with my daughter, my strange and tangential mind moved onto another young boy who grew up with heavy burdens: my mother's grandfather.

Ambrose "Amby" O'Connell had responsibility from an early age. His father had kept going on after going out for a "quart of milk." In the way of that time, Amby was lucky to have been given his father's job in the coal mine. He was nine-years-old. No fourth-grade primer for this boy—his path was to help feed a family.

Such is life.

He went on to be a well-respected man, a dragger man, the man who dragged others out of the mine following a cave-in or a fire. He also became the fire chief of his local area, a man who led other small-town saviors into the very heart of all that intended to destroy everyone: ruin, despair, death. Along these same lines, he was an early union organizer. Somebody forgot to tell him he "owed his soul to the company store," and he didn't believe it when they tried to influence him after the fact. Union supporters were having unfortunate accidents, and there was outright brutality in the streets of New Waterford, Dominion Beach, and Glace Bay, courtesy of the companies (and the Canadian government). Mr. O'Connell started a credit union in his house so that the miners would have a place to come for funds. Some place *not* owned by the Dominion Coal Company.

"A man's a man for a' that . . ."

I told my daughter that her great-great grandfather was one of the reasons that sociologists love to hang around Nova Scotia. And then I moved onto another strange and wonderful story . . .

Another Strange and Wonderful Story. MUMS is the acronym the women gave their union as they emerged from the battered women's shelter, empowered to take on all manner of injustice and brutality.

MUMS stands for Mothers United for Metro Shelter.

This was 1984. *Brave New World* was available, if only we had the map, and the wisdom to use it.

MUMS had a great start by six women who had joined together to protest the prejudicial and falsely inflated Halifax rental housing market. They held up traffic on the Alexander A. MacDonald Bridge one day, and handed out fliers describing the pitiful state of housing for poor women and children in Halifax. They described how they were dubbed the welfare bums, but how $700 out of the $900 they were "given" each month to support a family, really went to line the pockets of landlords. How hard it was to feed and clothe children on $200 a month. (Have you ever noticed the 'nickel-and-diming' that goes on? It'll be the death of us.)

MUMS were radical in that they suggested (aside from the fact that the bulk of the fund they were given was going to the fattest people in town) the true state of affairs implied they were in essence paid employees of the government, bringing up the next generation of wage slaves in the absence of that brutal "milk cow" they used to call their husbands. They were a union of mothers, employed by the government, enduring the full stigma of the hand out. No benefits except the health and happiness of their children, the sort you can fashion on the most meager of wages—a very hard job.

They called for a public demonstration of their powerlessness, and they gave a date for their intended act of civil disobedience. They planned to march on City Hall, hand the mayor an eviction notice, give him a bogus check for $900, and tell him to find new accommodations for his activities.

On the designated date, they set out from a site halfway down Gottigen Street, a place heavily damaged by munitions explosions in the various world wars. It was a place where the corpses of the Titanic washed up, along with their sad, water-logged possessions. These six women walked along the water front to City Hall, so purposeful, proud, and adamant.

On the way, they gathered others—folks watching from the sidelines, but invigorated by their passion. When they passed the docks next to the bridge separating Halifax from Dartmouth, the entirety of the union of dock workers joined them.

A half dozen women and several hundred men. The women served their eviction notice, and the Mayor, noting so many potential voters in his presence, made the necessary promises.

A rent-controlled apartment complex with a daycare.

The Mayor never made good on this.

But I told my daughter about this story to tell her about the people we come from, the places we've been. The dreams lost, the promise shown and denied. The ability of people to rise above the squalor. The hope of brotherhood and sisterhood.

I can't tell the story about those dock workers joining the *Mother's Union* without crying, and I did some serious boohooing when I told my daughter about them. Me, a silly middle-aged woman, crying while she sat on her living room floor in the middle of America, so far away from the fray.

And I cry now. But it's for the same reasons that I told my daughter as she patted my head and kissed me while I cried on the *Tree of Thanks* day.

"Sometimes, people are so good, and they have so much dignity, that they just break your heart."

I only wish I could've laughed.

"A Man's a Man for All That"

ROBERT BURNS, 1795

Is there for honesty poverty
That hangs his head, an' a' that;
The coward slave—we pass him by,
We dare be poor for a' that!
For a' that, an' a' that,
Our toils obscure an' a' that,
The rank is but the guinea's stamp,
The man's the gowd for a' that.

What though on homely fare we dine,
Wear hoddin grey, an' a' that?
Give fools their silks, and knaves their wine,
A man's a man for a' that.
For a' that, an' a' that,
Their tinsel show, an' a' that,
The honest man, tho' e'er sae poor,
Is king o' men for a' that.

Ye see yon birkie ca'd a lord,
Wha struts, an' stares, an' a' that;
Tho' hundreds worship at his word,

He's but a coof for a' that.
For a' that, an' a' that,
His ribband, star, an' a' that,
The man o' independent mind
He looks an' laughs at a' that.

A price can mak a belted knight,
A marquise, duke, an' a' that;
But an honest man's aboon his might,
Gude faith, he maunna fa' that!
For a' that, an' a' that,
Their dignities an' a' that
The pith o' sense, an' pride o' worth,
Are higher rank than
Then let us pray that come it may,
(As come it will for a' that,)
That Sense and Worth, o'er a' the earth,
Shall bear the gree, an' a' that.
For a' that, an' a' that,
That man to man, the world o'er,
Shall brothers be for a' that.

6

Success

The Aftermath of Survival

In dreams begins responsibility.
—W. B. YEATS, epigraph in *RESPONSIBILITIES
and Other Poems*

AT THE OUTSET, New City Writing was the Institute for the Study of Literature, Literacy, and Culture, a purposeful intervention in the workings of Temple University designed to expand the College of Arts and Sciences' support of progressive literacy practices in North Philadelphia. Within this context, New City's individual projects were tactical moments designed to infiltrate gaps within traditional literacy institutions and embed alternative writing practices. The ultimate goal, however, was always to create an enclave out of which such progressive work could be supported on a continual basis. During much of this time, the growth of New City Writing stood as a marker for our overarching success in creating such a strategic space.

When our work began in late 1990s, New City Writing's space consisted of one drawer of a single file cabinet. Eight years later, in addition to all the community partners and partnerships detailed in previous chapters, New City had its own carpeted office suite, a director (myself), office staff, graduate student assistants, work-study students, college faculty, part-time associates, and a publishing enterprise, New City Community Press. New City Writing had also raised approximately $2 million and, through Eli Goldblatt's efforts, participated in developing an endowment specifically for the writing program's community-based efforts. Strategically, then, the collective efforts of those involved had created a unique and established space from

191

which to develop and financially support university and community literacy partnerships aimed at larger social justice efforts.

During this same period, however, Temple University was also participating in an educational marketplace that was moving toward a more traditional and corporate sense of priorities and values. These larger pressures ultimately led to the rearticulation of the space in which New City Writing existed, calling into question its very existence within the university. These shifting winds of administrative priorities, particularly when it comes to community-based work, makes the situation of New City Writing all too familiar to those engaged in community efforts. As articulated more in hallway conversations than in scholarly discussions, community literacy and service-learning projects are often one of the first sites where institutional mission realignment and budget cuts occur. In such an environment, the question for many of us becomes, what type of partnership network can best respond to these shifting winds and ensure long-term survival of our community-based work?

In the following pages, I argue for the importance of composition and rhetoric programs that develop strategic spaces (as opposed to tactical interventions) to support community-based partnerships and progressive literacy programs. I want to argue that the existence of strategic spaces not only ensures the continuation of progressive literacy work in spite of any particular institutional shift, but also creates the possibility on a new civic space in which such work can grow and expand. For, ultimately, the real goal is not just transforming the university, but transforming the context in which progressive literacy politics can occur. And in this concluding chapter, I recount how New City Writing attempted to survive internal institutional realignments of its work and emerged as a collaborator in the production of this new civic space in Philadelphia.

Shifting Winds

In its opening moments, New City Writing benefited from a faculty tradition of community service embedded within a supportive administrative culture. The tradition grew from a faculty who believed in the university's working-class heritage and who imagined the university as a resource for supporting North Philadelphia's economic, cultural, and political develop-ment. As service-learning and community partnership paradigms emerged nationally, these faculty could situate such work within this tradition and expand it across departments and colleges. When New City began, then, dozens of faculty initiatives were already occurring in the surrounding com-munity. The ability of so many efforts to exist simultaneously was the result of a university culture that fostered a progressive entrepreneurial spirit. Indi-vidual faculty were actively encouraged to initiate community work, and the university's budget practices appeared open enough to allow for redirecting funds accordingly. It was a network of reciprocity.

It was this culture that allowed New City Writing. In a more structured environment, a new assistant professor such as myself would usually not be given the charge to create such an institute. Partnerships with the public schools, such as the *Urban Rhythms* project, would have to be vetted and assessed before starting; cost analysis would be conducted to determine long-term viability; standards for assessment would need to be created. A more articulated system might have also noticed that multiple university initiatives were occurring at the same location—with one initiative often being unaware of another. At one school, for instance, university faculty were implementing two separate mathematics programs. This lack of coordination, however, was perfectly suited for New City Writing to develop new initiatives because there appeared to be few bridges to cross before a project could begin.

Midway through my time at Temple University, however, the system began to morph. The progressive entrepreneurial culture was slowly being placed within a network that was better able to monitor how a particular initiative supported the university's overall agenda. A new president was hired; new budgeting systems were put into place; new oversight policies were announced. A more centralized system was created. Instead of support-ing multiple initiatives in multiple public schools, the university took on a formal partnership with a set of schools (in response to the aforementioned state takeover), acquiring stewardship of their success. A blue line map was created that highlighted Temple's zone of influence in North Philadelphia. Grants that fit into this zone would likely receive stronger support from the university. Indeed, this zone was now imagined as so integrated into the university that it was now patrolled by Temple University police.

For anyone engaged in community-based work, this attempt to ratio-
nalize and organize community engagement made sense. Although many
faculty benefited from the entrepreneurial system, many were also aware
that the benefits could be one-sided. Faculty could set a particular research
agenda, enter a neighborhood or school, perform their research, and leave.
No long-term institutional commitment was required or expected. As a
result, the image (and practice) of the university within the community
seemed chaotic or, at least, uncoordinated. At the time, neither I nor my
colleagues saw asking faculty to filter their work through a system of critique and evaluation as necessarily coercive. It might even be a good idea.
For this reason, there was genuine interest when these new initiatives were
announced at a university meeting.

The move to regularize community partnerships, however, was soon
recognized as a broader attempt to redefine student and faculty identity.
As discussed at various point in previous chapters, the new administration
was set on the goal of raising admission standards. Coupled with this effort
were repeated signals to faculty about the diminishing institutional value of
community-based work and scholarship. For instance, in the midst of this
shifting terrain, New City Writing was essentially told to stop raising funds.
The explanation given was that because many of the grants New City Writing received were coded as "service grants," they did not support a *research*
college's fund-raising needs, nor did they support themselves through over-
head return. Rather, they were perceived as taking faculty away from teaching in the classroom and from producing scholarship for academic journals.
That is, New City Writing grants were perceived as dedicating faculty time to
organizing community-based initiatives rather than to educating or commu-
nicating to its real clientele. Attempts to demonstrate how New City Writing was actually producing both research (such as journal articles, etc.) and
research-in-practice (public-school curricula, community publications, literacy programs, etc.) did not carry much weight in the emerging paradigm.

In saying this, I don't want to imply that community partnerships were
discounted. There was never a moment when administration or college representatives did not sincerely express their support for community involvement. Rather, the support for such partnership work was rearticulated as
distinct from scholarly work and placed within terms more similar to social

services. Under the new system, such work was "properly placed" outside of academic centers. For instance, Temple's new Office of Partnership Schools was not placed in the School of Education, but within the President's Office. There was to be a University Community Center, but no systemic faculty involvement in it. This new structure was not so much an abandonment of community partnerships as it was the beginning of a new community-partnership management system. New offices, new programs, and new hires would continue elements of community engagement; they would do so with diminished insight from faculty. In such a world, New City Writing's location within a writing program, within a department, within a college, no longer seemed appropriate. What counted as legitimate disciplinary work was being rearticulated away from the activities that had marked New City Writing and more toward traditional visions of the "professoriate"—a tradition that had animated the initial FIPSE grant discussions out of which New City Writing had emerged.

The purpose of such a new management structure was to return the professoriate to playing the role of "traditional intellectuals." As articulated by Gramsci, every economic system creates its own intellectuals. A certain percentage of these intellectuals will spend their time ensuring that the system is able to continue reproducing itself economically, and others—the traditional intellectuals—will spend their time enabling the continual reproduction of the system ideologically. As has been highlighted throughout this book, I, like Gramsci, believed that the working class could draw from their unique historical and personal experiences to develop intellectuals organic to their own interests—using these intellectuals to begin mobilizing for broader political and economic rights. To me, New City Writing represented an attempt to shift the resources of the university toward the support of communities developing their own organic intellectuals. That is, New City was aligned with the community against those elements that were attempting to control both the production of knowledge and the basis by which knowledge was defined as legitimate.

In the new managerial system, however, faculty were returned to the classroom as the primary location of their work within North Philadelphia. As admission standards were raised, however, the students in the classroom were less and less from the North Philadelphia community. The classroom became an island distinct from the streets around Temple. Without the encouragement or the support to be engaged with the surrounding neighborhoods (either through promised hires or merit pay), disciplinary and departmental identity soon returned to focusing on static notions of knowledge production. That is, by placing the responsibility to the surrounding community outside of the academic fields, the university and the liberal arts were able to take on a more traditional sense of their intellectual identity. Aesthetic questions could become decoupled from local economic and political concerns. In effect, the new management system relieved the pressure for faculty to be actively involved with community concerns. Although it would not be fair to say that the university abandoned its responsibility to a concept of the university as engaged citizen, it is fair to ask, to what extent does such a model allow faculty expertise and a university's knowledge-producing capacities to be placed in the service of local community needs? To what extent does this model support the development of local community-based intellectuals?

Here is where the history of New City Writing begins to intersect with larger narratives structuring community rights and higher education. Local, state, and federal governments currently often supply tax breaks, reduce environmental standards, and provide cheap land as a means to bring in jobs for resource-poor neighborhoods. Stricter standards and increased testing are introduced to schools in an effort to address middle-class anxiety about public education. Within the paradigm of corporate capital, the politicians are providing necessary and vital economic help. But this is only within the corporate capital paradigm. Missing from the corporate capital model, however, are community organizations' attempts to advocate for progressive and environmentally sound economic development.

It is at this nexus that faculty knowledge and skills become important. As local communities become weaker publics in relationship to the demands of corporate capital, there are fewer sources from which they can generate the data, strategies, and resources to imagine an alternative future for themselves. For instance, high-pollution industries (such as sewage plants) are pushed on neighborhoods as the best possible solution to economic decline. The option of microbusinesses, self-sustaining green gardens, and renewable-energy renovation options are often ignored. For such progressive and alternative models to be fully articulated and implemented within the local environment, I believe that university resources should be placed in the service of the emergent community vision. In an information age, the university's knowledge-producing aspects can serve a larger purpose than disciplinary formation.

Yet the increased corporatization of the university further facilitates community disempowerment. The production of knowledge is placed within a corporate logic that puts profits above people, cash over community values. The proof of this relationship has been recorded numerous times: scientists are unable to share the results of their research because it was funded by a corporation; universities sell patents on faculty-produced concepts to fill their own coffers; conservative donors support the creation of corporate-endowed chairs and conservative think-tanks. What each of these moments share is the concept of the university as more responsible to the needs of a global capitalism than to the needs of a local community (White and Hauck 2000).

In this framework, a managerial model that further removes faculty from active engagement with the community, that further removes the production of knowledge from the local community, further embeds the university more deeply in the conservative paradigm of learning and economics. In line with conservative attacks on humanities scholars for being politically active, faculty are increasingly being rearticulated in the role of traditional intellectuals—serving the interests of the mainstream economic powers either through actively endorsing the corporate paradigm or finding that their ability to critique corporate culture is muted.

In such a context, New City Writing represented a strategic intervention and alternative collaborative paradigm for faculty work and community/university partnerships within Temple University. As evidenced throughout the preceding chapters, in an emergent corporate and conservative culture, New City Writing had attempted to build a partnership model marked by a sharing of power between university and community scholars, a collaborative effort aimed at the production of community-based knowledge for local purposes. Over the course of eight years, New City Writing enabled university scholars to debate and organize with scholars organic to the local community. This interaction produced an agenda that could not rest comfortably in the corporatized university, where information was privatized or divorced from immediate needs. Indeed, the conceptual framework developed from New City Writing's partnership efforts necessitated a different set of actions from both university and political leaders.

The New City Writing intellectuals demanded in and through their work that those in power recognize that urban working-class communities in Philadelphia have "certain inalienable rights":

The Right to Be Transgressive

At a moment where a static national identity (European, English speaking, Christian) is the endpoint of a conservative national politics, New City intellectuals supported an urban identity that was consistently portrayed as multiple—drawing from many heritages and orientations, crossing many traditional boundaries. This multiple identity authorized alternative concepts of family, work, and social values divorced from the pursuit of profit. In its communal nature, this urban identity transgressed many of the current attempts to limit concepts of citizenship.

The Right to Their Own Language and Culture

It was clear that urban schools were not being structured to develop this transgressive identity or to interact effectively with its possibilities. Instead of creating curricula and writing that would highlight the broader community values from which such an identity grows, multiplying the influences from which it can develop, simplistic visions of multiculturalism were instantiated. More to the point, even this weakened vision of multicultural education became hemmed in by state and federal standardized-testing requirements. In the process, an alternative vision of literacy and education was being marginalized. Urban students, however, had a right to their own identity and culture. New City Writing's work was to create the educational space where this identity could flourish.

The Right To Their Own Economy

Urban identity is intimately wrapped up in the new globalism. The very diversity of languages, heritages, and religions in the urban environment is the result of global economic and political forces. Within the context of a global flattening of wages and benefits, it is even more important that urban communities gain more control of the local economy. Policies governing the role of new corporate businesses, such as Walmart, in the existing small-business network and neighborhood population must be negotiated, not dictated, to a community. The right to a living wage must be ensured. Community values must work to transcend global forces.

The Right to an Activist Government

Rights can be demanded and even acted upon. For rights to be institutionalized requires a government committed to supporting local needs over and against the demands of a corporate or conservative culture. The activists in *No Restraints* and *Espejos y Ventanas* clearly understood that community organizing within a weak public sphere (writing, publications, etc.) ultimately had to connect with efforts at altering the strong public sphere (legislation, etc.) This belief also came to represent New City's operating framework.

It can be argued, of course, that there is nothing "new" in these rights—that New City simply rediscovered the working poor's existing demands. This claim might be true, but it is true only because so much is still to be done. Its lack of originality should thus only increase our efforts. Moreover, what I have come to believe was valuable about the articulation of these rights at Temple University was the process by which the demand for these rights emerged. As discussed throughout this book, the belief in these rights grew from collaborative partnerships wherein each participant recognized and acted upon these rights through a series of community-based actions—of which only a small fraction are represented here. In this way, New City intellectuals and their allies were attempting to develop a theory and practice strategic in its local environment and immediate in its effects.

To some extent, despite the changing context of Temple University, New City had created a strategic space in line with the vision articulated in Tony Bennett's academic work. As quoted in the introduction, he wrote that cultural studies needed to be more

circumspect and circumstantial [in its calculations] about how and where knowledge needs to surface and emerge in order to be consequential. . . . [The] field of culture needs to be thought of as constituentively [*sic*] governmental [and] to suggest the need for forms of cultural theory politics that will concern themselves with the production and placing of forms of knowledge—of functioning truths—that can concretely influence the agendas, calculations, and procedures of those entities which can be thought of as agents operating within, or in relation to, the fields of cultural control. (1992, 32)

Although New City Writing was not a cultural studies institute in the strictest sense, it implemented Bennett's concepts within the particular confines of Philadelphia. Much of New City's work aligned with his belief that "one cannot calculate what the politics of a particular type of criticism are without taking into account the field in which it is likely to surface and have effects" (Bennett 1992, 28). Such an effort was evident in projects such as *Urban Rhythms* and the Philadelphia Writing Centers Project and in publications such as *Espejos y Ventanas* and *No Restraints*. These programs represented New City's successful past.

It was becoming clear, however, that there might not be such a successful future. New City Writing was quickly losing traction within the new university community-service paradigm. As already noted, gaining institutional support for grants was already an issue; curriculum emerged as another issue. In some ways, the initial decision to move away from a graduate certificate in cultural studies and toward community-based knowledge production was coming back to haunt New City Writing. Although we could point to a set of undergraduate classes, graduate students, and faculty partners, we did not have a recognizable academic "calling card," such as a minor, major, or certificate. Even if we had developed such calling cards, it was not clear that they would have been in line with the new academic vision of the university because they would have been too focused on the community to be strictly disciplinary. Our attachment to the university writing program could no longer prop up our academic credentials, either. The writing program was being revalued as the university attempted to burnish its academic credentials; basic writing, with its taints of remediation, was not part of the new environment. For the first time since its inception, then, New City Writing could no longer count on the dean's or upper administration's support. Things had not exactly collapsed, but they were in need of a profound reworking, for within two years of the new managerial paradigms, New City Writing, having completed most of its outside funding, found itself an embattled entity.

Here is where the importance of strategic space becomes most salient. If each of the tactical interventions described in previous chapters had been sponsored by an individual faculty, as is not uncommon, they would not have been able to withstand the new policies that reassigned faculty work, moved partnerships to nonacademic units, and shifted grant funds. That is, there would not have been sufficient pushback from a range of community organizations with sufficient strength to secure the possibility of continued work. New City Writing, however, had been part of an effort to create a strategic base of operations that had a stronger community foundation. Within this space, it had been able to work through many obstacles and to support numerous sustained partnerships, even when its partnering institutions made sudden policy changes or faced budget crises.

A review of the previous chapters in this book demonstrates this to be the case. When a public-school partner could no longer support its writing center, New City Writing was able to use its position to morph the singular center into the Writing Centers Project, thus providing multiple years of support for its partners. When community residents did not like the initial version of a publication, New City Writing could reprint it, thus gaining trust across numerous communities. When disability organizations wanted a means to form larger alliances, New City Writing could provide the support and venue for such work. Moreover, the support did not emerge just from the university outward: community partners supported our graduate students; they supported each other's programming and grant requests; they shared expertise about program development, staff training, and fund-raising. That is, New City Writing had become an organizational space and support network that was valuable to Philadelphia community organizations, and these organizations now wanted to fight for its continued existence.

The fight for New City Writing's organizational space, however, did not necessarily mean New City itself should survive in its current form. Continuing New City Writing within the confines of the disciplinary models being placed into the college and university did not seem sustainable over the long term. Producing such academic markers as a certificate or a minor might have forestalled some scrutiny or even garnered some short-term support, but it would not have helped New City's partners achieve the overarching goal of a fundamental rearticulation of the relationship between the university/political culture and the community. Further, within the new context, the curricular battles for an open and inclusive community-based pedagogy now needed to be fought within the confines of the English major. Disciplines were again the dominant paradigm. Bringing New City Writing into those debates would have entrenched it further in departmental and college politics and not altered the larger city or national politics that were shaping education in Philadelphia.

The question of whether New City Writing should continue was also implicated within larger political frameworks. If the "inalienable rights" that had informed our partnership work were actually to be implemented, community alliances would have to be built that actively lobbied the university and public-school system to take on a different political relationship to North Philadelphia, in particular, and to the working-poor in general. The brunt of New City Writing's time had been spent looking outward in an attempt to support local community organizing around issues of literacy and economics. Important work had been accomplished. With the shifting paradigm at the university and public schools, there would now have to be an effort to push these two entities to support the local community's larger goals—educational as well as economic and environmental. Traditional literacy institutions would ultimately have to be persuaded not only to expand acceptable writing practices, but to use their leverage to alter wage practices in local corporations, commit to supporting local knowledges and belief systems, and lobby for increased support from local government.

All the partners involved in New City Writing understood that the space that would allow this work to continue, that had marked the best of New City Writing, now needed to move off campus and be directly situated within the larger "public sphere." As important, everyone involved recognized that it would be by shifting outward to the public sphere that the community partners could help support grant applications that bypassed implicit college strictures against service grants. At this moment, the Knight Foundation, which had previously provided more than $600,000 in grant funds to New City Writing, had announced a new initiative to support community arts and education alliances. It was decided that New City Writing, through its press, would join its community partners in developing a proposal that would ensure that the ongoing partnership work could continue and expand. And as important, the partners would ensure that funds would be provided to New City Writing's administrative core while it attempted to ride out a negative university environment. In other words, the community partners took over the university space, demanding that Temple seek these funds and compelling Knight and Temple to back the continuation of the partnership. In doing so, the partners also made certain the survival of New City Writing for two to three more years.

As a result of these efforts, in 2004 the North Philadelphia Community Arts and Literacy Network (CALN) formally took over as the organizing point for progressive community-based literacy partnership work previously done under the rubric of New City Writing. Funded by a multiyear grant of $325,000 from the Knight Foundation, CALN was designed to build off the existing work of New City Writing and its partners and to create a set of community-based curricular models that would be implemented in the partners' public schools and community organizations. University faculty would continue to be supported in their efforts to bring academic research into alignment with community goals. Given New City Writing's commitment to the idea of *organic* intellectuals, however, this work would also entail expanding who could be considered a teacher within these programs. Community activists and artists would be offered internships to develop the classroom-management skills necessary to succeed in public-school/university classrooms, and public-school and university teachers would be trained in community-based arts. As each particular curricular site and teacher core developed, New City Community Press, now an independent nonprofit, would produce curricular materials for use in the schools and the community. Many of these initiatives would represent a more complete articulation of programs discussed throughout this book.

The original CALN partners would ultimately be expanded to include local labor representatives, university administrators, nonprofit organizations, and political representatives. CALN's ultimate goal would be to connect the production of community arts and education to public forums that serve as political venues for North Philadelphia to argue for increased economic and political rights. CALN would concentrate on creating a consistent public space where politicians would be able to hear alternative visions of a community and its values concerning what constitutes economic well-being. Like Linda Flower's work with Pittsburgh's Settlement House (Flower 2008), CALN would bring together faculty research, community activists, neighborhood residents, school children, college students, and public-school teachers around a common goal: to create a literacy and legislative environment within North Philadelphia that would support its residents' aspirations and ideals.

In this model, Temple University would be an institution to be lobbied. That is, the university would not be so much a community partner, but an organization that needed to reinvent itself as a community stakeholder. By attempting to change the political and social context in which the university existed, CALN would also attempt to change that institution's most recent behavior. We believed CALN could be the means by which to advocate actively for a different university, for only within such an environment where local knowledge is seen as vital to the institution's functioning would faculty, departments, and colleges be persuaded to be serious about their community responsibility. Only with strong administrative support would faculty have the ability to alter fundamentally the ways in which undergraduate and graduate programs are structured in their relationship to surrounding neighborhoods. Only by a budgetary commitment would hiring practices be changed to allow organic intellectuals from the community to teach within a program that focused on issues such as community literacy goals, local economic control, and political rights.

Such was the dream and the responsibility placed within CALN.

Whither New City Writing?

But what would be the role of New City Writing? Could it even be said to exist at this point? In one sense, the answer is a productive "no." If one imagines New City Writing's goal as helping to create a space where a progressive and collective literacy politics could be enacted, then this goal was achieved. Its continuation as an entity, in that sense, was probably less important than its role in helping to create CALN. That is, sometimes the true test of a program's success is the achievement of its own irrelevance. Much of New City Writing's work had been successfully moved into a collective partnership with community arts and literacy organizations. And this, I believe, was exactly what should have happened.

But it is not the end of the story. The value of a strategic space is that the transfer of one element of its work does not erase the residue of its initial desires or the human resources that those desires produced. Elements of New City might have moved on, but the institutional memory remained cathected with the desire for a different form of disciplinary and scholarly identity for those active in community/university partnerships. When at the outset of this book, I tried to characterize the moment of New City's birth, I focused on the reluctance of disciplinary faculty to endorse community-based work as scholarship. Unlike New City's opening moments, however, its eight-year history had created a cadre of faculty aligned with progressive literacy work, a literal network of community literacy partners, and an established track record of grant support. Within that context, it became possible at least to imagine how New City Writing might use "writing" to begin to foster an interdisciplinary and intercommunal study of writing that would support CALN's work.

What much of New City's work demonstrated was that *writing* is a term that seems to float across a variety of fields, institutions, communities, and populations. It seems to bring together academics and activists, teachers and legislators. Perhaps because *writing,* unlike *composition,* seems to be a key cultural term it authorizes conversations and work that transcends the narrow confines of a discipline or college identity. Within this frame, a programmatic effort to study writing would not be just a set of methods useful for textual analysis (à la cultural studies with vernacular texts or composition with student texts) or just a set of institutionally located pedagogies (whether in graduate seminars or first-year writing courses). Instead, an effort to *study writing* would name the potential framework by which academics, community activists, legislators, public-school educators, and others might develop effective writing practices that can be taught to community-based organizations and activists. Although such work might have been possible before CALN, there would have been no network through which to disperse such work. Joined with CALN, however, New City could inhabit a research and activist network that went *beyond the curriculum.* The study of writing could imply the possibility of real change.

For this vision of *writing studies* to succeed, however, we would have to work against the current climate within our university. Our focus would not be so much the traditional forms of undergraduate/graduate education, but the teaching of a new sense of expertise to new audiences who would enact their writing in nontraditional or new locations. For this reason, not all the faculty in the writing studies program would be writing specialists (i.e., composition or rhetoric scholars). Although disciplinary knowledge about the historical, theoretical, and cognitive aspects of writing instruction would be vital, equally important would be scholars in urban economics, race studies, and vernacular cultures. In addition, not all faculty need be (or should be) the standard Ph.D. model. Room would have to be made for policymakers, former legislators, and literacy activists. Community members who have spent a lifetime advocating for progressive literacy models would also be included as faculty. In short, rather than a disciplinary-based production of knowledge as the determining factor of who is qualified faculty, our goal would be to create a dynamic where individuals based in the academy and in the community, the theoretical and the concrete, would interact in the production of a writing studies uniquely tied to its local environment. Our faculty's efforts would be focused primarily on using writing instruction to support the creation of organic intellectuals, linked to organizational alliances, who could effectively advocate for a progressive sense of literacy and community rights.

In some senses, we had helped to create an alliance, but now we needed to generate the literacies and strategies that would allow such an alliance to succeed. And although the internal context was challenging, to say the least, the need for such an effort was clear. So with a sense that we had completed the first stage of our work, we began to look toward the future once again.

Epilogue: Success?

When choosing "Success" as the title for the final chapter, I struggled with whether to put a question mark after it. As I look back on the history of New City Writing, could I really claim success?

Several years have passed since the events described in this book took place, so some form of taking stock is possible. For instance, New City

Writing continues to exist (with Eli Goldblatt now serving as director); New City Community Press (which I now direct) has continued to publish the voices of local residents; literacy studies was established as a separate track within the English major at Temple University; CALN existed for the period of the grant before moving into different and emerging partnership models; and grant funds continue to support individual and collaborative work among CALN's partners. In 2005, I left Temple for Syracuse University to be part of the development of a writing major in which New City "writing studies" could comfortably exist. New City Writing and Syracuse University's writing program recently sponsored a national conference on the goals of "community-based literacy work." Partnerships and projects continue.

But are these the pillars upon which New City Writing's success should rest? Perhaps. Survival is certainly not a sign of failure. Nevertheless, I would like to suggest a different way to imagine success—one that speaks of a slightly different strategic goal. Looking back, I would highlight the following moments as equally indicative of New City Writing's success:

• Elementary students standing in line to insist on more time with university tutors

• High school students dragging chairs into an empty classroom in an attempt to reopen their writing center

• University students and U.K. working-class writers writing in support of the continuation of an organic literacy and publication network

• Community residents successfully protesting the depiction of their community, demanding and receiving a revised second edition of the book about them

• Disabled activists using writing to record the history of their struggle and disseminate it to community, university, and legislative leaders

To me, each of these moments speaks to the mobilization of individuals into a collective body committed to an expansive and politically progressive use of literacy. What I now see is that behind each partnership, each moment of institutional success and failure, countless individuals experienced the power that can be achieved by collectively disrupting the *norm* for the *possible*. The real success of New City Writing and its partners, then, was possibly the work of creating opportunities for individuals to collectively come together, to develop a dream for their school, neighborhood, and city, and to draw in institutional partners who also feel responsible for achieving that dream. Maybe each moment of collective protest was actually the sign of our success.

Beyond the ability to ensure survival for our particular work in the university, then, the true value of creating a strategic space for tactical incursions against conservative literacy policies is that it models collective action for those involved. In addition to any particular individual literacy skill developed, participants also gained the tools (protest lines, appropriation of existing space, community forums, etc.) to develop their own strategic spaces. Writing beyond the curriculum was not just about recognizing the literacy existent in the communities that surround the university and working to enable the articulation of that literacy into a collective worldview; it was also about teaching the organizational skills that will ensure the long-term recognition of that worldview.

As I complete this book, then, I can't help but remember that it was the organizational skills and collective vision of a working-class community that provided the resources necessary for me to attend the university during a time of economic disaster in Pittsburgh. It was also this collective vision that supported my family during years in graduate school. And it was the responsibility to this collective tradition that first led me to the work of New City Writing.

For all those reasons, I like to believe that New City Writing was also a participant in the continuation of this collective tradition.

What I know is that the work continues.

REFERENCES | INDEX

References

Adams, Carolyn, David Bartelt, David Elesh, Ira Goldstein, Nancy Kleniewski, and William Yancey. 1993. *Philadelphia: Neighborhoods, Divisions, and Conflicts in a Postindustrial City.* Philadelphia: Temple Univ. Press.

Adler-Kassner, Linda, Robert Crooks, and Ann Watters. 1997. *Writing the Community: Concepts and Models for Service-Learning in Composition.* Herndon, Va.: Stylus.

Anderson, Perry. 1976. "The Antinomies of Antonio Gramsci." *New Left Review* 100: 6–78.

Bartholomae, David. 1995. "Writing with Teachers: A Conversation with Peter Elbow." *College Composition and Communication* 46, no. 1: 62–71.

Bartholomae, David, and Peter Elbow. 1995. "Responses to Bartholomae and Elbow." *College Composition and Communication* 46, no. 1: 84–92.

Bennett, Tony. 1992. "Putting Policy into Cultural Studies." In *Cultural Studies,* edited by Lawrence Grossberg, Cary Nelson, and Paula Treichler, 23–37. New York: Routledge.

Berlin, James. 1987. *Rhetoric and Reality: Writing Instruction in American Colleges, 1900–1985.* Carbondale: Southern Illinois Univ. Press.

Bissinger, Buzz. 1998. *A Prayer for the City.* New York: Vintage Press.

Bizzell, Patricia. 1994. "'Contact Zones' and English Studies." *College English* 56: 163–69.

———. 2002. "Multiculturalism, Contact Zones, and the Organization of English Studies." In *Professing in the Contact Zone: Bringing Theory and Practice Together,* edited by Janice M. Wolff, 48–57. Urbana, Ill.: National Council of Teachers of English.

Bizzell, Patricia, and Bruce Herzberg. 1996. *Negotiating Differences.* New York: St. Martin's Press.

Blackwell, Tameka. 2002. "And the Sun Still Shines." In *No Restraints: An Anthology of Disability Culture in Philadelphia,* edited by Gil Ott, 105–17. Philadelphia: New City Community Press.

Brandt, Deborah. 2001. *Literacy in American Lives*. New York: Cambridge Univ. Press.

Breaking Bread: The Food Issue. 2001. An issue of *OPEN City: A Journal of Community Arts and Culture* (Sept.). Philadelphia: New City Community Press.

Brettell, Caroline. 1996. *When They Read What We Write: The Politics of Ethnography*. Westport, Conn.: Bergin and Garvey.

Cary, Lorene. 2006. *Free! Great Escapes from Slavery on the Underground Railroad*. Philadelphia: New City Community Press.

Certeau, Michel de. 1988. *The Practice of Everyday Life*. Translated by Steven Rendall. Berkeley and Los Angeles: Univ. of California Press.

Cohen, G. A. 1988. *History Labour and Freedom: Themes from Marx*. Oxford, U.K.: Clarendon Press.

Coles, Nicholas. 2001. "Joe Shakespeare: The Contemporary Worker-Writer Movement." In *Popular Literacy: Studies in Cultural Practices and Poetics*, edited by John Trimbur, 189–208. Pittsburgh: Univ. of Pittsburgh Press.

Cushman, Ellen. 1998. *The Struggle and the Tools: Oral and Literate Strategies in an Inner City Community*. New York: State Univ. of New York Press.

Deans, Thomas. 2000. *Writing Partnerships: Service-Learning in Composition*. Urbana, Ill.: National Council of Teachers of English.

DeFilippis, James, Robert Fisher, and Eric Shragge. 2006. "What's Left in the Community? Oppositional Politics in Contemporary Practice." *Community Development Journal* 44, no. 1: 38–52.

Elbow, Peter. 1995. "Being a Writer vs. Being an Academic: A Conflict in Goals." *College Composition and Communication* 46, no. 1: 72–83.

Federation of Worker Writers and Community Publishers (FWWCP). 1978. *Writing*. Brighton, U.K.: FWWCP.

———, ed. 1989. *Once I Was a Washing Machine*. Brighton, U.K.: FWWCP.

Flower, Linda. 2002. "Intercultural Inquiry and the Transformation of Service." *College English* 65, no. 2: 181–201.

———. 2008. *Community Literacy and the Rhetoric of Public Engagement*. Carbondale: Southern Illinois Univ. Press.

Fraser, Nancy. 1990. "Rethinking the Public Sphere: A Contribution to the Critique of Actually Existing Democracy." *Social Text* 25–26: 56–80.

Freire, Paulo. 2000. *Pedagogy of the Oppressed*. New York: Continuum International.

George, Diana. 2003. "Addressing Homelessness and Poverty Through Community Organizing and Social Activism." Public lecture, Temple Univ.

George, Diana, and John Trimbur. 2001. "Cultural Studies and Composition." In *A Guide to Composition Pedagogies*, edited by Gary Tate, Amy Rupiper, and Kurt Schick, 71–91. New York: Oxford Univ. Press.

Giroux, Henri. 1988. *Teachers as Intellectuals: Toward a Critical Pedagogy of Learning*. New York: Bergin and Barvey.

———. 2000. "Public Pedagogy as Cultural Practice: Stuart Hall and the 'Crisis of Culture.'" *Cultural Studies* 14, no. 2: 341–60.

Goldblatt, Eli. 2007. *Because We Live Here: Sponsoring Literacy Beyond the College Curriculum*. Creskill, N.J.: Hampton Press.

Gorka, John. 1994. "Gravyland." On *Temporary Road* (CD). High Street Records.

Gorzelsky, Gwen. 2005. *Language of Experience: Literate Practices and Social Change*. Pittsburgh: Univ. of Pittsburgh Press.

Gramsci, Antonio. 1985. *Selections from the Prison Notebooks*. Edited by Quintin Hoare and Geoffrey Nowell Smith. New York: International Publishers.

Green, Michael. 1996. "The Centre for Contemporary Cultural Studies." In *What Is Cultural Studies? A Reader*, edited by John Story, 49–60. New York: Arnold Press.

Greene, Rev. Nellie. 2002. "Sermon at Chestnut Hill United Methodist Church." In *No Restraints: An Anthology of Disability Culture in Philadelphia*, edited by Gil Ott, 37–42. Philadelphia: New City Community Press.

Guillory, John. 1993. *Cultural Capital: The Problem of Literary Canon Formation*. Chicago: Univ. of Chicago Press.

Hairston, Maxine. 1985. "Breaking Our Bonds and Reaffirming Our Connections." *College Composition and Communication* 36, no. 3: 272–82.

Hall, R. Mark, and Mary Rosner. 2004. "Pratt and Pratfalls: Revisioning Contact Zones." In *Crossing Borderlands: Composition and Post-colonial Studies*, edited by Andrea A. Lunsford and Lahoucine Ouzgane, 95–109. Pittsburgh: Univ. of Pittsburgh Press.

Hall, Stuart. 1982. "The Rediscovery of 'Ideology': Return of the Repressed in Media Studies." In *Culture, Society, and the Media*, edited by Michael Gurevitch, Tony Bennett, James Curran, and Janet Woollacott, 52–86. London: Methuen.

———. 1996. "Race, Culture, and Communications: Looking Backward and Forward at Cultural Studies." In *What Is Cultural Studies? A Reader*, edited by John Story, 337–43. New York: Arnold Press.

Harris, Joseph. 1996. *A Teaching Subject: Composition since 1966*. New York: Prentice-Hall.

Hart, Greg, Mary Ellen Mangino, Zoeanne Murphy, and Ann Marie Taliercio, eds. 2008. *Working: An Anthology of Writing and Photography*. Philadelphia: New City Community Press.

Heath, Shirley Brice. [1983] 2006. *Ways with Words: Language, Life, and Work in Communities and Classrooms*. New York: Cambridge Univ. Press.

Hebdige, Dick. 1979. *Subculture: The Meaning of Style*. New York: Methuen.

Herzberg, Bruce. 1994. "Community Service and Critical Teaching." *College Composition and Communication* 45, no. 3: 307–19.

Hoggart, Richard. [1957] 1991. *The Uses of Literacy*. New York: Transaction.

Hyatt, Susan Brin. 2002. "Service Learning, Applied Anthropology, and the Production of Neo-liberal Citizens." *Anthropology in Action* 8: 6–13.

Liberating the Literary World. 2003. *Federation Magazine* 26 (special issue).

Lukacs, Georg. 1971. *History and Class Consciousness: Studies in Marxist Dialects*. Translated by Rodney Livingstone. Cambridge, Mass.: MIT Press.

Lyons, Mark, and Leticia Roa Nixon, eds. 2004. *Espejos y Ventanas / Mirrors and Windows: Oral Histories of Mexican Farmworkers and Their Families*. With an afterword by Jimmy Santiago Baca. Philadelphia: New City Community Press.

Maguire, Paddy, Roger Mills, Dave Morley, Rebecca O'Rourke, Sue Shrapnel, Ken Worpole, and Stephen Yeo. [1982] 2010. *The Republic of Letters: Working Class Writing and Publishing*. Edited by Dave Morley and Ken Worpole. London: Comedia. Reprint. Syracuse, N.Y., and Philadelphia: Syracuse Univ. Press and New City Community Press.

Marx, Karl. 1977. *Capital*. Vol. 1. Translated by Ben Fowkes. New York: Vintage Books.

Mathieu, Paula. 2005. *Tactics of Hope: The Public Turn in Composition*. Portsmouth, N.H.: Boyton-Cook.

Montero, M. Kristina, ed. 2007. *Soul Talk: Urban Youth Poetry. A Writing Project Featuring Syracuse City School District Students*. With an introduction by Luis J. Rodriguez. Philadelphia: New City Community Press.

Ott, Gil, ed. 2002a. *No Restraints: An Anthology of Disability Culture in Philadelphia*. Philadelphia: New City Community Press.

———. 2002b. "What It Is, an Introduction." In *No Restraints: An Anthology of Disability Culture in Philadelphia*, edited by Gil Ott, 9–14. Philadelphia: New City Community Press.

Parakrama, Arjuna. 1990. *Language and Rebellion: Discursive Unities and the Possibility of Protest*. London: Katha.

Parks, Stephen. 2000. *Class Politics: The Movement for the Students' Right to Their Own Language*. Urbana, Ill.: National Council of Teachers of English Press.

Parks, Stephen, and Eli Goldblatt. 2000. "Writing Beyond the Curriculum: Fostering New Collaborations in Literacy." *College English* 62, no. 5: 584–607.

Pfister, Joel. 1996. "The Americanization of Cultural Studies." In *What Is Cultural Studies? A Reader*, edited by John Story, 287–99. New York: Arnold Press.

Pollard, Nicholas. 2003. "Liberating the Literary World." In *Liberating the Literary World*, special issue of *Federation Magazine* 26: 3.

Pratt, Mary Louise. [1991] 2005. "Arts of the Contact Zone." In *Ways of Reading*, edited by Dave Bartholomae and Anthony Petrosky, 517–30. New York: St. Martin's Press. Originally published in *Profession* 91: 33–40.

Readings, Bill. 1996. *The University in Ruins*. Cambridge, Mass.: Harvard Univ. Press.

Rogers, Olive. 1989. "Once I Was a Washing Machine." In *Once I Was a Washing Machine*, edited by the Federation of Worker Writers and Community Publishers (FWWCP), 34. Brighton, U.K.: FWWCP.

Rose, Mike. 1990. *Lives on the Boundary*. New York: Penguin.

Rubin, Gayle. 1975. "The Traffic in Women: Notes on the 'Political Economy' of Sex." In *Toward an Anthropology of Women*, edited by Rayna R. Reiter, 157–210. New York: Monthly Review Press.

Said, Edward. 1983. *The World, the Text, and the Critic*. Cambridge, Mass.: Harvard Univ. Press.

Scott, James C. 1985. *Weapons of the Weak: Everyday Forms of Peasant Resistance*. New Haven, Conn.: Yale Univ. Press.

Seitz, James. 1999. *Motives for Metaphors: Literacy, Curriculum Reform, and the Teaching of English*. Pittsburgh: Univ. of Pittsburgh Press.

Shor, Ira. 1992. *Culture Wars: School and Society in the Conservative Restoration*. Chicago: Univ. of Chicago Press.

Shorr, Lori, and Benjamin Herold. 2002. *Agreeing on What Matters*. Philadelphia: Office of School and Community Partnerships.

Shusterman, Richard. 1997. "Ghetto Music." *Urban Rhythms* 1, no. 1. Available at http://www.temple.edu/ur/home.

Smitherman, Geneva. 1986. *Talkin and Testifyin: The Language of Black America*. Detroit: Wayne State Univ. Press.

Soley, Lawrence. 1999. *Leasing the Ivory Tower: The Corporate Takeover of Academia*. Cambridge, Mass.: South End Press.

Spellmeyer, Kurt. 1989. "Foucault and the Freshman Writer: Considering the Self in Discourse." *College English* 51, no. 7: 715–29.

———. 1996. "After Theory: From Textuality to Attunement with the World." *College English* 58, no. 8: 893–913.

Spivak, Gayatri. 1985. "Scattered Speculations on the Question of Value." *Diacritics* 15, no. 4: 73–93.

"Students' Right to Their Own Language." 1974. *College Composition and Communication* 25, no. 3: 1–32.

Sullivan, Frank, Arabella Lyon, Dennis Lebofsky, Susan Wells, and Eli Goldblatt. 1997. "Strong Composition, Strong Student Needs: Dialectics of Writing Program Reform." *College Composition and Communication* 48, no. 3: 372–91.

Sze, Lena, ed. 2004. *Chinatown Live(s): Oral Histories from Philadelphia's Chinatown*. Photographs by Rodney Atienza. Philadelphia: New City Community Press.

Trimbur, John. 1994. "Review: Taking the Social Turn: Teaching Writing Post Process." *College Composition and Communication* 45, no. 1: 108–18.

Urban Rhythms: A Journal on Music and Culture. 1997--99. Vol. 1, nos. 1–4. Available at http://www.temple.edu/ur/home.

Villanueva, Victor. 1993. *Bootstraps: From an American Academic of Color*. Urbana, Ill.: National Council of Teachers of English Press.

Von Schmetterling, Erik, M.D. 2002. "What Is Disability?" In *No Restraints: An Anthology of Disability Culture in Philadelphia*, edited by Gil Ott, 15–22. Philadelphia: New City Community Press.

Welch, Nancy. 2008. *Living Room: Teaching Public Writing in a Privatized World*. Portsmouth, N.H.: Heinemann.

Wells, Susan. 1996. "Rogue Cops and Health Care: What Do We Want from Public Writing?" *College Composition and Communication* 47, no. 3: 325–41.

White, Geoffry D., and Flannery C. Hauck. 2000. *Campus, Inc.: Corporate Power in the Ivory Tower*. Amherst, N.Y.: Prometheus Books.

Williams, Raymond. [1958] 1989. "Culture Is Ordinary." In *Resources of Hope: Culture, Democracy, Socialism*, 5–14. London: Verso.

Willis, Paul. 1981. *Learning to Labor*. New York: Columbia Univ. Press.

Woodin, Tom. 2005. "Building Culture from the Bottom Up: The Educational Origins of the Federation of Worker Writers and Community Publishers." *Journal of the History of Education Society* 34, no. 4: 345–63.

Yeats, W. B. *RESPONSIBILITIES and Other Poems*. London: Macmillan, 1916.

Index

Index